Bringing Back the Social into the Sociology of Religion

Studies in Critical Research on Religion

Haymarket Books is proud to be working with Brill Academic Publishers (www.brill.nl) to republish the *Studies in Critical Research on Religion* book series in paperback editions. This peer-reviewed book series offers insights into our current reality by exploring the content and consequences of power relationships under capitalism, and by considering the spaces of opposition and resistance to these changes that have been defining our new age. Our full catalog of *SCRR* volumes can be viewed at https://www.haymarketbooks.org/series_collections/6-studies-in-critical-research-in-religion.

Bringing Back the Social into the Sociology of Religion

Critical Approaches

Edited by
Véronique Altglas
Matthew Wood

Haymarket Books
Chicago, IL

First published in 2018 by Brill Academic Publishers, The Netherlands.
© 2018 Koninklijke Brill NV, Leiden, The Netherlands

Published in 2019 by
Haymarket Books
P.O. Box 180165
Chicago, IL 60618
773-583-7884
www.haymarketbooks.org
info@haymarketbooks.org

ISBN: 978-1-64259-075-3

Distributed to the trade in the US through Consortium Book Sales and
Distribution (www.cbsd.com) and internationally through Ingram Publisher
Services International (www.ingramcontent.com).

This book was published with the generous support of Lannan Foundation and
Wallace Action Fund.

Special discounts are available for bulk purchases by organizations and
institutions. Please call 773-583-7884 or email info@haymarketbooks.org for
more information.

Cover design by Jamie Kerry and Ragina Johnson.

Printed in United States.

Library of Congress Cataloging-in-Publication data is available.

10 9 8 7 6 5 4 3 2 1

This book is a tribute to Matthew Wood (1970–2015) who passed away before seeing this work completed or having the time to fulfil many promising intellectual endeavours.

We were lucky to be your wife, friends and intellectual companions.

∴

Contents

Series Editor Preface

In this edited volume, Véronique Altglas and Matthew Wood take aim at what they call a "religious sociology" – that is, a sociology of religion which is sympathetic not only with various manifestations of religiosity but is indeed funded by, aligned with and does research in support of institutional religion. They place a "critical sociology of religion" into opposition to it – one which in their conception is "highly reflexive" and breaks with the normative evaluations of religious traditions by being not only social scientific but secular. Indeed, in "bringing the social back in," they attempt to make the sociology of religion more sociological, a position from which the contemporary subfield has gone astray from its classical foundations. The essays in this book fan out in this direction, critically approaching the religious groups who they study and using frames such as Margaret Archer's critical realism and Pierre Bourdieu's cultural sociology to analyze them.

Warren S. Goldstein, Ph.D.
Center for Critical Research on Religion
www.criticaltheoryofreligion.org

List of Illustrations

Figure

Tables

Notes on Contributors

Véronique Altglas
is Lecturer in Sociology at Queen's University Belfast. Her book, *From Yoga to Kabbalah: Religious Exoticism and the Logics of Bricolage*, was chosen by the International Society for the Sociology of Religion as the best book in 2017.

Peter Doak
is Lecturer in Sociology at Ulster University. He completed his doctoral research at Queen's University Belfast, where he taught for several years. His research focuses on the use of urbanism as a vehicle of ethno-political conflict transformation.

Yannick Fer
holds a PhD. in Sociology (EHESS, 2004). He is a CNRS researcher at the Centre Maurice Halbwachs (Paris), specialist in Pentecostal/Charismatic movements. His most recent publication is a volume on Protestantism in Paris, coedited with G. Malogne-Fer (2017).

Gwendoline Malogne-Fer
holds a PhD. in Sociology (EHESS, 2005). Working on gender and religion, she has done extensive fieldwork in Polynesian Protestant churches. She has notably coedited a book on Gender and Pentecostalism with Y. Fer (2015).

Christophe Monnot
is Assistant Professor of Sociology of Protestantism at the University of Strasbourg. He works on religious congregations and religious diversity. He recently published (2018) *Congregations in Europe* at Springer, co-authored with Jörg Stolz.

Eric Morier-Genoud
(Ph.D SUNY-Binghamton) is a lecturer in African and Imperial history at Queen's University Belfast, Northern Ireland. He has written extensively on religion and on politics in Southern Africa and the Portuguese-speaking world.

Alix Philippon
holds a PhD from the Institute of Political Studies (Sciences Po), Aix-en-Provence, France, where she is currently Assistant Professor in sociology. She has authored two books on Islam, including *Sufism and politics in Pakistan*, Paris, Karthala, 2011.

Matthew Wood

(*1970–2015*) was lecturer in Sociology at Queen's University Belfast. His work is particularly influential for the study of New Age, spirituality, and the epistemology of the sociology of religion. It includes *Possession, Power and the New Age* (*2007*).

Introduction: An Epistemology for the Sociology of Religion

Véronique Altglas and Matthew Wood

This volume is based on a symposium at Queen's University Belfast in 2014, featuring papers delivered by academics from the United Kingdom, France and Switzerland. The aim of the symposium was to diagnose and address current weaknesses in the sociology of religion in specific areas of study and national contexts, in order to develop a more robust sociological approach, one that returns the social to the heart of enquiry and engages with contemporary ideas, debates and theories central to cognate disciplines such as Anthropology, Politics, and History. The contributors to the symposium explored how "bringing the social back" into the social study of religion makes possible a more adequate sociological understanding of such topics as the emotions, the self, religious practices, and the construction of beliefs and discourses. Based on original empirical research and making use of a range of methods, ranging from quantitative to ethnographic and documentary, they developed this approach by engaging with social theory and addressing a range of different religious traditions and regions of the world: for example, Sufism in Pakistan, the Kabbalah Centre in Europe, Brazil and Israel, African Christian missions in Europe, and Evangelical Christianity in France and Oceania.

The symposium originated in the contributors' eagerness to reflect on the current state of the sociology of religion and, in particular, on the challenges affecting their subfield. There is currently more scholarly interest in religion than there has been for many decades, with Smilde speaking of a "period of paradigmatic reflection" (2010). Responding to this, sociologists of religion have begun to re-appreciate their subject matter, with many attempting to fundamentally rethink it. These attempts include: placing rational choice theory at the heart of the sociological explanation of religious activity and organisations (starting with Stark and Bainbridge, 1987); positing a domain of spirituality alongside that of religion (Heelas and Woodhead, 2005); viewing religion as a form of cultural consumption (Gauthier and Martikainen, 2013); arguing that

---

*	We are particularly grateful to Jim Beckford for his constructive feedback on this chapter. It also greatly benefited from comments by our colleagues at Queen's University Belfast, Rossella Ciccia, Teresa Degenhardt, Peter Doak, Jonathan Heaney, Cate McNamee, and Robert Miller. Their contributions improved this work.

contemporary societies are entering a post-secular phase in which the relationship between religion and areas of public social life is significantly altered (for example, Bosetti and Eder, 2006); and viewing religion in terms of how it is experienced in everyday life, as "lived religion" (McGuire, 2008).

These re-orienting attempts have had significant impacts on the sociology of religion, but we argue that each impact has, to a greater or lesser extent, been detrimental to the sociological understanding of religion. Each potentially represents the re-introduction of one or more epistemologically problematic antinomies: the self and society; subjective and external authority; practice and discourse; empowerment and disempowerment; the material and the non-material; the private and the public; consumption and production; and, last but not least, religion and society. For example, rational choice theory tends to view the world as composed of individuals exercising rational judgements and sees social contexts merely as their background. The sociology of spirituality argues for a distinction between some activities in which people exercise their own authority and others in which they are subject to external authorities. The idea that religion consists of cultural consumption elides the issues of value and meaning entailed by consumption, as well as the processes of distinction at play. The sociology of post-secularity views religion as an autonomous actor in society, able to re-formulate its relations with society in different historical epochs. The view of religion as a discourse or communication emphasises its free-floating or autonomous nature, suited to present conditions, such as globalisation or technologically advanced societies. And the focus on "lived religion" seeks to understand religion through private individual and domestic practices rather than in broader contexts of power relations. Certain concepts, from either other scholars or those people or groups being studied, are adopted in a scientifically non-reflexive manner, thereby confusing sociological analysis and emic folk models.

By repeating the antinomies that sociology has constantly battled against, these various approaches cannot epistemologically question the basis of their theories. In fact, underlying this volume's contributions is a shared concern for the epistemological challenges that affect the contemporary social study of religion. While addressing a wide range of case studies and topics in different regions of the world, the authors all point out issues of normativity, positionality, reflexivity, and criticality affecting the accuracy of our understanding of religious life.

Part of this diagnostic and on which the chapters shed light, in various ways, is an inadequate appreciation of the *social constitution* of religion. Kapferer's diagnosis of some recent influential strands in social anthropology neatly captures the phenomenon to which we are drawing attention:

> [There is] a shift away from a concern with social relational and int‐
> tive structures, as well as institutional and organizational formations ...
> [t]he complexities of their internal dynamics, their structuring processes,
> and the forces of their effects on human action within and beyond them.
>
> KAPFERER, 2005: 1–2

Put otherwise, the various recent attempts to re-orientate the sociology of religion encourage a shift away from "the social" in one or both of two ways: by inflating agency and subjectivity at the expense of concerning themselves with social relations and interactions and the contexts in which these take place, and/or by treating religion as a phenomenon in and of itself rather than as socially instituted and organised. Both strands of research show a lack of attention to social power. In such studies, one generally looks in vain for a representation and discussion of what people are doing together in specific relations and organisations that involve broader interactional and institutional configurations of social power. As such, we argue this shift from the social represents a turn away from the sociological method itself.

Another significant feature of these attempts to re-orientate the sociology of religion that reveals their shift away from "the social" is their failure to connect meaningfully with main sociological debates, such as the renewed interest in social class formations, the management of social diversity, racial and ethnic theories, the nature of individualisation and reflexivity in contemporary societies and emotion and embodiment. When main sociological ideas or theorists are referred to, little attention is paid to the debates surrounding them – with relatively superficial references to the individualisation and subjectivisation theses, to the nature of cultural consumption, to gender and the construction of womanhood, and to functional differentiation (even though this idea is central to the formation of the sociological study of religion). Furthermore, these attempts are often dismissive and/or even contemptuous of sociology, consistently setting up a naive view of the discipline as deterministic and reductionist, one that does not engage with the complexity of current sociological debates but implicitly misrepresents mid-20th century Parsonian or Marxian sociology. Thus, many contributions to this volume engage with social theories that have been productive for sociological thinking but remain marginal or are paid only lip-service in the sociology of religion – such as those of Bourdieu, Goffman, and Elias – enabling a re-connection to themes in classical social theory.

A last feature of the authors' diagnostic, something reflected in all contributions, is their identification of a tendency towards normative analysis within the social study of religion. This is reflected in the underlying celebration of forms of religion that are held to be growing, for example, in discussions of "spirituality" or in descriptions of some forms of religion as "progressive" or as representing a "revolution" or "resurrection" (Heelas, 2008).[1] One indication of such normativeness is the pursuit of an argument in clear contradiction to the available evidence, as seen in counter-evidential claims of a spiritual revolution, for example, that Christianity in Britain is being resurrected (Heelas and Woodhead, 2005). Tellingly, Heelas and Woodhead fail to observe – in their own dataset, no less – that initial regular churchgoing is a determinant factor of participation in "spiritual" and holistic practices. Accordingly, "spirituality" seems a religious sensibility of individuals who have left churches and, therefore, a consequence of secularising trends, not a growing subjective culture, seriously questioning the plausibility of a "spiritual revolution" (Wood, 2009: 245). In other words, this normative tendency generates a distorted understanding of the social world, describing what some scholars would like it to be, not what it actually is. Bruce provides a telling example of a quantitative project, whose flawed methodology and interpretation of data led its authors to conclude religiosity was growing among British university students (Bruce, 2014: 34), in contradiction to the results of existing large-scale surveys (Voas and Crockett, 2005). By and large, the claim of a return of religion often reflects an ideological posture linked to the social positioning of the scholars themselves, in both the academic *and* the religious field (Robertson, 1994: 128). Given this turn, it is no surprise that the sociology of religion is increasingly intertwined with the interests of governments and religious organisations, including their funding and conferring of markers of prestige. Such embroilments seriously weaken the scientific autonomy of the sociology of religion, reducing it to the handmaiden of broader political agendas and powers. For instance, Smilde and May's (2010) research on publication within the sociology of religion underscores a clear correlation between positive normative findings about religion and research funding. Religious funding is not related to these positive and normative findings, any more than public funding. However, they say funding from private religious organizations is linked to a support of "classic 'religious sociology,' in which religious scholars use sociology to engage religion, warts and all, in order to improve religious institutions and practices" (Smilde and May 2010: 25).[2]

---

1   A similar "teleology of progressive politics," as Mahmood (2005: 9) calls it, is found in the tendency to seek and hence find empowerment for women in conservative religions (Brasher, 1998; Griffith, 1997; Masken, 2009).

2   We have addressed the epistemological challenges related to the ways funders' and stakeholders' interests increasingly frame social research problems elsewhere (Wood, 2014).

Thus, it is perhaps not surprising that even as sociologists of religion see their object of study becoming increasingly socially significant, they sense a crisis looming in the subfield (Cadge, Levitt, and Smilde, 2011: 437–438; McKinnon and Trzebiatowska, 2014: 1; Smith et al., 2013). And yet, this is not new. American and European sociologists of religion have long underlined the "self-referential" (Robertson, 1994: 128) and insular nature of the sociology of religion. "It has not played a role in or constituted a part of any major theoretical debate in modern sociology," writes Turner (1991: 3), and, conversely, other fields of sociology, as well as social theory, have paid little attention to the significance of religion as an object of study (Beckford, 1989: 13–17; Davie, 2007: 249; Hervieu-Léger, 1997: 24; Luckmann, 1967: 18). The study of religion rarely features in general sociology peer-reviewed journals, while, at the same time, "there is also a dearth of sociology in much superficially social scientific writing about religion," deplores Bruce (2014: 38) in reference to the British academic context.

Our book reflects both this sense of crisis and a desire to contribute to the understanding of religion in contemporary society. Engaging with the social study of religion from various methodological and theoretical perspectives and drawing on different case studies, its chapters aim to suggest a more critical understanding of religion. The notion of a critical sociology of religion has been used in various ways. Goldstein (2009) understands it in reference to the Frankfurt School, or, more widely, neo-marxism. In this sense, a critical study of religion would focus on the roles religion plays in relation to oppression and emancipation; a value-based approach would weight religion in relation to values such as democracy, freedom, equality, justice, inclusion, and so forth (Goldstein, 2009: 141). Our understanding of a critical sociology of religion is different. As this introductory chapter makes clear, we find issues with a normative evaluation of one's object of studies on epistemological grounds. To put it simply, we agree with Bruce who considers that whether religion is good or bad is a theological question not a sociological one (2015: 210). We also wonder to what extent the association of "positive" effects of religion in relation to such values above might denote a Euro-American liberal, middle-class, and male-centred standpoint, oblivious to itself. This would lead, pardocially, to an uncritical (and hence, paradoxically, uncritical).

We understand a critical sociology of religion, as having four key features that sharply contrast with religious sociology. First, it is critical in the sense that it aims to break from the beliefs of the religious field itself – in particular, the pro-religion standpoint, but not only that one. Second, this non-normative endeavour requires a highly reflexive approach, through which students of religion reflect on their relationship with their objects of studies and, more largely, how this relationship affects the knowledge they are producing on religion. Third, a critical sociology of religion avoids sacralising (and hence insulating) its object as religious sociology does. Rather, it envisages religion as socially constructed and as a prism through which to understand the social beyond the narrow description of religion for itself, making it a social phenomenon that needs to be studied in conjunction with other social trends and facts – the family, authority, work, ethnicity, health, and so forth. This is about bringing back the social into the study of religion. Fourth, this critical agenda for the sociological study of religion implies the decompartmentalisation of the subfield by engaging with sociological debates and other subfields, thus making significant contributions to the discipline as a whole.

Book Content

Peter Doak's theoretical chapter furthers the Introduction's critique of a renewed religious sociology by focusing on Margaret Archer's argument for the introduction of transcendence into social theory. Archer has not expressed any interest in the sociology of religion in her writing, but her theoretical work is central to critical realism, an increasingly influential school of thought within sociology that has made inroads within the study of religion with scholars such as Christian Smith (2010). In addition, her argumentation has deep implications for the study of religion (and, in fact, for sociology as a whole), making Doak's theoretical critique of Archer's admission of transcendence particularly relevant. Situating Archer's work within critical realism, the chapter underlines the epistemological deficiencies of Archer's model of man. In particular, it underscores the ways her theoretical framework is uncritically shaped by situated and culturally specific representations, which reflects her personal identity and trajectory as a social actor but, more importantly, obfuscates the understanding of human beings' relations to the world and to transcendence.

Gwendoline Malogne-Fer focuses on the controversies stirred up in 2012–13 by the "marriage for all" bill in France. She explores the Christian churches' positions and discourses on the subject. She analyses the academic discourses and shows how some sociologists of religion uncritically reiterated what were religious arguments and justifications within the academic field. This leads her to ponder sociology of religion's incomplete autonomy vis-à-vis its own object, a problem that might become more acute as political discourses on religions' positive contributions to public life are legitimated and taken for granted.

Drawing on empirical research conducted on New Religious Movements that are unconventional versions of Hinduism and Judaism, Véronique Altglas furthers the critique of a central paradigm within the sociology of religion according to which religion in modernity – particularly when it is called "spirituality" – is increasingly the object of a free and voluntary individual choice. Drawing on her fieldwork, she demonstrates why social actors' assertions of their self-authority cannot be taken for granted as an accurate description of the social world. Instead, she suggests understanding individualism as a way of regulating social actors through individual responsibility and self-discipline. The chapter explains how the conflation of emic and etic discourses leads scholars of "spirituality" to uncritically confuse social actors' beliefs about their own freedom with an analysis of the social world. Altglas argues that this epistemological flaw springs from intellectuals' ideological assumptions about freedom, suggesting the need for a more reflexive understanding of such a situated ideal.

Matthew Wood revisits his fieldwork in London Methodist churches in order to engage in a critical reflection on congregational studies. Arguing that this perspective derives from theological presuppositions, he underscores the emphasis on worship, a tendency to see worship as an individual activity, and, finally, the central role given to theology to explain worship and congregational features. This leads the sociology of religious congregations to decontextualise worship and downplay the significance of some of their organisational features, as well as their social interactions. In contrast, he argues for the importance of committees and committee meetings. These are under-researched within the sociology of religion, yet Wood shows they are vital to a proper understanding of issues of power, legitimacy, and contestations within congregations, especially those that are ethnically diverse, such as the London Methodist churches he has studied.

Christophe Monnot's chapter starts with the following question: do academics contribute to a masking of the dynamics of power at work in the religious field by becoming specialists of one religion instead of looking at interactions and distinctions between groups and congregations? The chapter draws on a quantitative analysis of Christian congregations in Switzerland and focuses on worship as a marker of the cultural distinction between congregations. Showing the significance of such investigation, he reflects on sociology's lack of interest in distinction strategies and practices among religious groups. Monnot also warns us against cultural homology within our own field of research. This blinds us to logics of distinction and leads us to participate in struggles in the religious field through normative portrayals of religious agents.

The book turns to the study of religious emotions with Yannick Fer's chapter. The renewed interest in the social study of emotion is scarcely noticeable in the sociology of religion, he argues, mainly because of the predominance of classical interpretations of emotion, through an "irrationality-regression" paradigm. Discussing academic analyses of emotions within Pentecostalism, he shows how these analyses contribute to logics of classification and (dis)qualification that say less about religious emotions than academics' positionality within the scientific and the religious fields. By drawing on mainstream social theory, these emotions can be understood as part of wider social trends, such as the ideology of the communication society described by Neveu (2001), or set within an Eliasian framework, as a process of informalisation of emotions (Wouters, 2007).

Taking a social historical perspective, the chapter by Eric Morier-Genoud explores the notions of "reverse" or "return mission," terms conceived to capture the ways African and Asian migrants engage in Christian proselytism in Euro-American societies. While fashionable in theology and social sciences, these notions are normative, vague, and over-simplistic. Morier-Genoud argues they are unhelpful to understand migration patterns and dynamics of global Christianity, mainly because they confuse missionaries' programs and discourses with actual social trends. They optimistically assume the revitalisation of the North's evangelising endeavours by a postcolonial emancipated South, yet continue to display a sense of paternalism towards the young missions from Asia and Africa.

In the final chapter, Alix Philippon draws on her research on Islam in Pakistan to reflect on axiological neutrality within the social sciences. Academic and political discourses have, over the last 15 years, constructed a polar opposition between, on the one hand, fundamentalist, political, and violent forms of Islam, and on the other hand, an apolitical, tolerant and mystical one – Sufism. This essentialised categorisation has led academics and, consequently, political actors to present Sufism as the "good Islam" that needs to be supported against Islamic terrorism. Yet the Pakistani case study presented in Philippon's chapter shows that Sufi orders can politically and militarily mobilise for the establishment of an Islamic State. The chapter also ponders the political implications of such normative constructions, when instrumentalised for neocolonial ends by western countries or for political benefits by Muslim regimes.

Overall, the contributions do not converge on a single topic, methodology, or theoretical framework. Rather, through a range of empirical or theoretical approaches, they all strongly emphasise the need for a reflexive approach and call for a complete sociology of the sociology of religion. The remainder of this Introduction aims to initiate such an endeavour. We begin by sketching the outlooks of the subfield's peculiar historical development, most notably its difficult emancipation from a "religious sociology." This, in our view, is the source of the sociology of religion's insularity and epistemological weaknesses:

we wish to underscore this point because of the growing attempts, both from within and outside the sociology of religion, to redefine the subfield towards a return to this religious sociology. We go on to explore these attempts, exposing their serious epistemological consequences and effects. We conclude the chapter by reasserting the need for a robust and critical sociology of religion.

Development of Sociology of Religion

To begin with, the sociology of religion's development helps us understand why this subfield is prone to particular epistemological challenges. One of its main features is that it was preceded by other scholarly investigations and discourses on religion (Beckford, 1989: 15), through which religious institutions maintained and reproduced a symbolic monopoly on the knowledge of religion. It is therefore not surprising that 20th-century theologians and church administrators saw in the emerging social sciences a potentially useful "ancillary science." On the one hand, their analytical and supposedly reductionist approach was distrusted, but on the other, descriptive social studies undertaken by insiders could inform religious institutions of the changing socio-cultural environment they were operating in and help them adjust evangelising and pastoral activities accordingly. Many sociology of religion societies were founded by churches, thereby limiting the interests of the former to issues of church administration. Because of this collusion of interests, the sociological research conducted on religion had, by and large, until into the second half of the 20th century, a very narrow scope, leading Luckmann to comment: "The definition of research problems and programs is, typically, determined by the institutional forms of traditional church organization" (1967: 18).

When we look back at the theoretical significance of religion in sociology's foundational works, we realise Luckmann was one of the first – with Brothers (1964) in the British context – to deplore the "regressive" and parochial nature of the religious sociology in the post-war period. Although flourishing, it was devoid of theoretical significance. It was by emancipating itself from its own object that a sociology of religion – and not a sociology *for* religion (Robertson, 1985: 357) – was made possible. Religious institutions became disinterested in sociology when it proved, in its critical and theoretical features, ineffectual for institutional purposes. This was related to the fact that this sociology was gradually undertaken by non-members of the clergy, eager to develop a scientific study of religion beyond the concerns of religious organisations themselves, through the development of secular academic societies, university departments, and specialist scientific journals (Blasi, 2014; Conway, 2011; Dobbelaere, 1999, 2000; Martin, 1999; Voyé and Billiet, 1999).

While these features of the sociology of religion are widespread internationally, they take different forms according to national contexts. These forms, however, have this in common: in various national and regional contexts, the sociology of religion has remained, at least in part, institutionally isolated from other sociological fields. In Northern Europe, the sociology of religion is closely associated with church-affiliated scholars and research groups. In the United Kingdom, and also in the United States according to Smith et al. (2013: 912), the study of religion has been concentrated in religious studies departments, often with roots in theological programs and divinity schools. Essentially, scholars with a religious standpoint who differentiated themselves from what they saw as "secular sociology" created American professional organisations and societies for the study of religion. They underwent deconfessionalisation as they became increasingly professionalised (Blasi, 2014: *passim*). However, for Williams and Josephsohn, the subfield remained "an enclave for sociologists personally sympathetic to religion" (2013: 63), in part because most American sociologists did not consider religion a significant object. In the UK, religion caught sociologists' attention relatively late (Banks, 1969: 61). Today's British sociology of religion is organisationally dominated by scholars from religious studies and theology, as indicated by their institutional affiliations. Bruce observes that among those attending and presenting their work at the British Sociological Association Sociology of Religion Study Group, sociologists represent a minority and are clearly outnumbered by theologians and those working in religious studies (Bruce, 2014: 33–34, 2015: 208–209). Publicly funded research on religion has been undertaken in the recent years by scholars in these latter two fields rather than by sociologists, with significant implications for the nature of the knowledge produced and disseminated about religion (Bruce, 2014: 33–34, 2015: 208–209).

By contrast, religious studies does not exist as a subfield in France, arguably explained by the specific French process of separation of church and state. Aiming at reclaiming its authority over higher education, the Third Republic founded a section for the study of religion in *Ecole Pratique des Hautes Etudes* in 1886 to replace the faculty of Catholic theology in the Sorbonne (Lassave, 2014, 2015). However, paradoxically, as they concentrated the scientific study of religion in the *Ecole Pratique*, these distinctive institutional arrangements may have contributed to the isolation of the sociology of religion. Gwendoline Malogne-Fer in this volume underscores that by developing "religious sciences" alongside rather than within humanities and social sciences, the subfield has become prone to "re-confessionalisation." It is also striking that, while

Durkheim's (1971) theory of religion constituted a deliberate break from theology (i.e., through the argument that religion is socially constructed and is about worshipping society), a Durkheimian sociology of religion has not developed in France. It is instead a sociology of Catholicism, led by Gabriel Le Bras (1891–1970), a professor of history of canon law. Le Bras established a sociology of religion research group in 1954 (*Groupe de Sociologie des Religions*), stimulating large, quantitative studies of participation rates amongst the French population (Poulat, 1999: 65). In her chapter, Malogne-Fer explains that setting a group researching religion outside universities meant the sociology of religion did not become a subfield internal to general sociology in France. The implications are substantial: French sociology of religion gives more attention to its object than to approaches and methodologies pertaining to sociology. This might have been reinforced by the fact that many in the first generation of French sociologists of religion were former Catholic clergy. This led Bourdieu, in his address to the French Association for the Sociology of Religion in 1982, to address the ambivalent nature of this subfield of sociology in France. For the most part, as argued by Malogne-Fer, the French sociology of religion is a subfield "continually reinforced by academics who advocate the irreducible distinctiveness of the 'religious' object."

From, and Back to, Religious Sociology

In a nutshell, the sociology of religion has evolved from the emancipation of a religious sociology and reflects the concomitant secularisation of educational and academic institutions. At the same time, however, it struggles to establish itself as a convincing domain of sociological study – at least in the European context, as there is a thriving section on the sociology of religion in the American Sociological Association. Part of our diagnostic is the question of whether this specific trajectory of the subfield is not still affecting it and the ways it approaches its object(s) of study. Thus, it might well be that the transition from religious sociology to sociology of religion is an unfinished process. Or worse yet, we may witness attempts to return to religious sociology, with sacramental, post-secular and Christian sociologies promoted as chances to renew and enhance the sociological study of religion by admitting, one way or another, that religion cannot be fully grasped as a social fact.

   Here, we address this return to religious sociology, for it is perhaps becoming normalised within the contemporary study of religion. Indeed, while this discourse might be more commonly found in the works of theologians, some scholars who identify themselves as sociologists endorse and develop its arguments, including Archer (2004), a prominent social theorist. Our concerns seem substantiated by Smilde and May's analysis of publications within the sociology of religion between 1978 and 2007. They find "clear evidence of the emergence of a 'strong program' in the sociology of religion," that is to say, "a steady increase of research that portrays religion as an independent variable having causal impact, accompanied by a steady decrease of research portraying religion as a dependent variable caused by something else" (Smilde and May, 2010). This "strong program" that plays up the social significance of religion is directed related to "pro-religiousness" (Smilde and May, 2010), leading Williams to comment "religion is good for you" (2008: 3). Ultimately, the renewed celebration of religious sociology needs consideration from sociologists of religion,[3] because the penchant for religious sociology generates serious epistemological difficulties that replicate the early sociology-*for*-religion's flaws and which are underlined by the chapters in this volume.

Let's first consider the arguments supporting a religious sociology, before we discuss their epistemological and social implications for the scientific study of religion. The arguments come from a range of disciplines, from theology to sociology, but they converge along three lines of reasoning. The first relates to the assumption that there is a "secular" sociology, distinct from a religious one. In the second, the former argument's inherent flaw – i.e. secularity – is considered to prevent it from appropriately investigating religion as an object of study. In the final line of reasoning, reintegrating transcendence, the divine or the sacred is believed to correct the flaws of "secular" sociology.

The idea that the sociological study of religion is inherently flawed is explained by Gregory:

> The rejection of confessional commitments in the study of religion in favour of social-scientific or humanistic theories of religion has produced not unbiased accounts, but reductionist explanations of religious belief and practice with embedded secular biases that preclude the understanding of religious believer-practitioners.
>
> GREGORY, 2006: 132

Because it is prejudiced against religious affiliation or belief, the "social scientific" approach does not allow the researcher to grasp people's religious lives. The challengers of the "secular sociology" often refer to the discipline's historical and cultural roots to underscore its ideological bias. With Comte and

---

3   Beckford (2014) developed a critique of Milbank's arguments in the F.D. Maurice unpublished lectures he presented at King's College London (see references).

Durkheim, for instance, sociology developed in a positivistic intellectual environment that celebrated science and reason which, it was believed, would triumph over dark superstition and religion as we continued to progress in the modern era. Marxism added its touch to the critique of religion by presenting it as an ideology that conceals and maintains domination. In other words, references to the founders of sociology are made to underscore the discipline's inherent prejudice against religion, and it is often implied or stated that these features pervade the contemporary sociological study of religion.

Indeed, a common assumption in these works and beyond is that sociologists studying religion are generally atheists. According to Rodney Stark, "Until very recently, *nearly all* social scientists who studied religion did so from antireligious motives and premised their work on atheism – and many still do" (Stark, 2003: 4); emphasis added). As suggested here, this alleged personal standpoint would make such sociologists adverse to their object of study – an obvious hindrance for its understanding. Stark continues, "Even if they abide by the agnostic assumption, social scientists are unlike to grasp the human side of phenomena for which they have no empathy" (5).

Furthermore, sociologists' lack of personal experience of, and empathy for, belief leads them to see religiosity as a "deformation" (Smith, 2012: 166) and, therefore, to pathologise religious life. Their alleged anti-religious standpoint also makes them oblivious to the pervasive and universalistic nature of religion and prone to announce (wrongly) the decline of religion in contemporary Euro-American societies (Gregory, 2006: 132; Keenan, 2003: 27; Varacalli, 1990: 260). By and large, the advocates of a religious sociology envisage this presupposed atheism as a deficiency. For Smith, "those who study 'believers' are often those without this extra-human supplement: they are 'just' human, that is, 'secular'" (2012: 166). Making the unreferenced claim that "a majority of people do report instances of spiritual awareness in various surveys," Archer argues, "Perhaps others have 'turned their heads away,' which is not how 'to develop an ear'" (2004: 73). Archer therefore invites these unsophisticated scholars to start "refining [their] spiritual sensibility" (71).

Another argument centres on the flaws of what is called "secular" sociology, and perhaps this one is the most surprising. By focusing on social and cultural facts, sociology is believed to be unable to understand religion and, more broadly, the human world in its entirety. The implication is that sociology is limited, especially when it aims to study religion, because it does not consider the existence of the divine or the fundamental interactions between human beings and transcendent actors. For Archer, for example, sociology's anthropocentrism and sociocentrism have an "epistemic fallacy" – the fallacy that we can understand the human world by focusing on human subjects and social factors, while dismissing relations with the supernatural and how they affect these subjects (Archer, 2004: 67). Needless to say, we find it surprising that a sociologist states the impossibility for the discipline to produce sound knowledge about the human world because of its stress on the social. We would expect to read such arguments in the writings of theologians, not in those of social theorists. In this regard, Milbank, one of the most vocal critics of the sociology of religion, simply pushes Archer's fallacy argument further by "casting doubt on the very idea of there being something 'social' ... to which religious behaviour could be in any sense referred" (Milbank, 2006: 102). Therefore, and in contrast to theology, "sociology of religion cannot claim to be a true metadiscourse about religion" (Milbank, 2006: 110). In the end, by distinguishing the religious from the social, the theologian and the social theorist seem to agree that sociology cannot scientifically explore religion.

From this reasoning, Archer and other challengers of "secular" sociology infer that religion would be better understood if its scientific study integrated transcendence in one way or another – this transcendence being, more often than not, implicitly conceived in a Christian perspective. Archer, for instance, would like to see sociology adopting the point of view of critical realism for the following reason: "It does not assume that all our relations with reality are socially derived, and therefore it does not rule out the possibility of authentic relations with the divine in advance" (Archer, 2004: 64).

Keenan takes Douglas' analytical definition of sacrament as an assertion of the factual pervading existence of the supernatural, hoping this will "add theoretical value to the sociological ambition to make critical sense of the elementary forms of the moral and social life" (Keenan, 2003: 20–21). Accordingly, by admitting the existence of the divine, a "post-secular" (Johansen, 2013; Smith, 2012), "sacramental," "theological" (Keenan, 2003), or "Christian" sociology (Milbank, 2006: 382) would display a valid and more solid epistemology:

> The methodological agnosticism should be abandoned in favour of, for example, genuine atheism, agnosticism, Christian beliefs or Buddhist cosmologies, as legitimate horizons for the production of knowledge. And the sociologists could, instead of taking for granted that "the social" is the natural framework for our argumentation ... take it on as a priority task to show the work being done in the name of the idea of "social reality" – where it originates and emanates, what purposes it serves – and argue why it should be privileged as the context sine qua non for the academic work.
>
> JOHANSEN, 2013:12

In Response

Such assessments of the sociological study of religion call for a response. Our aim is certainly not to contest the legitimacy of any critical engagement with the subfield and its potential limitations – not least because this is precisely what this volume intends to do. Yet this response is vital because, as we show below, the epistemological difficulties that the authors of this volume underscore in their contributions is implied by this religious sociology. To put it simply, we believe an ambivalent and unreflexive relationship with religion as an object of study and with the religious field is core to the subfield's epistemological weaknesses.

For a start, the critique of the sociology of religion draws on a series of unsubstantiated claims and a relatively superficial knowledge of the subfield it aims to evaluate. As a result, the suggestions made to redress the sociology of religion's alleged secular bias are either obsolete or unspecific about, firstly, how exactly one inserts transcendence into social research and, secondly, what the methodological, theoretical or epistemological benefits of doing so might be. All these observations, in our view, shed light on the highly ideological nature of what pertains to religious rhetoric, not to scientific argumentation. In the next section, we underline the epistemological costs of such a perspective.

The detractors of the "secular" sociology of religion often say sociologists of religion have a secular or anti-religious standpoint. The implicit assumption might be that one has to be an atheist to focus – wrongly – on the social expression of religion. However, there is today no comprehensive sociology of the subfield that would confirm this statement about sociologists of religion's irreligiosity. In fact, the accounts of sociologists of religion's socialisation and relations to their object of studies, in both Anglo-Saxon (Hjelm and Zuckerman, 2013) and European francophone regions (Lambert, Michelat, and Piette, 1997), underscore highly diverse personal and intellectual trajectories. These personal accounts, in addition, do not reflect a dislike of or contempt for religion. Unsurprisingly, as in any other field, sociologists of religion express a deep scientific interest in their object and, more often than not, a strong sense of empathy towards the participants in their research. Ultimately, some critiques seem more prone to dismiss today's sociology of religion for having a "secularist humanist bias" than to provide evidence or examples to establish the existence of such bias. In the works criticising the sociological study of religion, it is hard to find a critical review of contemporary sociological studies that discusses how the conducted research, its theoretical framework, methodology or interpretation of data explains away religion.

For the most part, these works display a superficial and out-dated knowledge of the sociological study of religion; therefore, they lack what is required for an appropriate critical overview. Archer's chapter mentioned above, for instance, despite having its argumentation geared towards sociology's inability to grasp religion, makes no reference to any sociological studies of religion (Archer, 2004). As Beckford notes, the critique of sociology's understanding of religion is often based on hasty generalisations referring to Durkheim's functionalism or Marxism's materialism (Beckford, 2014). When cited, targets are selective, dated, and sometimes misunderstood. Consider, for example, the following piece from Keenan:

> Within the contemporary sociology of religion, the emerging "new paradigm" gives short shrift to tired old reductionist models where religion is explained away in terms of anxiety, fear, psychopathology, deprivation, evil intent, malign contagion, infantilism, cognitive handicap and so on, a litany that those who have gone through the portals and initiation rites of secular social sciences will be familiar with (Bruce, 2000; Stark and Finke, 2000). This movement from the sociology of irreligion and secularity to the sociology of religion and religiosity (Hervieu-Léger, 2000; Lyon, 2000) opens up choices for students of society and culture in which the "theological" option becomes, in some eyes, a plausible hermeneutic.
>
> KEENAN, 2003: 27

We cannot think of any work within the sociology of religion of the past 60 years that would understand religiosity as an abnormality, nor how authors such as Bruce, Stark, and Finke could be associated with such an approach. Moreover, the decision to group these three authors in the sociology of irreligion and secularity, while Lyon and Hervieu-Léger are categorised as sociologists of religiosity, is bewildering. Bruce is openly opposed to rational choice theorists, not least because their theoretical framework leads them to argue secularisation is a self-limiting process that engenders religious revivals and new religious movements, while Bruce could be seen as a "hard line" proponent of the secularisation thesis (Bruce 2000; Stark and Bainbridge, 1985). Keenan also seems to ignore that Hervieu-Léger, while interested in the possibility of religious innovations, has pursued an in-depth analysis of the effects of secularisation on French Catholicism. More largely, Hervieu-Léger's intellectual endeavours have focused on contemporary religion's deregulation and fragmentation (Hervieu-Léger, 1999, 2000, 2001; Hervieu-Léger and Champion, 1986). Finally, while critical yet not totally dismissive, one of Lyon's main publications regards secularisation itself (1987). Overall, these five sociologists of religion describe *both* the growth of irreligiosity and the pluralisation of religious life in contemporary societies.

The lack of knowledge about the sociology of religion is unfortunate because it leads to significant inaccuracies and misunderstandings. In the critique of the "secular" sociology, secularisation, sometimes seen as a normative desire of presumed atheist scholars rather than an analytical framework, is often thought to be the (impossible) death of religion. Those holding this assumption are oblivious to the various social trends described in theories of secularisation – the differentiation of social spheres, rationalisation, or the privatisation of religion which, again, accounts as much for religion's loss of social significance as for religious diversity and innovation in Euro-American societies (Tschannen, 1991). Generally speaking, the common argument that the "secular" sociology of religion is mainly about secularisation does not reflect the review of the publications in the subfield, addressing religious experiences, practices, beliefs, emotions, healing, embodiment, and so forth.

A more thorough knowledge of the contemporary sociology of religion might prevent some advocates of a religious sociology from reinventing the wheel by proposing new turns within the discipline that are, in fact, foundational. Gregory, in his critique of the reductionist theories of religion, seems to believe scholars of religion "impose their own metaphysical convictions" on those they study; he suggests these scholars should instead focus on the question "What did it mean to them?" (Gregory, 2006: 132). Considering the bearing of Weber's comprehensive methodological principle (i.e., a focus on individuals' motives to understand their behaviours) on sociology, it is surprising (and, again, un-evidenced) to have someone presuppose that social scientists do not consider seriously social actors' religious beliefs and ideas. Archer postulates sociology is unable to grasp religion because it would be oblivious to possible relations between human beings and transcendence, but, in fact, there is an ontological approach within the social study of religion (Piette, 2015; Vasquez, 2014) that aims at observing moments of worship in terms of interactions between human beings and divinities, where the presence of divinities is postulated simply in order to understand the situation of worship. Smith tells us this particular sociology has not envisaged religion as both embodied and practiced, nor has it envisaged the existence of secular liturgies (2012: 162). He therefore proposes to "sketch a methodological paradigm for a 'post-secular' sociology that is attuned to worship rather than (just) belief and is thus primed to recognize religion in practice and institutions that we generally consider 'secular'" (Smith, 2012: 162). The focus on texts and doctrines is certainly a feature of theology and religious studies; but in this regard, it contrasts with the sociology and the anthropology of religion which have long developed classical theories of rituals (Turner, 1995; Van Gennep, 2010), or envisaged religion as lived (McGuire, 2008), as material culture (Vasquez, 2010) or as embodied (Mellor and Shilling, 1999; Csordas, 1996), to name a few. On "religion beyond religion," so to speak, Smith might be interested in classical discussions of "invisible religion" (Luckmann, 1967) or "civil religion" (Bellah, 1976).

To finish, consider the proposition by advocates of a post-secular, religious or sacramental sociology that we need to redress the sociology of religion by re-introducing the supernatural. For Archer, "there are certain ways of being-in-the-world that remain incomprehensible without the admission of transcendence" (2004: 80) – and she makes it clear that the understanding of religion as socially constructed precludes this. Yet Archer does not develop her assertion by telling readers what the belief in transcendence would allow us to understand, or how or why. Nor does she seem to recognise that conceptions of transcendence are highly diverse and vary according to historical and cultural contexts. Peter Doak, in this volume, points to Archer's assumption that relations between God and human beings are universal and notes that, in fact, her statement that God is love could not be more socially situated. He furthers his argument by showing that Archer's specific references to concepts and authorities within the religious field reveal, instead of universalism, a clearly Catholic situation of the social theorist. In contrast to Archer, Luckmann argues that the ways transcendences are organised and interpreted depend on social structures, the authority of specific social actors, and social interactions. They are therefore shaped by social, historical and cultural contexts (Luckmann, 1990). What Luckmann also illustrates is that, contrary to what Archer asserts, transcendence can be investigated by social scientists. Such investigations show, one more time, contrary to what is often claimed, reductionism is only one of the many ways in which sociology has addressed transcendence (Garrett, 1974).

To introduce the supernatural into sociology, Johansen contends sociology should embrace Christian or Buddhist cosmologies, for example, as "legitimate horizons for the production of knowledge" (Johansen, 2013: 12), but what that means for social theory or the implications for the design and conduct of research in practice is not addressed. Keenan's "sacramental sociology" would allow its practitioners to "awaken to the hope-filled light that illuminates rules, roles and relationships when perceived in the perspective of sacred history" (Keenan, 2003: 30). But apart from defining social researchers as believers in the supernatural – or comforting those who already are believers – like other critics, Keenan leaves her readers to their own devices to determine the implications for empirical research and social theory. Smith argues for a "normative post-secular methodology," a "more dynamic and nuanced anthropology in order to undergird social scientific study" (Smith, 2012: 164), but this methodological turn falls short after the acknowledgement of the existence of transcendence, as "(t)his might simply require that these disciplines relinquish any Enlightenment claim to unbiased neutrality that is usually associated with the requirement of 'secular' scholarship" (176). In a nutshell, the core proposition of this post-secular sociology, and of religious sociology more generally, is to renounce claims of scientific neutrality and to embrace religious – and more often than not Christian – beliefs as a better way to investigate religion (Archer, 2004: 75; Milbank, 2006: 382). Yet this proposition is devoid of any discussion of how the acceptance of the existence of the divine would benefit or change social research at an epistemological, methodological, theoretical, or analytical level.

Overall, the weaknesses of the argumentation of the advocates of a return to religious sociology all point to the ideological nature of the debate. The celebration of religious, Christian, or post-secular sociologies of a new religious sociology resonates with the ways intellectuals have recently attempted to bridge their religious commitments with academic research. Schmalzbauer's (2003) research on journalism and higher education in the United States describes the ways Catholics and Evangelicals in sociology, history, and political sciences (interestingly, two prominent scholars working on religion, Greeley and Marsden, are case studies for his work) have brought their religious commitments into academic research by rejecting the reductionism of social sciences, in particular, the idea of reality as a social construction. They invoke post-modernism, post-positivism, and multiculturalism to reject the principle of value-free science and to argue for the introduction of religious views in academic approaches prone to blend theology and social theory.

When it comes to the sociology of religion, we could analyse the promotion of a renewed religious sociology as revelatory of a struggle for symbolic power in the intellectual field. This struggle is clear in Milbank's defence of theology as a social science (Milbank, 2006: 382) and his intention to "reassert theology as a master discourse" which, tellingly, he also calls a Christian sociology (6). In the same vein, Keenan's advocacy of a "theological" or "sacramental sociology" seems to respond to his belief that "sociology usurped the throne of theology as queen of the sciences" (Keenan, 2003: 28). Ultimately, we could argue that the enterprise simply comes down to a subversion of sociology as a scientific discipline.

When Sociology becomes Religious: Epistemological Implications

As underscored above, those who are proposing to acknowledge the existence of the supernatural within sociology are hazy when it comes to the practical, methodological implications of conducting research in this perspective, not to mention the exact benefits of such an approach for the sociological study of religion. We, however, think it necessary to ponder on these, not least because such a religious sociology poses some serious epistemological problems – the inspiration and backbone of this volume.

Because "secular sociologists" are said to be prejudiced against religion in such a way that they are unable to understand the beliefs and religious sensibility of others, the advocates of religious sociology suggest that those social scientists with a believer's standpoint necessarily have a better understanding of religion. As we already have pointed out, there is no evidence that sociologists of religion are mainly atheists, and their lack of understanding of their object is simply assumed without any reference to contemporary studies in the subfield. More importantly, it is a fundamental mistake to use one's subjective experience to inform the interpretation of one's data. Such researchers project their own socially-situated experience onto that of their research participants, in short, authenticating their experience by assuming it is similar to that of the people they study. Indeed, by overlooking the ways their cultural background, gender, class, ethnicity, age, and other social factors have shaped their subjective experience, representations, and beliefs, they simply replicate discourses reflecting their own social positioning. For instance, sociologists of de-traditionalisation and individualisation have been criticised for the ways their social theories generalise their personal experience as white, mature, male, and privileged scholars into general explanations of the social world. In other words, a lack of reflexivity about one's own social positioning leads to flawed social theory and analysis.

The advocates of religious sociology vividly illustrate this epistemological flaw by projecting their own religious beliefs into the social study of religion. It is explicit in Milbank's idea of what his "Christian sociology" should aim at: "[It should] tell again the Christian mythos, pronounce again the Christian logos, and call again for Christian praxis in a manner that restores their freshness and originality" (Milbank, 2006: 383). In other words, his sociology is about a normative reassertion of what Christian beliefs and ideas are *in his view*. It speaks to the theologian's appreciation of Christianity, but does not tell us what Christianity might be for, for instance, a priest, a lay Christian, a woman, a Senegalese or Indian Christian, a Pentecostal, a Catholic, or a Presbyterian. Archer suggests that to understand the relations between the divine and the human, our starting point should be "the belief that God is love, the quintessence of unconditional love" (2004: 75). She goes on to claim the universality and timeless nature of "love," ignoring that the deeply culturally rooted notion of "love" in Christian theology does not necessarily coincide with other cultures' and religions' understanding of humans' relation to the divine. She seems blind to the fact that bonds or attachments are conceived differently in different cultural and historical contexts and might not, therefore, correspond to a notion of love whose meaning she takes for granted. In his chapter, Doak suggests Archer is oblivious to the power relations in which she is involved herself: "We can only presume that this authentic relation with (the recognisably Christian understanding of) the divine is superior to inauthentic relations with multiple (or no) gods, which appear to be denied the ontological status of the Christian God in her account." Archer also speculates on what "unbelievers" think: if they stopped doubting God's existence, she says, "they would admit that previously they had invested their loving in something inherently less worthy which failed to satisfy" (Archer, 2004: 76). If Archer presumes "atheist" sociologists do not understand religion, the least we can say is her understanding of individuals who do not believe in God is incredibly unrefined. Unsupported by any research or evidence, it is a normative projection of her own personal religious convictions, generalised as explanations of individuals' behaviours, self, and emotions, leaving in its entirety the question of what others may actually experience.

The knowledge we draw from our subjective experience as social actors is non-reflexive about the ways in which it is partial and socially situated. It is spontaneous, self-evident knowledge – and, as such, it is very powerful. Sociology, in contrast to common sense, aims to "defamiliarize the familiar" (Bauman, 1990: 15). A social science that does not break with this common-sense knowledge is condemned to take for granted the very beliefs and representations it aims to explore. This is why breaking with this common sense is foundational to sociology – Durkheim (1982) made this break with "pre-notions" a pillar of his *Rules of Sociological Method*. Not doing so unavoidably sets limits on the sociological investigation of religion, as explained by Le Bras: "There are sectors that the Catholic forbids himself to explore: those of Revelation. While the myths of archaic peoples are an invention...of the tribe or of the clan, Christian mysteries are dictated by God to Man, who limits himself only to translating it into his language" (quoted in Willaime, 1995: 43). We could easily conclude that religion cannot be fully studied from such a point of view, either because the individual is not ready to investigate what he/she, as a social actor, holds as unquestionable, or because his/her contemptuous positioning hinders the understanding of others' religious lives. Undoubtedly, an insider's knowledge can be valuable, yet scientists gain from their active distancing and detachment from the presuppositions associated with the subjective experiences of those being researched and their awareness of how preconstructions associated with social actors' different positions may relate to one another within fields of power (Wood and Altglas, 2010).

Through its hierarchical approach to Christian and the "tribe's" religious systems of beliefs, Le Bras' statement illustrates that talking from a religious point of view makes scholars prone to unconscious investment in a religion's quest for legitimacy when they are close to this religion and to disqualification when they are distant from it. Bourdieu calls this the *illusio*: "[*Illusio* is] the belief associated with belonging to the religious field..., in other words, the investment in this game, associated with specific interests and profits characteristic to this field and the particular stakes it offers" (Bourdieu, 2010: 3). The *illusio* generates confusion between the emic and etic discourses, that is to say, when the accounts of individuals and collective social actors are conflated with what should be their sociological analysis. Véronique Altglas' chapter underscores that this conflation is found, for example, in academics' assertion that individuals exert absolute freedom of choice in "spirituality," simply because they say so. She argues many scholars have uncritically reiterated social actors' understanding of spirituality by describing an autonomous believer who freely chooses practices and beliefs according to personal desires, free from social norms and constraints. Such scholars neglect the moral imperatives about self-actualisation so pervasively expressed by "spiritual" seekers and leaders; they also ignore the fact that spirituality is thought of, and practiced as, a discipline of the self whereby the latter becomes the locus of conformity to collective values and incentives. Similarly, in his chapter Matthew Wood addresses sociology of religion's tendency to reiterate insiders' understanding of religion through the study of congregational life. Wood notes a tendency to focus on worship and to conceive worship as an individual and subjective activity. This leads sociology to decontextualise worship and to downplay the significance of other important organisational features of congregations, including their social interactions.

Christophe Monnot tackles the epistemological issue of the *illusio* too. He contends that by specialising in the sociology of Catholicism, Islam, or Evangelicalism, for instance (and this is too often the case), scholars of religion accept the ways religious actors define the religious field and become oblivious to the relations *between* these religious actors. And yet these relations are crucial to the understanding of the making of religious cultures: by creating distinctive religious cultures, religious groups and denominations position themselves in relation to each other in the religious field. In other words, delimitations of religious denominations and groups are not to be taken for granted but are to be understood as part of the larger struggles for symbolic capital that structure the religious field. Taking for granted self-definition and categorisation of religious actors leads social scientists to participate in their struggles for symbolic capital. Bourdieu claims this "double play" is particularly noticeable amongst "Catholics who study Catholicism, Protestants who study Protestantism, Jews who study Judaism" (Bourdieu, 2010: 6). Monnot's chapter suggests that the homology between scholars' habitus and the symbolic capital of particular religious groups, if not addressed in a reflexive manner, affects the ways they think about cultural differences between religious denominations, for instance, by considering "the cultural indicators used by the *nobilis* as natural and those used by other religious groups as bizarre or singular," here indicating scholars' positioning in the religious field rather than an actual scientific understanding of this field. In other words, the case studies presented in this volume shed light on the ability of scholars' positioning to affect their understanding of the religious object.[4]

The *illusio* is also at play in the study of religious emotion. Through a review of the ways sociology has addressed the issue, in his chapter Yannick Fer demonstrates that the "categorisation and (dis)qualification" of religious emotions, reflects scholars' position both within the academics and the religious fields. The study of Pentecostalism constitutes a case in point. Pentecostalism has been described as an emotional form of religion that derives from "pure" experience; it is not organised by a system of beliefs in a given institutional context. Pentecostalism's association with "pure," uncontrolled emotions and irrationality is reinforced by the fact that Pentecostal churches initially spread among the poorest social strata and/or within traditional societies. Thus, the understanding of Pentecostalism as an elementary, subjective, and illiterate religion, Fer argues in his chapter, tells us more about scholars' own socialisation and positioning than about the social world they aim to study.

---

4   Neitz (2013) discusses the ways researchers' positioning affects research aims, methodology, and analysis, through a four-cell location matrix, by relating scholars' position to the social significance and legitimacy of the religion they study. We address the question of researchers' standpoint through a Bourdieuian framework: how they might become active players in the struggle for symbolic power within the religious field and the implications for the knowledge hereby produced. We feel this conceptual framework provides a more dynamic, multi-dimensional approach to the relations between researchers and their object and is particularly fruitful for showing the ways these are tied up with epistemological considerations of the *illusio* and reflexivity (Wood and Altglas, 2010). We nevertheless agree with Neitz on the need for more reflexivity within the sociology of religion.

Double Play: Social and Political Implications of the *Illusio*

By and large, detachment is required, because the sociologist's uncritical align-
ment with positions taken by religious actors will inevitably lead him or her
to participate in religious contestations and stakes, whether or not he/she
affirms or denies having a religious identification with those being studied. As
a sociologist, Bourdieu says, one "condemns oneself to play the socially and
psychologically [but not sociologically] profitable double play that allows one
to accumulate the profits of (apparent) scientificity and of religiosity" (Bourdieu, 2010: 6). The "double play" mentioned by Bourdieu concerns researchers
who, for instance, ally their analyses with those produced by people occupy-
ing a particular position within the religious field. This is noticeable in the far
too common tendency to evaluate positively – hence normatively – the contribution of religion to society, also observed by Bender et al. (2013), Smilde
and May (2010), and Williams and Josephsohn (2013), leading to "theoretical
impoverishment" within the studies of religion (Williams and Josephsohn,
2013: 63). This is also what Gwendoline Malogne-Fer in this volume points
out when discussing some of the works of French sociologist of religion Jean-
Paul Willaime. Willaime has often defended religion's positive role, claiming,
for example, that expressions of faith are "a chance for democracy," although
here he refers to Christianity, while making it clear that religious expressions
are not equal (Willaime, 1995). And indeed, it is not possible to be religion's
"caretakers" (McCutcheon, 1997) without participating in the struggles of the
religious field itself.[5] Malogne-Fer's chapter on the ways French sociologists of
religion intervened in the social controversies swirling around the "marriage
for all" bill demonstrates the weaknesses of sociological analyses when they
reiterate the religious field's norms. Here, a normative distinction between
Lutheran-Reformed Protestants and Evangelicals becomes an objective truth
and is used as a means to understand responses to same-sex marriage. Not
only does Malogne-Fer demonstrate that this is an inaccurate analysis, but she

---

5   A more specific example is found in Bourdieu and de Saint Martin's (1982) criticism of the
     ways French sociologist Émile Poulat portrays the diversity of social origins and political
     ideas inside the French Catholic Church as insignificant. For Bourdieu and de Saint Martin,
     who conducted research into the French Catholic Episcopate, Poulat is "totally in accordance
     with the representation the body of clerics has and wants to give of itself," so that his analysis
     functions as an academic version of the Church's official discourse (Bourdieu and de Saint
     Martin, 1982: 40). By contrast, the two sociologists outline the various actors' contrasting so-
     cial trajectories, competition and power, their analysis contrasting sharply with the picture
     of the Catholic Church as a unified body as presented not only by the Church itself to its
     members, but also by Poulat.

also shows such a distinction contributes to legitimate a specific and dominant Protestant organisation, aiming to present itself as moderate, if not progressive, in contrast to Evangelicals, deemed more conservative and expected to remain at the periphery of French Protestantism.

A double play is not sociologically profitable because, as demonstrated by these contributions discussed above, those who take part in a social struggle are tied to a certain unquestioned stance (again, the *illusio*), involving the preconstructions inherent in a field of social action. This is the reason why Bourdieu, in his address to sociologists of religion, demands they make a choice between "whether he [sic] wants to understand the struggles in which religious things are at stake, or to take part in these struggles" (Bourdieu, 2010: 2).[6] In this volume, Eric Morier-Genoud discusses the social effects of concepts informed by theology by examining the concepts of "reverse" and "return mission." Whilst embraced by immigrant Christians to assert the legitimacy of their missionary work, "reverse" and "return mission" are also used by established religious institutions in the North to maintain their dominance over the former and control their religious activities as sources of missionary skills and orthodoxy. Morier-Genoud claims these terms are performative and help maintain unequal power relations between religious organisations in a not so much postcolonial context.

Alix Philippon's chapter on Sufism in Pakistan sheds more light on the implications of normative studies of religion that participate in the struggles of the religious field itself.[7] It illustrates Smith et al.'s statement that "sociologists

---

6   The double play is well illustrated in Regnerus' (2012) study of same-sex parenting in which he argues the children of same-sex couples tend to be less successful in adulthood than others. This understandably elicited responses from critics who underscored that such a conclusion was largely derived from poor methodological choices and flawed sampling methods (Cheng and Powell, 2015: 615). The study was funded by two conservative organisations with ties to specific political causes, including the prohibition of same-sex marriage. One of the reviewers of Regnenus' article had ties with one of these organisations. Unsurprisingly, however flawed this research may be, it has been used by social actors to defend an anti-LGBT agenda in the United States and beyond (Flaherty, 2013; Kolovitch, 2012). Although Regnenus maintains the objectivity of his research, he has testified against same-sex marriage in several legal cases (Regnerus Fall Out, 2013).

7   Another example, Beaman's critique of the "new normal" (i.e., we all have religious or spiritual needs, an idea defended by the advocates of religious sociology), sheds light on the questionable practical and regulative consequences of assumptions about religion's significance and universality, including the following: an essentialized or flat understanding of religious identity categories; an "unnatural" foregrounding of religion; a reinvigoration of a Christian religious "normal"; and a colonizing discourse of religious freedom that acts as a guardian of the universal values embodied by religion (Beaman, 2013: 145).

have ... paid insufficient attention to how the study of religion has itself participated in and authorized the discourses of colonialism and 'Orientalism,'"
and, by doing so, have participated in power relations (Smith et al., 2013: 911).
For example, the polar opposition of "bad" (fundamentalist hence violent) and
"good" (Sufi hence non-violent) Islams has had adverse effects. As Philippon
points out, "The radicalisation process and the recourse to violent modes of
action can take place within movements officially promoted because they are
considered 'Sufi' (i.e., tolerant, peaceful, moderate etc.)."

Conclusion: For a Critical Social Study of Religion

Paul Chambers, an officer of the British Sociological Association's Sociology of
Religion Study Group, writes that the difference between "religious sociology"
and "sociology of religion" is "a distinction that most sociologists of religion
would reject" (Chambers, 2008: 25). That is, in our view, a bewildering claim
made on behalf of social scientists committed to the study of religion. We
claim there is no proper religious sociology, no more than a religious geometry
or a religious thermodynamics.[8] The notion of religious, Christian, or sacramental sociology, as discussed by several authors cited above, is a fundamental
epistemological misunderstanding in the sense that the sociology of religion is
not driven by religious values or standpoints but by scientificity. More importantly, religious sociology is presented by its supporters as a (better) sociology
that will not reduce religion to the social. This is a contradiction in terms, since
sociology, as a discipline, will study religion as part of the social construction
of the reality human beings live in. It is certainly not the only way to investigate
the human world; this is, however, what the discipline of sociology implies.
Therefore, a research that investigates religion and calls itself sociology while
refuting the principle that religion is studied as socially constructed, would be,
in our view, a subversion of sociology itself.

By this, we mean that the ways social actors define or perceive religion (for
example, Archer's claim that "God is love") are the result of historical and
cultural factors. Asad (1993) has underscored the significance of power in the
construction of religious truth, but the relations between religion and power
are actually something the advocates of religious sociology are prone to forget.
In passing, this is illustrated by the role played by religious sociology in Ireland,
where the Catholic Church has shaped many of the country's social policies.

---

8   "If Sociology is a name given to a science, then the expression 'Christian Sociology' is as im-
    proper as would be the title 'Christian Geometry' or 'Christian Thermodynamics'" (Walker,
    cited in Swatos, 1984: 18).

Peter Doak, in this book, evokes Irish "clerical sociologists," serving both the state and the Church, recording modern life's cultural decline and moral corruption, and, hence, making the Catholic Church the solution to all evils. We can only surmise the social and political implications of such a religious sociology in a national context which was so influenced by religious institutions until very recently. By exerting their authority, Asad tells us, specific individual and collective actors have shaped norms, beliefs, and practices throughout the centuries (Asad, 1993). The exertion of power is what gives religious symbolism its strength. Therefore, by asserting what religion is, or is not, academics play a part in the symbolic struggle of religious figures and institutions. And since the meaning of religion is "a continuous process of negotiation, reproduction and challenge," Beckford considers sociologists should instead observe a) the ways the ideas related to religion are used, contested, or legitimised in specific social contexts, and b) how these ideas have concrete effects on practices and behaviours – his research on religion in prison being a case in point (Beckford, 2003: 197, 193).

Furthermore, it is precisely when sociology explains religion outside itself that it makes incommensurable contributions to social theory. Max Weber's *Protestant Ethic and the Spirit of Capitalism* (1904), for instance, shows how a system of belief (here, Calvinism's asceticism) can affect attitudes and behaviours outside the realm of religious practices and beliefs themselves, such as work ethics or a quest for profits. Weber was obviously interested in religion, but only insofar as it represented a lens through which he could view the development of capitalism and, beyond that, the rationalisation process characterising Euro-American societies. This is by no means a sociology *for* religion. Similarly, Emile Durkheim (1971) explored religion as a way to sociologically understand cohesion and solidarity: religion is seen as a system of beliefs and practices whose social role is to bind individuals together. Religious rituals are thus understood as a way to worship society. In a nutshell, classical sociology investigated religion not for itself or within itself, but always in relation to other spheres of human life and for an understanding of other social processes – economic behaviours or social cohesion for Weber and Durkheim who, respectively, integrated the study of religion into theories of social change and modernity. This is probably what inspires Robertson to say: 'It is not the sociologist of religion per se but rather the sociologist treating religion as part of a larger set of problems who may well be seen as most relevant to the discipline as a whole' (Robertson, 1985: 358).

We believe, however, that a solid sociology of religion is possible, if it distances itself from the religious field's game and associated beliefs. The sociology of religion would gain significance and widen its scope by using its object as a means to understand the social world at large. This entails reintegrating the social – power and authority, social classes, ethnicity, embodiment and emotions, interactions and practices – into the study of religion. Re-inserting the concept of the social into the heart of its enquiries requires the sociology of religion to engage directly and consistently with debates within social theory and other sociological subfields, rather than being diverted to non-sociological ones in religious studies or theology. It also requires paying attention to epistemological issues that mark out what counts as social science and what does not, especially in terms of making a break from pre-notions, pursuing scientific reflexivity, and rejecting a normative agenda. Consequently, it means controlling interdisciplinarity so it is limited to those approaches that are social scientific – specifically, a convergence of sociology, social anthropology, and history is required, as seen in approaches a century ago. Indeed, many working in these disciplines view the boundaries between them as marked by distinctions between research methods rather than epistemologies.

Ultimately, we cannot stress enough the importance of reflexivity for a *critical* sociology of religion. Reflexivity is necessary as a deliberate rupture, both with the subjective presuppositions taken for granted by those being studied and with the researcher's scholarly presuppositions, to allow sociology to reach scientificity.[9] It entails thinking about the conditions in which we produce sociological knowledge and how this knowledge is affected by these conditions; otherwise, we may simply produce a knowledge serving the interests of certain social groups and institutions. One of the most critical tasks of sociology, Bourdieu tells us, is to reveal and analyse the instrumental uses of scientific knowledge (2013). The promotion of a religious sociology might well be one of them.

References

Archer, Margaret. 2004. "Models of man: the admission of transcendence." In *Transcendence: critical realism and God*, edited by Margaret Archer, Andrew Collier, and Douglas V. Porpora, 63–81. London: Routledge.

---

9   Interestingly, in the collective book *Le religieux des Sociologues*, French-speaking sociologists of religion evoke their choices of objects of study, their methodological choices, and their intellectual itinerary but rarely touch on how their biographical trajectories may have affected their research. This is stressed in the chapters of two discussants, Bréchon (1997: 245) and Tschannen (1997: 242, 244), the latter noting that a sociology of the sociology of religion in France is missing. Their Anglo-Saxon counterparts (Hjelm and Zuckerman, 2013), with some exceptions, are relatively similar in this regard. While the authors were asked to reflect on how their religious socialisation (or lack of) may have influenced their approach of religion as a sociological object, few of those featured in the volume address the issue.

Asad, Talal. 1993. *Genealogies of religion*. Baltimore: Johns Hopkins University Press.

Banks, Joe. 1969. "The sociology of religion in England." In *Readings in the sociology of religion*, edited by Joan Brothers, 61–68. Oxford; London: Perhamon Press.

Bauman, Zygmunt. 1990. *Thinking sociologically*. Oxford: Blackwell.

Beaman, Lori G. 2013. "The will to religion: obligatory religious citizenship," *Critical Research on Religion* 1: 141–157.

Beckford, James A. 2014. "Religion and sociology: a marriage made in heaven or hell?" F.D. Maurice unpublished lectures given at King's College London, 18–20 March, accessed 27 May 2016 from http://www2.warwick.ac.uk/fac/soc/sociology/staff/beckford/jimbeckforfhomepage/.

Beckford, James A. 2003. *Social theory and religion*. Cambridge: Cambridge University Press.

Beckford, James A. 1989. *Religion and advanced industrial society*. London: Routledge.

Bellah, Robert. 1976. "Civil religion in America," *Daedalus* 96: 1–21.

Bender, Courtney, Wendy Cadge, Peggy Levitt, and David Smilde, eds. 2013. *Religion on the edge: de-centering and re-centering the sociology of religion*, New York: Oxford University Press, Routledge.

Blasi, Anthony J. 2014. *Sociology of religion in America: a history of secular fascination with religion*. Leiden: Brill.

Bosetti, Giancarrio, and Klaus Eder. 2006. "Post-secularism: a return to the public sphere," *Eurozine* 17 August, accessed 1 April 2016 from http://www.eurozine.com/articles/2006-08-17-eder-en.html.

Bourdieu, Pierre. 2013. "In praise of sociology: acceptance speech for the gold medal of the CNRS," *Sociology* 47(1): 7–14.

Bourdieu, Pierre. (1987) 2010. "Sociologists of belief and beliefs of sociologists," *Nordic Journal of Religion and Society* 23(1): 1–7.

Bourdieu, Pierre, and Monique de Saint Martin. 1982. "La sainte famille: l'épiscopat Français dans le champ du pouvoir," *Actes de la Recherche en Sciences Sociales* 44(1): 2–53.

Brasher, Brenda. 1998. *Godly women: fundamentalism and female power*. New Jersey: Routledge.

Bréchon, Pierre. 1997. "Variations conclusives: de l'itinéraire à la pratique." In *Le Religieux des sociologues : trajectoires personnelles et débats scientifiques*, edited by Yves Lambert, Guy Michelat and Albert Piette, 245–254. Paris: L'harmattan.

Brothers, Joan B. 1964. "Recent developments in the sociology of religion in England and Wales," *Social Compass* 11(3–4): 13–19.

Bruce, Steve. 2015. "A British perspective on the critical sociology of religion: a response to Mary Jo Neitz," *Critical Research on Religion* 3(2): 206–216.

Bruce, Steve. 2014. "What sort of social theory would benefit the sociology of religion?" In *Sociological theory and the question of religion*, edited by Andrew McKinnon and Marta Trzebiatowska, 38–48. Aldershot: Ashgate.

Bruce, Steve. 2000. *Choice and religion: a critique of rational choice theory*. Oxford: Oxford University Press.

Cadge, Wendy, Peggy Levitt, and David Smilde. 2011. "De-centering and re-centering: rethinking concepts and methods in the sociological study of religion," *Journal for the Scientific Study of Religion* 50(3): 437–449.

Chambers, Paul. 2008. "Sociology of religion study group conference: religion and youth," *Network: Newsletter of the British Sociological Association* (Autumn): 25–26.

Cheng, Simon, and Brian Powell. 2015. "Measurement, methods, and divergent patterns: reassessing the effects of same-sex parents," *Social Science Research* 52 (July): 615–626.

Conway, Brian. 2011. "Catholic sociology in Ireland in Comparative Perspective," *The American Sociologist* 42: 34–55.

Csordas, Thomas J. 1996. *The sacred self: a cultural phenomenology of charismatic healing*. Berkeley: University of California Press.

Davie, Grace. 2007. *The sociology of religion*. Los Angeles; London: Sage.

Dobbelaere, Karel. 2000. "From religious sociology to sociology of religion: towards globalisation?" *Journal for the Scientific Study of Religion* 39(4): 433–447.

Dobbelaere, Karel. 1999. "CISR, an alternative approach to sociology of religion in Europe: ACSS and CISR compared." In *Sociologie et religions: des relations ambiguës / sociology and religions: an ambiguous relationship*, edited by Liliane Voyé and Jaak Billiet, 79–89. Leuven: Leuven University Press.

Durkheim, Émile. 1982. *The rules of sociological method and selected texts on sociology and its method*. London: Macmillan.

Durkheim, Émile. 1971. *The elementary forms of the religious life*. London: Allen and Unwin.

Flaherty, Colleen. 2013. "Controversy continues over gay parenting study," *Inside Higher Education*, August 2, accessed 28 June 2016 from https://www.insidehighered.com/quicktakes/2013/08/02/controversy-continues-over-gay-parenting-study.

Garrett, William R. 1974. "Troublesome transcendence: the supernatural in the scientific study of religion," *Sociological Analysis* 35(3): 167–180.

Gauthier, François, and Tuomas Martikainen. 2013. *Religion in consumer society*. Aldershot: Ashgate.

Goldstein, Warren S. 2009. "The case for a critical sociology of religion." In *Crisis, Politics and Critical Sociology*, edited by Graham Cassano and Richard Dello Buono, 135–142. Leiden: Brill.

Gregory, Brad S. 2006. "The other confessional history: on secular bias in the study of religion," *History and Theory* 45(4): 132–149.

Griffith, R. Marie. 1997. *God's daughters: evangelical women and the power of submission*. Berkeley: University of California Press.

Heelas, Paul. 2008. *Spiritualities of life: new age romanticism and consumptive capitalism.* Oxford: Blackwell.

Heelas, Paul, and Linda Woodhead. 2005. *The spiritual revolution: why religion is giving way to spirituality.* London: Blackwell.

Hervieu-Léger, Danièle. 2001. *La religion en miettes ou la question des sects.* Paris: Calmann-Lévy.

Hervieu-Léger, Danièle. 2000. *Religion as a chain of memory.* Cambridge: Polity Press.

Hervieu-Léger, Danièle. 1999. *Le pèlerin et le converti.* Paris: Flammarion.

Hervieu-Léger, Danièle. 1997. "De l'utopie à la tradition: retour sur une trajectoire de recherché." In *Le religieux des sociologues: trajectoires personnelles et débats scientifiques,* edited by Yves Lambert, Guy Michelat, and Albert Piette, 21–32. Paris: L'Harmattan.

Hervieu-Léger, Danièle, and Françoise Champion. 1986. *Vers un nouveau christianisme?* Paris: Les éditions du Cerf.

Hjelm, Titus, and Phil Zuckerman, eds. 2013. *Studying religion and society: sociological self-portraits.* New York: Routledge.

Johansen, Birgitte S. 2013. "Post-secular sociology: modes, possibilities and challenges," *Approaching Religion* 3(1): 4–15.

Josephsohn, Thomas J., and Rhys H. Williams. 2013. "Possibilities in the critical sociology of religion," *Critical Research on Religion* 1(2): 123–128.

Kapferer, Bruce. 2005. "Introduction: the social construction of reductionist thought and practice." In *The retreat of the social: the rise and rise of reductionism,* by Bruce Kapferer, 1–18. Oxford: Berghahn Books.

Keenan, William J.F. 2003. "Rediscovering the theological in sociology: foundation and possibilities," *Theory, Culture & Society* 20(1): 19–41.

Kolowich, Steve. 2012. "Is the research all right?" *Inside Higher Education,* 13 July, accessed 28 June 2016 from https://www.insidehighered.com/news/2012/07/13/ut -austin-scrutinizes-ethics-controversial-same-sex-parenting-study.

Lambert, Yves, Guy Michelat, and Albert Piette, eds. 1997. *Le religieux des sociologues: trajectoires personnelles et débats scientifiques.* Paris: l'Harmattan.

Lassave, Pierre. 2015. "France: re-founding the sociology of religion." In *Sociologies of religion: national traditions,* edited by Giuseppe Giordan, and Anthony J. Blasi, 232–267. Leiden: Brill.

Lassave, Pierre. 2014. "Les sociologues des religions et leur objet," *Sociologie* 5(2), accessed 1 April 2016 from http://sociologie.revues.org/2175.

Luckmann, Thomas. 1990. "Shrinking transcendence, expanding religion?" *Sociological Analysis* 50: 127–138.

Luckmann, Thomas. 1967. *The invisible religion.* New York: Macmillan.

Lyon, David. 2000. *Jesus in Disneyland: Religion in Postmodern Times.* Cambridge: Polity Press in association with Blackwell Publishers Ltd.

Lyon, David. 1987. *The steeple's shadow: on the myths and realities of secularization.* Grand Rapids: Eerdmans Publishing Company.

Mahmood, Saba. 2005. *Politics of piety: the Islamic revival and the feminist subject.* Princeton: Princeton University Press.

Martin, David. 1999. "Sociology and the Church of England." In *Sociologie et religions: des relations ambiguës / sociology and religions: an ambiguous relationship,* edited by Liliane Voyé and Jaak Billiet, 131–138. Leuven: Leuven University Press.

Maskens, Maité. 2009. "Identités sexuelles pentecôtistes: féminités et masculinités dans les assemblées bruxelloises," *Autrepart* 49: 65–82.

McCutcheon, Russell T. 1997. "A default of critical intelligence? The scholar of religion as public intellectual," *Journal of the American Academy of Religion* 65(2): 443–468.

McGuire, Meredith. 2008. *Lived religion: faith and practice in everyday life.* New York: Oxford University Press.

McKinnon, Andrew, and Marta Trzebiatowska. 2014. "Introduction: thinking theoretically in the sociology of religion." In *Sociological theory and the question of religion,* by Andrew McKinnon and Marta Trzebiatowska, 1–14. Farnham: Ashgate.

Mellor, Philip, and Chris Shilling. 1999. *Re-forming the body: religion, community, modernity.* London: Sage.

Milbank, John. 2006. *Theology and social theory: beyond secular reason,* 2nd ed. Malden; Oxford: Blackwell.

Neitz, Mary Jo. 2013. "Insiders, outsiders, advocates and apostates and the religions they study: Location and the sociology of religion," *Critical Research on Religion* 1(2): pp. 129–140.

Neveu, Erik. 2001. *Une société de communication?* Paris: Montchrétien.

Piette, Albert. 2005. "God and the Anthropologist. The Ontological Turn and Human-Oriented Anthropology," *Tsantsa* 20: 34–44.

Poulat, Emile. 1999. "La CISR de la fondation à la mutation." In *Sociologie et religions: des relations ambiguës / sociology and religions: an ambiguous relationship,* edited by Liliane Voyé and Jaak Billiet, 57–78. Leuven: Leuven University Press.

Regnerus, Mark. 2012. "How different are the adult children of parents who have same-sex relationships? Findings from the New Family Structures Study," *Social Science Research* 41(4): 752–770.

Regnerus Fall Out. 2013. "The story," accessed 28 June 2016 from http://www.regnerus fallout.org/the-story.

Robertson, Roland. 1985. "Beyond the Sociology of Religion?" *Sociology of Religion* 355–360.

Robertson, Roland. 1994. "Religion and the global field," *Social Compass* 4(1): 121–135.

Schmalzbauer, John. 2003. *People of faith: religious convictions in American journalism and higher education.* Ithaca: Cornell University Press.

Smilde, David, and Matthew May. 2010. "The emerging strong program in the sociology of religion," Social Science Research Council, accessed 8 December 2017 from https://tif.ssrc.org/2010/02/08/the-emerging-strong-program-in-the-sociology-of-religion/.

Smith, Christian. 2010. *What is a person? Rethinking humanity, social life, and moral good from the person up.* Chicago: University of Chicago Press.

Smith, Christian, Brandon Vaidyanathan, Nancy Tatom Ammerman, and Meredith Whitnaw. 2013. "Roundtable on the sociology of religion: twenty-three theses on the status of religion in American sociology – a Mellon working-group reflection," *Journal of the American Academy of Religion* 8(4): 903–938.

Smith, James K.A. 2012. "Secular liturgies and the prospects for a 'post-secular' sociology of religion." In *The post-secular in question: religion in contemporary society,* edited by Philip S. Gorski, David Kyuman Kim, John Torpey, and Jonathan Van Antwerpen, 159–184. New York: New York University Press.

Stark, Rodney. 2003. *One true god: historical consequences of monotheism.* Princeton: Princeton University Press.

Stark, Rodney, and William S. Bainbridge. 1987. *Theory of religion.* Bern: Lang.

Stark, Rodney, and William S. Bainbridge. 1985. *The future of religion: secularization, revival and cult formation.* Berkeley: University of California Press.

Stark, Rodney and Roger Finke. 2000. *Acts of Faith: Explaining the Human Side of Religion.* Berkeley, CA: University of California Press.

Swatos, William H. 1984. *Faith of the fathers: science, religion and reform in the development of early American sociology.* Bristol: Windham Hall Press.

Tschannen, Olivier. 1991. "The secularization paradigm: a systematization," *Journal of Scientific Study of Religion* 30(4): p. 395–415.

Tschannen, Olivier. 1997. "Constructions sociales et sociologiques du religieux : état des lieux d'une discipline en mutation." In *Le Religieux des sociologues : trajectoires personnelles et débats scientifiques,* edited by Yves Lambert, Guy Michelat and Albert Piette, 239–244. Paris: L'harmattan.

Turner, Brian S. 1991. *Religion and social theory,* London: Sage.

Turner, Victor. 1995. *The ritual process: structure and anti-structure.* New York: Aldine de Gruyter.

Van Gennep, Arnold. 2010. *The rites of passage.* London: Routledge.

Varacalli, Joseph A. 1990. "Catholic sociology in America: a comment on the fiftieth anniversary issue of 'Sociological Analysis,'" *International Journal of Politics, Culture, and Society* 4(2): 249–262.

Vasquez, Manuel A. 2014. "The crisis of sociological representation: toward an ecological sociology of religious efficacy," BSA Sociology of Religion Study Group Annual Conference, 2–4 July, Bristol.

Vasquez, Manuel A. 2010. *More than belief: a materialist theory of religion.* Oxford; New York: Oxford University Press.

Voas, David, and Alasdair Crockett. 2005. "Religion in Britain: neither believing nor belonging," *Sociology* 39: 11–28.

Voyé, Liliane, and Jaak Billiet. 1999. "Introduction: sociology and religions: patterns of encounter." In *Sociologie et religions: des relations ambiguës / sociology and religions: an ambiguous relationship*, edited by Liliane Voyé and Jaak Billiet, 9–22. Leuven: Leuven University Press.

Weber, Max. (1904) 1992. *The protestant ethic and the spirit of capitalism*. London: Routledge.

Willaime, Jean-Paul. 1995. *Sociologie des religions*. Paris: Presses Universitaires de France.

Williams, Rhys H. 2008. "From the editor," *Journal for the Scientific Study of Religion* 47: 1–4.

Williams, Rhys H., and Thomas J. Josephsohn. 2013. "North American sociology of religion: critique and prospects," *Critical Research on Religion* 1(1): 62–71.

Wood, Matthew. 2014. "Lessons from *The Wire*: epistemological reflections on the practice of sociological research," *Sociological Review*, 62: 742–759.

Wood, Matthew. 2009. "The nonformative elements of religious life: questioning the 'sociology of spirituality' paradigm," *Social Compass* 56 (2): 237–248.

Wood, Matthew, and Véronique Altglas. 2010. "Reflexivity, scientificity and the sociology of religion: Pierre Bourdieu in debate," *Nordic Journal of Religion and Society* 23(1): 9–26.

Wouters, Cas. 2007. *Informalization: manners and emotions since 1890*. London: Sage.

CHAPTER 1

Protestant Churches and Same-Sex Marriage in France: "Theological" Criteria and Sociological Approaches

Gwendoline Malogne-Fer

Introduction

The reflection presented here was born from my personal questions about the academic study of religion, including the place of non-believer scientists in the field of the French sociology of religion and the potential influence of researchers' religious beliefs and belonging on sociological analyses. My own research on Polynesian Protestantism questions the relevance of the classical academic boundary between sociology and anthropology. The *grand partage* of the earth into distinct "cultural areas" (Lenclud, 1992) still prompts researchers studying non-western societies to adopt an anthropological approach. Anthropology has historically focused on non-Christian religions, with Christianity assigned to sociology, at least until the more recent development of an anthropology of Christianity (Coleman and Hackett, 2015; Robbins, 2004). Yet for me and for many other researchers of my generation who received no religious education, Protestantism is as "exotic" as a non-Christian religion.

The advice given me by my first thesis supervisor, an anthropologist, was to "look beneath the Christian varnish" to discover the true Polynesian culture and beliefs; to me this was difficult to apply, as it implied a "true Christianity" with which I lacked familiarity. In addition, such an unveiling would be difficult in Tahiti and its neighbouring islands, as Christianity has been present since the end of the 18th century. I turned to the sociology of religion, but ended up facing new difficulties related to the eurocentric nature of many paradigmatic concepts that have contributed to the distinctive identity of this discipline in France since the 1960–70s, notably, the theory of secularisation and the concept of religious modernity and its various reformulations, such as ultra-modernity, advanced modernity, or late modernity (for a critical analysis, see Obadia, 2014). I also had methodological and epistemological issues with the use of concepts with Christian origins, which can be understood in both a secular and a religious sense and owe part of their success to their polysemy.

My argument here is that the sociology of religion in France is not simply a branch of sociology, but a discipline whose specificity is continually reinforced by academics who advocate the irreducible distinctiveness of the "religious" object. Even if the diversity of theoretical approaches represents an intellectual richness conducive to debate, the risk is that the alleged specificity of the religious object ultimately means that an irreducible part of religion will always elude the scope of sociological analysis.

This chapter draws on the confrontational debates triggered in 2012–2013 by the "marriage for all" bill (same-sex marriage) and considers the way these debates were analysed from a Protestant and a sociological point of view. The debates revealed tensions within French society, as well as within the sociology of religion, more specifically, the sociology of Christianity. Although I focus on two articles by Jean-Paul Willaime, the following reflection should not be read as a critique of the work of this eminent sociologist of Protestantism; in fact, his insights furthered my own doctoral research on women's accession to the pastorate and the professionalisation of this ministry. Rather, my objective is to draw on a case I previously studied[1] to highlight the divergent approaches coexisting in the sociology of religion.

To understand what was at stake in the debate on same-sex marriage and the commitments of actors in both academic and religious fields, we need to review the chronology of events and the stances of the various Christian churches on the issue. The notion of "field" elaborated by Bourdieu is particularly relevant to understand the relationships of power and the strategies involved in the positions adopted by religious, political, and academic actors (Obadia, 2014: 299–300; also Bourdieu, 1971).

The debate on the "marriage for all" bill highlighted a convergence of views on this kind of issue by Protestant and Catholic churches. At the beginning of the 2000s, Willaime noted the significant convergence of Protestants and Catholics in matters of sexual ethics (Willaime, 2002) during the debate on same-sex civil union (civil solidarity pact, PACS). This convergence contrasted sharply with the context of the 1970s, when Catholic and Protestant churches showed strong divergences. There were also clear divergences at the time within the various Protestant faiths: the Lutheran-Reformed churches, dominant in the French Protestant Federation, argued in favour of contraception, decriminalisation of abortion, and recognition of divorce, while Evangelicals

---

1 In a presentation with V. Aubourg at the Congress of the French Sociology Association (2013) and in a recent publication (Malogne-Fer, 2017), I explained the use of social sciences by Catholic and Protestant churches in the debate on same-sex marriage.

were more conservative. Despite the more recent move towards convergence, many in religious and academic fields still see this as an unbridgeable gap.

This chapter explains the evolution of Protestant churches' positions on same-sex marriage and seeks to shed light on the convergence of views, on the one hand, between Catholic and Protestant churches and, on the other hand, between the different Protestant streams. It questions the relevance of a strict distinction between Lutheran-Reformed Protestants and Evangelicals as a sociological key to analysing Protestant attitudes towards same-sex marriage. It shows why intra-Protestant "theological" criteria do not provide a sufficient sociological explanation: there is a risk of reproducing theological criteria as they are elaborated in the Protestant field without examining the social and institutional stakes of these distinctions. Finally, the chapter turns to a controversy between two major sociologists of religion during the debate on same-sex marriage to illustrate the tensions generated by an incomplete process of secularisation of the sociology of religion in France.

Protestant Stances on the "Marriage for All" Bill

French Protestant churches have two different federations. The French Protestant Federation (FPF), established in 1905, includes churches from all denominational backgrounds, but its leaders are mainly Reformed and Lutheran ministers. Its mission is to represent French Protestantism and Protestant actors to state authorities. Since 2010, the FPF has faced competition from the *Conseil National des Évangéliques de France* (CNEF), which has a doctrinal basis and attracts approximately 70 percent of Evangelicals in France.[2] Both federations took stances on the bill; even though their arguments differed, their official statements show both federations – as well as numerous Protestant churches – were against same-sex marriage.

On 13 September 2012, the CNEF and the Assemblies of God (the main Pentecostal denomination within the CNEF) released two quite different statements on same-sex marriage. The CNEF's statement begins with a reminder that its position rests on biblical ethics but goes on to make a different type of argument: it notes the need for a large and democratic debate and cites the difference between men and women which "has always been a fundamental fact of anthropology," with marriage considered a "foundation that structures society." Not least, it is in the best interests of the child to be brought up by

---

2   The distinction between these federations is less clear at the church level, as nine church unions are simultaneously affiliated with both.

a father and a mother (CNEF, 2012). In contrast, the Assemblies of God formulate their arguments in biblical terms:

> The biological difference between men and women has existed since
> creation. Male and female sexual identities are the timeless foundation
> of the couple, which makes marriage, procreation and family possible....
> By their doctrine, the Assemblies of God remain strongly committed to
> respect for ethical biblical values, as expressed in the first point of their
> theology, where the Bible is presented as the unerring rule of faith and
> behaviour for the assembly, as well as for each Christian.[3] (addfrance.org/
> communique-de-presse.html)

Pastor Thierry Le Gall, in charge of the communications of both the Assemblies of God and the CNEF, differentiates the statements as follows:

> The Assemblies' statement is a little bit timeless and outside society, to
> say: this is what we believe and will always believe; the discourse is more
> spiritual, and that's what we wanted to emphasise. The CNEF discourse is
> societal; it's a stance taken within the society.
>
>   Interview, PASTOR THIERRY LE GALL, 28 August 2013, côtes-d'armor

The CNEF's argumentation strives to appropriate a "discourse under constraints" (Fassin, 2001) and borrows expressions from the vocabulary of the
social sciences to gain political legitimacy. Le Gall explains:

> When we started thinking about this statement, the specification was
> to translate Evangelical thought in terms acceptable by civil society. It
> was made for media first, then for political leaders and also for Evangeli-
> cals; this can explain its form and its low profile.... And this statement
> has been a gateway for us, to be heard and received in the institutional
> spheres.... Even if this statement was not perfect, it brought us visibility
> for the first time; ... it enabled us to be heard in Parliamentary settings,
> to express our position and get better identified as an established body
> that has something to say and represents about 600,000 voters today in
> France.
>
>   Interview, PASTOR THIERRY LE GALL, 28 August 2013, côtes-d'armor

Opinions on same-sex marriage are usually diverse amongst the Lutheran-
Reformed churches and the leaders of the FPF, but public stances do not

---

3   Unless otherwise indicated, the translations are my own.

reflect this diversity. On 27 August 2012, Laurent Schlumberger, President of the French Reformed Church, said in internal correspondence that a process of collective reflection was still going on within the church. Therefore, he asked those ministers supporting the blessing of same-sex couples to remain silent until the conclusions of the working group led by theologian Isabelle Grellier were released.[4] In September 2012, a pastor working at the FPF head offices explained to colleagues that the FPF would not take any official stance on the issue; the diversity of opinion amongst churches within the FPF was too strong to reach a common position. But on 2 October 2012, Claude Baty, President of the FPF, declared to *Le Monde* that his federation opposed the government's project, not for theological reasons, but for anthropological ones: "'Marriage for all' suggests a false equality. Heterosexual and homosexual couples, this is not the same thing."[5]

Ten days later, on 13 October 2012, the council of the FPF endorsed the position of its President in a new statement:

> It is not a question of putting homosexuality and same-sex marriage at the core of theological debates; the issue is fundamentally social and collective. It's about the way a society perceives and builds itself, and the symbols that structure the field of its identity. In this perspective, we need to say clearly that distinctions made between homosexuality and heterosexuality don't reflect an outdated moralism, but rather a deeply-felt need of the society. Society requires to be structured, both symbolically and concretely, by the representation and the acceptance of an original and fundamental difference that shapes our deepest interiority, in bodies and ways of being.... Marriage is not a celebration of love, a display of feelings, but rather a social organisation that contributes to structure relations by symbolising the difference between generations, sexes, between marriageable and non-marriageable people.... The FPF thinks that the current project of "marriage for all" brings confusion into the social symbolical order and doesn't help structuring families. This is not a question of morality but of anthropology and symbol.
>
> FPF, 2012

---

4 Addressed to the presidents of local church councils, it said: "The Church is not committed to the blessing of same-sex couples.... A reflection is still going on. If choices should be made and the position of the Church should evolve, this would be as a last resort the prerogative of the national synod to take such decision."

5 http://religion.blog.lemonde.fr/2012/10/02/le-gouvernement-ne-veut-pas-de-debat-sur-le-mariage-pour-tous.

The statement had not been subject to long discussions. In fact, it borrows most of its arguments from a text on homosexuality entitled "A few elements to reflect on homosexuality," published by the ethical commission of the FPF in 1994. This suggests that for the FPF, the terms of the debate on same-sex marriage had not significantly changed over 20 years. Its reflections remained strongly influenced by the national context and did not mention the positions adopted by the Protestant churches of Northern Europe in favour of same-sex marriage or the blessing of same-sex couples (in Denmark, the Netherlands, Norway, and Sweden). Rather, the FPF appropriated the so-called "anthropological" arguments developed by the Catholic Church.

Reasons for Using "Anthropological" rather than "Biblical" Arguments

How can we explain the disappearance of all or part of the biblical arguments and the emphasis placed on allegedly "anthropological" arguments? What kind of resources were selected from the social sciences to support the Protestant stances on same-sex marriage?

Euphemising biblical arguments while emphasising "anthropological" ones can be understood as a way to comply with the constraints of political commitment in a secular state and as a strategy to legitimate the churches' participation in the public debate, in a partly de-Christianised French society. Thus, for Catholic and Protestant institutions, the use of non-biblical arguments allowed a kind of generalisation facilitating the mobilisation of a larger circle than committed Christians, so that they did not appear simply as groups defending specific interests and convictions. This non-confessional vocabulary also enabled individuals to be recognised not only as church members but also as concerned citizens engaged in major social debates.

Fassin remarks that the "anthropology" to which religious actors referred during the debate on civil union was quite different from the academic discipline, because it aimed to re-establish a transcendent truth:

> In fact, anthropology is requested to say simply but with authority that there are men and women – the order of heterosexuality, based on the order of gender differences.... This is what speaking about an anthropological transcendence means: just as religion could once stand above politics, today in a "democratic and secular" society, some people would like to place anthropology above politics.
>
> FASSIN, 2001: 96

The mobilisation of these "anthropological" arguments was part of an adjustment of religious convictions to the social context. To speak with legitimacy, religious authorities needed to elaborate a discourse that took into account, on the one hand, the legal prohibition of homophobic language (Fassin, 2001), and, on the other hand, the French regime of *laïcité*, not to mention a double process of diversification and individualisation of moral norms.

The Catholic Church had been working on developing such a discourse since the 1970s and updated it in the 1990–2000s during the debate on civil union. In her study of Catholic opposition to the "theory of gender" – initiated by the Vatican in 1995 and appropriated by the French episcopate in 2005 – Beraud shows how the Catholic hierarchy turned to "human sciences, and particularly to psychoanalysis and law, in a quest of invariants, of universal and intangible norms" (Beraud, 2011: 234–235). An interdisciplinary working group, made up mostly of lay peoples, was established:

> The request was explicit. "Today, how does one say that homosexuality is a tragedy?" wondered Cardinal Philippe Barbarin, Archbishop of Lyon. "Bring us some "biscuits" [good arguments] on this," he said to Jacques Arènes, a Catholic lay person and psychoanalyst. The program was clearly stated: "We have to highlight a discourse on differences as a component of human being and self-realisation through a vocabulary drawn from anthropology and human sciences, which is the most acceptable today."
>
> BERAUD, 2011: 234–235

In other words, the use of psychoanalysis and anthropology was officially promoted as part of a strategy to dress up an unchanged Catholic doctrine in new rhetorical clothes.

Protestant actors drew on this rhetoric for purposes of intra-Protestant competition and distinction. The stance of the FPF underlines the influence of this Catholic discourse and the effect of the reshaping of the Protestant institutional field – especially with the creation of the CNEF – on the federation. Interestingly, the FPF's position against same-sex marriage does not reflect its internal diversity and is actually quite similar to the CNEF's position. The use of "anthropological" arguments was intended to distance the FPF from Evangelicals and their biblical arguments. But these "anthropological" arguments do not draw on any anthropological or sociological work; the anthropology mentioned by the FPF is not an academic discipline but a concept referring, in a normative and non-descriptive way, to human beings as a whole.

The working file "Church and Homosexuality" (subtitled "Symbolic significance of publicly established things") issued by the Lutheran-Reformed

Communion in 2002, to which the FPF still refers today, proposes three kinds of approaches to the issue of same-sex marriage: a biblical approach, a psychoanalytical approach, and a psycho-sociological approach. The authors from the human and social sciences mentioned in the document are Freud, Lacan, theologian and Pastor Jean Ansaldi (1987), and Pastor Antoine Nouis. The third part, "To take the psycho-sociological approach some steps further" includes excerpts from the writings of Michel Johner (a professor of ethics at the Evangelical Theological Faculty of Aix-en-Provence who opposes the blessing of same-sex couples) and Tony Anatrella, a Catholic priest and psychoanalyst whose virulent and homophobic stances contrast with the tone of the statements made by Protestant churches and their federation. Rather than being a reflection based on marriage as intrinsically linked with procreation, the argumentation of the FPF in this working file establishes a hierarchy of sexualities in which homosexuality is described as inferior, because of its "essential impossibility to procreate."[6] To avoid any contradiction that might undermine the relevance of this theory, the leaders of the FPF do not refer to the social sciences' studies on homosexual parenting or to the social sciences more generally. In fact, the main intellectual influence appears to have been the conservative discourse of the Catholic Church.

In addition to their distinctive "anthropological" arguments, the leaders of the FPF presented their position on same-sex marriage as an illustration of the democratic functioning and the inclusiveness of their federation, thus differentiating it from the CNEF by casting itself the only federation to comprise the whole diversity of Protestantism. Claude Baty explains:

> What could be feared on such a sensitive issue was a confrontation between Evangelicals and Lutheran-Reformed Protestants. This text [the statement issued by the FPF] has been voted without hesitation by both of them, underlining the existence of a fruitful dialogue within the Protestant federation. With all the diversity of its members, the federation took a stance against the "marriage for all" not for religious reasons but for matters of social, symbolical and anthropological structuring.
>
> BATY, 2012

Theological Differences and Scientific Categories

In summary, the two national Protestant federations took stances against same-sex marriage and advanced "anthropological" arguments inspired by

---

6   Quoted in *L'homosexualité: éléments de réflexion*, Ethical Commission of the FPF (1994).

Catholic rhetoric. The CNEF, seeking political recognition, adopted this position to make an Evangelical voice heard in the public space, while preserving the possibility for its members to emphasize biblical arguments. For the FPF, still the only federation recognised by political authorities, the use of "anthropological" arguments served two purposes: first, to distance itself from the biblical argumentation usually put forward by Evangelicals by using more consensual arguments; second, to secure its status as the exclusive representative of Protestantism in the political arena, by emphasising its democratic and inclusive functioning.

The distinction between the two federations and more generally between (liberal) Lutheran-Reformed Protestants and (conservative) Evangelicals on issues of sexual morality needs to be carefully specified. The statements released by these federations during the debate on same-sex marriage took place in a particular political and historical context. Recent debates on the blessing of same-sex couples, and the reactions that followed the 2015 decision of the United Protestant Church to allow such blessing under some conditions suggest that while there are liberals amongst Reformed Protestants, conservatives are present in all Protestant streams: Reformed, Lutheran, and Evangelical.[7] Therefore, a relevant sociological framework of analysis cannot be based on intra-Protestant theological distinctions alone.

Additional sociological data show that opinions on the topic vary according to age and gender. Women as a whole are more in favour of "marriage for all" than men.[8] In addition, intergenerational gaps are important in such issues, regardless of religious affiliation, and Lutheran-Reformed church members in France constitute an ageing population. Quantitative analyses also reveal significant differences between pastors and ordinary church members: when asked if "same-sex couples should be able to get blessed by churches," 36 percent of Protestants answered positively in 2010, compared to only 26 percent of Protestant pastors. To the question "Should the right to abortion be advocated?" 72 percent of Protestants answered positively, compared to 54 percent of their pastors. These differences suggest personal opinions are not uniquely

---

7 In June 2014, the union of Protestant churches in Alsace and Lorraine decided, as no consensus could be reached, to make no decision on the blessing of same-sex couples and refused to examine this question again in the following three years. The decision of the national synod of the United Protestant Church in May 2015 generated a significant movement of internal opposition, called the "attestants" (testifying Protestants).

8 IFOP survey, 2012 (93 and f.). To the question "Do you think homosexual couples in France should have the right to marry?" 63 percent of all respondents and 43 percent of Protestants said "yes." Amongst Protestant respondents, 53 percent of the women said "yes" and 38 percent of the men; 51 percent of the respondents under 35 supported same-sex marriage, while the over-65s strongly opposed it, with only 35 percent answering "yes."

determined by religious identities; social positions also play a role. Within a single church, pastors are *ex officio* in charge of reminding parishioners of sexual ethical norms, while church members who have to cope with these norms tend to be less normative. From the perspective of the sociology of social movements, the debate on same-sex marriage also underlines the strong mobilising capacity of the Catholic Church, in contrast to the small impact of Protestants, who represent approximately two percent of the French population.[9]

How can we explain the prominent role of intra-Protestant distinctions, specifically between Lutheran-Reformed Protestants and Evangelicals, in French academic analyses of the debate on same-sex marriage? Part of the answer lies in the relationships between sociologists of Protestantism and Protestantism itself. This sensitive issue is rarely discussed in publications, workshops, or conferences. In his conclusion to the proceedings of a symposium of the French Association for the Sociology of Religion (AFSR) on "The Religion of Sociologists," Bréchon remarks that the challenge consists in

> asking sociologists to publically expose the links that may exist between their convictions and their theories.... It is clear that readers will not find in this volume any sensational confession. I have to say that those who spoke about the influence of their personal beliefs or ideological convictions mostly mentioned the years of their youth.
>
> BRÉCHON, 1997: 245–246

With one exception, "no one has really taken the risk to conduct a self-analysis for the present days" (Bréchon, 1997: 245–246).

In fact, the point is not so much the beliefs of the sociologists of religion, but their interests in the religious field (Bourdieu, 2010: 2). Thus, emphasising the difference between Lutheran-Reformed Protestants and Evangelicals as the key to understanding Protestant stances on same-sex marriage tends to transform an alleged difference into a scientific and "objective" truth. Such an analytical framework serves not only scientific interests but also, objectively, the interests of the FPF's leaders and their strategy of distinction.

In November 2013, in an article entitled "Protestant diversity and homosexuality in France," Willaime presented the positions of the FPF and the CNEF on same-sex marriage as an illustration of this "difference," understood as an opposition between moderate and conservative Protestants: "On the marriage

---

9   The President of the FPF did not call for demonstrations, and many Evangelicals were reluctant to join Catholics in these demonstrations, presented by most media as Catholic initiatives.

for all, the FPF adopted… a position which can be described as moderate. In the Evangelical Protestant world…, a marked opposition to same-sex mariage is dominant" (Willaime, 2013: 82–83). In the article, Willaime mentions two elements to demonstrate the moderation of the FPF's stance: the kind of argumentation used and the decision-making process. First, he points to the FPF's defence of the institution of marriage "not from a moral point of view, but from the perspective of a Christian anthropology sensitive to the symbolical and structuring dimensions of social fundamental institutions" (Willaime, 2013: 82–83). The notion of "Christian anthropology" does not refer to the academic field but to the definition promoted by the Catholic Church, and the diffusion of this notion since the 1990s has caused sociologists and anthropologists to criticise a Catholic misappropriation of the social sciences (Fassin, 2001). For example, sociologist of religion Hervieu-Léger points out that the "anthropology" to which the Catholic Church refers should be understood not as a discipline of the social sciences "that explores the diversity of family and kinship patterns in space and time" but as a family model built by the Catholic Church itself (Hervieu-Léger, 2013). Moreover, the debate on "marriage for all" has produced, as Rochefort remarks, a paradoxical scheme, as "conservative religious actors use secular discourse, while dissent theologies innovate through reinterpretations of religious heritage" (Rochefort, 2014: 229).

Second, Willaime points to the decision-making processes of the FPF. The stances taken were, according to him, preceded by extensive consultation of local churches. But the statement made by the President of the FPF in October 2012 was not preceded by any consultation; the consultation he mentions was, in fact, conducted in 2002, when the working file "Church and Homosexuality" issued by the Lutheran-Reformed Communion was distributed in local churches.

This selective interpretation can be understood as a reprise in the academic field of the arguments posited by the FPF leaders in terms that legitimated and reinforced the dominant position of this federation within the Protestant field. In the intra-Protestant competition for representativeness, an academic discourse emphasising the opposition between a conservative Evangelicalism (represented by the CNEF) and a moderate, inclusive Protestantism (represented by the FPF and Lutheran-Reformed Protestants) can hardly be seen as neutral. Of course, Evangelicals are more conservative than Lutheran-Reformed Protestants, but the increasing conservatism of Protestant churches affiliated with the FPF should be included in the picture. Finally, the Catholic use of "anthropological" rather than biblical arguments is a rhetorical strategy that aims to defend a body of doctrine. The use of this same "anthropological" argument within the academic field seems more problematic as it introduces – and tends to legitimate – religious categories into the sociological analysis of religious facts.

The controversy between Willaime and Hervieu-Léger during the debate on same-sex marriage sheds light on these epistemological issues and underlines the tensions generated by the incomplete secularisation of the sociology of religion in France – an essential part of the history of this academic discipline.

From Religious Sciences to the Sociology of Religion (and Vice Versa)

The new academic discipline called "religious sciences" was officially recognised in 1886 with the establishment of the fifth section of the *Ecole pratique des hautes études* (EPHE). It took place in a specific historical context and raised epistemological and methodological issues that French historians of Catholicism (Langlois; Poulat and Poulat [1966]) and Protestantism (Cabanel) have analysed in detail. As Langlois explains, the education policy of the third Republic and the secularisation of teaching programs and staff dominated the context. In 1880, the government re-established the state monopoly on university education and supressed funding for the faculties of Catholic theology. Two options were possible: the creation of chairs in history of religion in the main French universities or the establishment of a few chairs concentrated in one prestigious Parisian institution. The second option was preferred. That same year, a university chair in history of religions was created at the Collège de France, with the aim of delivering generalist and comparative teaching (Langlois, 2002). The first holder of this chair was Albert Réville, a liberal Protestant. According to Langlois, this choice brought to the study of religious facts "the most indisputable scientific legitimacy (Collège de France/EPHE) but under a model that avoided human sciences, developed in the universities, where the scientific study of religions also had its place" (Langlois, 2002).

What exactly were these "religious sciences" elaborated in France at the end of the 19th century? For one thing, the new discipline distanced itself from theology by opting for a scientific methodology: the historical approach. A second distinctive feature was the strong presence of liberal Protestants amongst the teachers and researchers:

> For a quarter of a century, we find a very strong core of Protestants, even pastors or former pastors, most of them closely linked with the new Parisian faculty of Protestant theology, which appears to be the main recruitment pool of the masters and disciples of the young science.
>
> CABANEL, 1994: 34

Albert Réville (a former pastor) was amongst them, as were his son Jean Réville and Maurice Vernes (also a pastor's son). The latter finally left the faculty after having elaborated an agnostic and extremely liberal approach. In effect, he contributed to the first criticism of religious scientists; in his view, they should restrict themselves to collecting and classifying data. To this, Jean Réville responded: "Dissecting documents [requires] knowing by experience what a religious feeling or a religious thought is. Put in other words, even the most erudite person in the world would never offer anything else than a mummy instead of a living organism" (Reville, 1886).

As Cabanel remarks, religious feeling is "at the core of the French-Dutch – or we may say Protestant – conception of religious sciences" (Cabanel, 1994: 60). This implies a vigorous opposition to any hostile, ironic or condescending approaches to religion. This idea that "religious feeling" and the personal religious dispositions of the researcher will determine his/her ability to understand religious facts led Durkheimian sociologists to suspect these religious sciences of being based on non-scientific premises. Durkheim aimed to study religious facts rather than religion and criticised the promoters of religious sciences of "wanting to express straightaway the content of religious life" (Cabanel, 1994: 61) instead of approaching this content through a careful study of the external forms of religious phenomena such as services, rituals and practices. In Durkheim's view, "the so-called religious phenomena consist in compulsory beliefs, linked with well-defined practices oriented towards objects given by these beliefs" (Cabanel, 1994: 61). Similarly, Mauss strongly criticised Tiele's introduction to religious sciences as turning away from scientific methods in favour of general considerations: "When you try to reach them [the deeper and more intimate conditions of religious life] straightaway, through a simple introspection, your own prejudices, personal and subjective impressions take the place of things" (quoted by Cabanel, 1994: 62).

Simply stated, the sociological school advocated an analysis of religious phenomena as natural and objective things with social functions and refused to consider the philosophical, psychological or theological approaches of the religious sciences as relevant. This led Albert Réville to denounce the "exaggerations of the sociologists" who gave a determinant role to the social context in their study of individuals (Cabanel, 1994: 63).

Langlois argues that the choice to establish a fifth section at the EPHE dedicated to the religious sciences instead of several chairs in French universities contributed to the development of "a model of avoidance of human sciences" and the lasting isolation of this discipline (Langlois, 2002). He notes that the creation, in 1956, of the *Groupe de sociologie des religions* (GSR) by the CNRS followed a similar pattern. The objective was to develop the sociology of religion within "prestigious" institutions, at the margins of universities;

as a consequence, the sociology of religion did not become a branch of general sociology. This means that sociologists of religion preferred to base the coherence of their discipline on its particular – "religious" – object, rather than on a sociological methodology shared with other branches of sociology. By so doing, they reinforced in the sociological field the impression that studying "religion" is a specific task, as if the object studied should rub off on the methodology to be used.[10]

This isolation of "religious sciences," only taught at the faculty of Protestant theology in Strasbourg and at the EPHE in Paris, was further reinforced in 1975 when the fourth section "Economic and social sciences" left the EPHE to form a new, independent institution: *Ecole des hautes études en sciences sociales* (EHESS), which now comprises historians, sociologists, anthropologists and political scientists. Sociology of religion is today a declining discipline, mainly taught at the EPHE and the EHESS (Lassave, 2014). In 1998, the GSR was split into two research centres: *Groupe sociétés, religions, laïcités* (CNRS-EPHE) and *Centre interdisciplinaire des faits religieux* (CNRS-EHESS).

The incomplete process of secularisation of the discipline tends to resurface in this context of decline and isolation, with the need for religious erudition considered an "admission ticket" by the defenders of the specificity of this academic subfield. And the criticism Willaime (as director of studies in religious sciences at the EPHE and sociologist of Protestantism) levels at Hervieu-Léger (director of studies at the EHESS and sociologist of Catholicism) should be resituated in this field configuration. Without getting into all the details of their biographies and the reasons for their involvement in the sociology of religion, both sociologists have been part, in one way or another, of the churches they study. Williaime, who was a holder of a Ph.D. in religious sciences from the faculty of Protestant theology in Strasbourg, chose to write his thesis on "The Profession of Pastor," "as if to distance himself from the profession for which his previous training in theology destined him" (Lassave, 2014). Meanwhile, Hervieu-Léger conducted her first fieldwork on Catholic student missions while she was herself part of this protest movement in the university setting (Lassave, 2014).

During the demonstrations against the same-sex marriage bill, Hervieu-Léger published a text in the newspaper *Le Monde*, in which she expresses her surprise that the Catholic Church uses "anthropological" rather than biblical arguments to oppose same-sex marriage: "In this debate on marriage for all, it comes as no surprise that the Catholic Church makes its voice heard.

---

10 There is an exception in this process of isolation; since the 1990s, the history of religion has found a place in the context of the democratisation of university education.

How the Church carefully avoids any reference to a religious interdiction is more surprising" (Hervieu-Léger, 2013). Then she underlines the weakness of the arguments put forward by the Catholic Church:

> The arguments used by the Church – the end of civilisation, the loss of foundational landmarks of human beings, the threat of the familial cell's dislocation, the confusion of sexes, etc. – are the same as those once used to criticise the professional involvement of women outsides the domestic household or to fight against the establishment of divorce by mutual consent.
>
> HERVIEU-LÉGER, 2013

Finally, Hervieu-Léger remarks that same-sex marriage is one of many examples of the diversity of contemporary familial patterns characterised by the demand for equality and the dissociation of marriage and religious affiliation. Without denying the legitimacy of the Catholic Church to speak on the bill, she regards its arguments as unconvincing and concludes that "on these various issues, a word which places emphasis on freedom is expected" (Hervieu-Léger, 2013).

This critical approach to the Catholic institution is in line with her previous work on the "exculturation" of Catholicism, defined as a loosening grip of Catholicism on French society (Hervieu-Léger, 2003). The process of exculturation implies the Catholic Church is facing disaffection with its traditional activities; it also means the Church must now elaborate values and norms that make sense in a society where an increasing proportion of individuals have no Catholic culture at all. The use of "anthropological" arguments by the Catholic Church could, in such a context, be seen as a way to cope with exculturation. But Hervieu-Léger gives little consideration to these efforts as she questions "the capacity of the Church to nurture and elaborate... collectively shared representations whose religious origin might remain identifiable in the French society today" (Hervieu-Léger, 2003: 131).

In 2014, Willaime published a text in *Transversalité*, a publication of the Catholic Institute of Paris. In this text, he develops his criticism of the stance taken by Hervieu-Léger and provides his ongoing reflections on the definition of "religion" and the specific methodology of the sociology of religion. He ends with a vibrant call for better public recognition of the role of religion in society. The text uses two repertoires; while employing an ostensibly sociological approach, it nonetheless advocates the political involvement of churches in society. In several passages, it echoes the controversies that opposed, more than a century before, sociologists and promoters of "religious sciences." In other words, these debates remain relevant today, and Willaime's definition of religion as a particular object of study that requires a specific approach seems in line with the heritage of the religious sciences. His warning about the risk of "reductionist tendencies that marked the history of sociology" (Willaime, 2014: 114) can be read as an implicit criticism of the Durkheimian sociological school. He is especially critical of "the approaches that tend to limit themselves to the study of the non-religious factors of religion... and reduce the sociological study of religion to the analysis of the social activities in which they are manifested, for example the various forms of ritual practices" (Willaime, 2014: 114). The definition of religion he proposes makes religion an object of study that is not reducible to the sociological approach:

> I consider religion as a symbolic activity which has its own consistency; that is to say that while religion is socially determined – in many ways –, it remains relatively independent from these determinations.... This could be summarised by saying that, in its own way, religion makes society (by creating links), makes truth (by building legitimacy) and that historical processes are always evolving. What matters to me is reflecting the singularity of this social activity, while staying within a sociological framework. This entails recognising that this activity can't be reduced to any other forms of activities.
>
> WILLAIME, 2014: 115–116

Defining "religion" also means drawing the boundaries of a discipline – the sociology of religion. And as religion is defined here more by its essence than its social expressions, the risk is that this object constructed by and for the sociology of religion might end up being similar to the "culture" studied by classical anthropology. This implies the same limits as those underlined by Bensa in *La fin de l'exotisme*, where he shows the epistemological consequences of defining culture as an encompassing entity that exists beyond and outside individuals, and as a radical otherness that anthropologists have the task of defining. To find their disciplinary object in social reality, these anthropologists tend to exaggerate the homogeneity of culture, to minimise the temporal dimension of the social facts they study, and to consider actors as individuals governed by an encompassing reality:

> But it is clear that the discourse [of the anthropologist] which takes on the air of "I was there" rarely produces a chronicle of what really happened "there." This kind of dodge probably comes from the dualist scheme which supposes the existence, as the saying goes, of a "good god

behind the wardrobe," that is to say an elsewhere more significant that the social relations implemented and observable in the frame of a given experience.

BENSA, 2006: 10

The definition proposed by Willaime also echoes debates in France in the 1960–70s, in the context of the institutionalisation of the sociology of Catholicism. Thus, Henri Desroche, a former Catholic priest who left the Dominican order in 1951, says religion should not escape – even partially – the sociological analysis:

> I tend to think that no area of the religious domain should be closed to the sociological investigation. The history of gods is part of the history of men.... Put in other words, there is not a part of religion accessible to the sociological approach and another set apart for the sole religious approach.
>
> DESROCHE, 1968: 131

To this, Desroche adds: "It would be a mistake to interpret Durkheim as a purely and simply 'reducist' .... Society and religion function in a complementary manner to form a total act" (Desroche, 1968: 61–62).

In addition, the sociology of religion as defined by Willaime requires researchers studying religion to have specific "dispositions" following Bourdieu's understanding of a disposition as something larger than belief (2010). He doesn't criticise Hervieu-Léger for not being a Christian believer (she was once involved in the Catholic Church) but for not believing enough in the Catholic institution. From his perspective, she is disrespectful when she says the Church has lost the battle against "marriage for all" or when she states "same-sex marriage obviously does not mean the end of civilisation," thus contradicting the official discourse of the Catholic Church. Rather, by publicly and explicitly contradicting the arguments of the Church, she gives the impression of personally breaking with her object of study, so that her point of view remains radically external and sociological. Paradoxically, this exteriority is precisely what Willaime considers at odds with the epistemological and methodological requirements of sociology:

> According to Danièle Hervieu-Léger, the opposition of the Catholic Church to same-sex marriage represents – and this is not purely hypothetical... – "the path towards the end of Catholicism in France." Nothing less! I was struck by the predictive character of my colleague's stance

(even if, like anyone else, she owns the right to defend a militant point of view based on her political and religious convictions). *The question I asked myself was whether a sociologist should put the religious group she studies on trial like this* and deliver such a prediction. Personally, this is not how I see the position of the sociological analysis.

WILLAIME, 2014: 128, emphasis added

The conflicting views expressed by these two sociologists who both have a Christian background are probably partly based on the gendered dimension of the debate on same-sex marriage. They may also be explained by the different ability of the Catholic Church and the Lutheran-Reformed churches to manage internal diversity and critics. But beyond this difference of opinion, the kind of arguments put forward should elicit our attention. When Willaime regrets that a sociologist criticises the church she studies, he means sociologists cannot properly study a religion without having a kind of sympathy with it. The lack of loyalty to the institution studied (to which, in this case, the sociologist is supposed to belong) appears to him to be a methodological bias. The risk of such a perspective is that it may imply no critical approach to religion can be legitimate within the sociology of religion, especially when non-believing or non-practising sociologists develop it. More generally, according to Willaime,

> The [Marxist-inspired] scheme has strongly influenced a part of sociology which is still dominated, in the name of "liberation," by the criticism of religion, and considers religions as traditions on the way to becoming totally obsolete. Such an approach is unable to overcome a disqualification of its object while intending to study it, and this obviously creates a bias in the analysis.
>
> WILLAIME, 2014: 115

By equating a critical perspective on religion with a militant approach that "disqualifies" the object of study, he minimises the inherently critical dimension of sociology. By redefining the sociology of religion, he tends, in fact, to disqualify sociologists who don't believe enough in "their" church – the church they study.

The debate on the beliefs of the sociologists of religion is an old one, as illustrated in the opposition between Durkheim and Réville at the start of the 20th century and its regular reappearance throughout the century (Desroche, 1968: 20; Wach, 1947). In 1980, a presentation given by Bourdieu at a conference of the French Association for Social Sciences of Religion revived this debate, despite meeting with strong resistance:

> The question is not to know, as we often pretend, whether those who practise sociology of religion have faith or not, nor even whether they belong to the Church or not. Leaving aside the problem of faith in God, in the Church, and in all that the Church teaches and guarantees, it is about posing the problem of investment in the object, of adherence linked to a form of belonging, and of knowing what belief, understood in this sense, contributes to determine the relationship to the scientific object, to determine the investments in this object and the choice of this object.
>
> BOURDIEU, 2010: 2–3

It seems Willaime interprets the criticism levelled by Hervieu-Léger against the Catholic Church as a lack of "adherence linked to a form of belonging," while the definition of axiological neutrality he defends implies sociologists should, at least in part, share the *illusio* of the religious institutions they study. In this perspective, the essential critical approach comes not from sociological methods but, more importantly, from religious faith: "Religions, by the very fact that they refer to an elsewhere, to one form or another of the beyond, invite us to decentre our gaze, to keep a critical distance from the world, the secular" (Willaime, 2014: 120). Willaime goes on to defend a very positive view on the role of religion in society:

> Religions today constitute sub-cultures, groups to identify with, providing landmarks and perspectives to the individual. They are meaningful and structuring minorities which offer fraternal communion and resources for hope in a global society dominated by instrumental and market relationships, and marked by concerns about the more or less radical relativisation of the foundational models of modern society.
>
> WILLAIME, 2014: 126

The purpose becomes the rehabilitation of religion in the public space, with this expression of religious faith seen as a "chance for democracy… at a time when the democratic life is dominated by opinion and the sensational… and the political life faces globalisation and the emotional democracy of opinion" (Willaime, 2014: 126).

Willaime doesn't really specify in this text which particular religious expressions might be included in this vision of democratic life, even though he makes it clear that "all religious expressions are not equal" (Willaime, 2014: 124). Nevertheless, Christianity as a whole seems to be the main implicit reference underlying this defence of the legitimacy of religious public and political expression in ultramodern, postsecular and disenchanted societies.

This positive view of religion goes with a pessimistic view of social relationships (to be re-enchanted by religion) and democratic regimes (which religion
needs to protect from their own excesses): "Against totalitarian drifts and human rights violations, Christianity, even if it has been slow to adopt the logic
of the defence of human rights, also represents a resource of awareness and
ethical mobilisation" (Willaime, 2014: 127).

While religions are, at least in part, defined as social organisations, it is as if
they are located outside social and political life and, therefore, preserved from
the ills affecting ultramodern societies. It is difficult to understand how religions presented as preserved – or even disconnected – from social dynamics
could have an influence on these same social dynamics. Is it because religion
is defined as "a symbolic activity which has its own consistency" (Willaime,
2014: 115–116) that it is protected from the harmful effects of social dynamics? The legitimacy of religious intervention in the public space is built on
a strong bipolarisation of religion and society, making it difficult to understand how churches could become involved in society without losing their
specificity.

It is not clear what kind of fieldwork and empirical data these general
reflections draw on. But the perspective outlined by Willaime is evident: on
the one hand, he makes a vibrant call for the greater visibility of and respect for
a religious conservative stance in the public space and in politics, and on the
other, he defends a sociology of religion as posited by sociologists who believe
in "their" church – the one to which they attend and/or study. Willaime also
sees the reference to "an elsewhere" as the core of religion, and his definition of
the social role of religion focuses on the ontological distance which separates it
from the secular world. In such conditions, it seems quite complicated for non-
believing sociologists who base their research work on empirical observation
in this "secular world" to find the "good god behind the wardrobe," as Bensa
writes (2006: 10) – an elsewhere supposedly more meaningful than the social
relations observed through fieldwork.

Conclusion

The debate on "marriage for all" and the stances adopted by Protestant churches and sociologists examined in this chapter show the kind of difficulties the
sociology of religion faces today. The use of "anthropological" rather than biblical arguments in the religious field and the uncritical reprise of religious categories in the academic field comprise a double movement which jeopardises
the sociology of religion's autonomy vis-à-vis religious discourses. The reprise

of Catholic arguments promotes an approach to social facts in religious terms, even as it reinforces the churches' strategy of presenting religious convictions as scientific truths. The fact that "anthropological" arguments mask biblical arguments reintroduces religious logics into a discipline, which is tempted to remain anchored in a restrictive definition of "religious sciences," thus distancing it from the critical debates of the more general social sciences. Invoking "anthropological evidence" can be interpreted as an attempt to escape the "rules of systematic discussion and general criticism" that should organise scientific exchanges (Bourdieu, 2010).

The conclusion of Willaime's article in *Transversalités* can thus be read as an attempt to cut short any scientific discussion on same-sex marriage, by reducing the contribution of anthropology to a form of cultural relativism, while asserting the legitimacy of a moral religious norm:

> Why should the fact of "being in conflict with all that anthropologists describe of the variability of familial and kinship patterns in time and space" be regarded as a problem? ... Because other models exist, it doesn't mean that they must be considered as valuable. And because a great diversity exists in time and space, it doesn't necessarily mean, unless we deliberately choose to support relativism, that we have to celebrate this diversity from a normative point of view.
>
> WILLAIME, 2014: 132

In an article where he questions the sociological relevance of the "religious" object, Michel remarks that even in widely secularised societies, religion retains a specific status. More than other objects, religion inspires attitudes of reverence and conformism, most notably

> because, as Proust wrote in *Swann's Way*, "The facts of life do not penetrate to the sphere in which our beliefs are cherished; as it was not them that engendered those beliefs, so they are powerless to destroy them; they can aim at them continual blows of contradiction and disproof without weakening them."
>
> MICHEL, 2003: 161

As sociology values the objective observation of facts, sociologists are necessarily confronted by the effects of beliefs when they turn their attention to religious facts. This should inspire them to elaborate a critical analytical framework for the study of subjective religious experiences and to carefully reflect on their own relationship with religious truth.

This well-known difficulty associated with the scientific study of religion has been increased by new interactions between the scientific, religious and political fields, as implied in the debate on the concept of post-secular society (Stavo-Debauge and Roca I Escoda, 2016). The idea that the symbolic resources offered by religions make a specific contribution to public debate paves the way for new kinds of religious mobilisations and places the social sciences of religion in an awkward situation. While they can have an interest in the social revaluation of their object of study in public debate, such sociologists can't uncritically accept the strategies of religious actors who seek the recognition of a particular legitimacy based on a transcendent truth.

References

Baty, Claude. 2012. "Le marriage pour tous," *Réforme*, 18 October, accessed 23 October 2016 from http://reforme.net/une/societe/positions-protestantes-mariage-homo sexuels.

Bensa, Alban. 2006. *La fin de l'exotisme: essais d'anthropologie critique*. Toulouse: Anacharsis.

Béraud, Céline. 2011. "Les autorités catholiques face à la question du genre." In *Sacrées familles ! Changements familiaux, changements religieux*, edited by Martin Gross, Séverine Mathieu, and Sophie Nizard, 229–239. Toulouse: Editions Erès.

Bourdieu, Pierre. 2010. "Sociologists of belief and beliefs of sociologists," translated by Véronique Altglas and Matthew Wood, *Nordic Journal of Religion and Society* 23(1): 1–7.

Bourdieu, Pierre. 1971. "Genèse et structure du champ religieux," *Revue Française de Sociologie* 12(3): 295–334.

Bréchon, Pierre. 1997. "Variations conclusives: de l'itinéraire à la pratique." In *Le religieux des sociologies: trajectoires personnelles et débats scientifiques*, edited by Yves Lambert, Guy Michelat, and Albert Piette, 245–254. Paris: L'Harmattan.

Cabanel, Patrick. 1994. "L'institutionnalisation des sciences religieuses en France (1879–1908): une entreprise protestante?" *Bulletin de la Société de l'Histoire du Protestantisme Français* (Jan-Fev-Mars): 33–80.

Coleman, Simon, and Rosalind Hackett, eds. 2015. *The anthropology of global Pentecostalism and evangelicalism*. New York; London: New York University Press.

Conseil National des Évangéliques de France (CNEF). 2012. "Mariage entre personnes de même sexe et homosexualité: un mauvais choix de société," accessed 23 October 2016 from lecnef.orfg/documents-pdf/func-startdown/49/.

Desroche, Henri. 1968. *Sociologies religieuses*. Paris: Presses Universitaires de France.

Fassin, Éric. 2001. "La voix de l'expertise et les silences de la science dans le débat démocratique." In *Au delà du PaCS: l'expertise familiale à l'épreuve de l'homosexualité*, edited by Daniel Borrillo and Éric Fassin, 87–110. Paris: Presses Universitaires de France.

Fédération protestante de France. 2012. "Déclaration du Conseil de la Fédération protestante de France à propos du 'mariage pour tous'," 12 oct. 2012 (www.protestants .org/?id=33257).

Hervieu-Léger, Danièle. 2013. "Mariage pour tous: le combat perdu de l'Eglise," *Le Monde*, 12 January.

Hervieu-Léger, Danièle. 2003. *Catholicisme, la fin d'un monde*. Paris: Bayard.

Langlois, Claude. 2002. *Aux origines des sciences religieuses en France: la laïcisation du savoir (1810–1886), Actes du séminaire du fait religieux*. Paris: Éduscol.

Lassave, Pierre. 2014. "Les sociologues des religions et leur objet," *Sociologie* 5(2): 191–206.

Lenclud, Gérard. 1992. "Le grand partage ou la tentation ethnographique." In *Vers une ethnologie du présent*, edited by Gérard Althabe, Daniel Fabre, and Gérard Lenclud, 9–38. Paris: Éditions du M.S.H. (coll. Ethnologie de la France, cahier 7).

Malogne-Fer, Gwendoline. 2017. "Les sciences sociales au secours des Églises protestantes: l'exemple du 'mariage pour tous'." In *Science et religion*, edited by Claude Dargent, Yannick Fer, and Raphaël Liogier, 125–150. Paris: CNRS Alpha.

Michel, Patrick. 2003. "La religion, objet sociologique pertinent?" *Qu'est-ce que le religieux? Religion et politique, Revue du MAUSS* 22(2): 159–170.

Obadia, Lionel. 2014. "Paradoxes, utopies et cécités du modernisme en religion: le cas du bouddhisme de France," *Archives de sciences sociales des religions* 167: 295–314.

Poulat, Emile, and Odile Poulat. 1966. "Le développement institutionnel des sciences religieuses en France," *Archives de sciences sociales des religions* 21(1): 23–36.

Réville, Jean. 1886. "L'histoire des religions," *Revue de l'Histoire des Religions*, 14: 357–359.

Robbins, Joel. 2004. *Becoming sinners: Christianity and moral torment in a Papua New Guinea society*. Berkeley: University of California Press.

Rochefort, Florence. 2014. "'Mariage pour tous': genre, religions et secularisation." In *Qu'est-ce que le genre?* Edited by Laurie Laufer and Florence Rochefort, 213–283. Paris: Payot.

Stavo Debauge, Joan, and Marta Roca i Escoda. 2016. "Le post-sécularisme nuit-il aux femmes et aux homosexuel-el-s?" In *Revue sextant dossier Habemus Gender! Déconstruction d'une riposte religieuse*, by Joan Stavo Debauge and Marta Roca i Escoda, 59–74. Bruxelles: Éditions de l'Université de Bruxelles.

Wach, Joachim. 1947. "La sociologie et la religion." In *La sociologie au XXᵉ siècle*, edited by George Gurvitch, 417–447. Paris: Presses Universitaires de France.

Willaime, Jean-Paul. 2014. "Pertinence de l'impertinence chrétienne dans l'ultramo-
dernité contemporaine? Un point de vue sociologique sur la condition chrétienne
aujourd'hui," *Revue Transversalités* 131: 113–132.

Willaime, Jean-Paul. 2013. "Diversité protestante et homosexualité en France." In
*Normes religieuses et genre: mutations, résistances et reconfiguration, XIXᵉ–XXIᵉ
siècle,* edited by Florence Rochefort and Maria Eleonora Sanna, 71–86. Paris:
Armand Colin.

Willaime, Jean-Paul. 2002. "Entre éthique de responsabilité et éthique de conviction:
l'éthique sexuelle en débat dans le protestantisme français des années 1970–2000."
In *Religion et sexualité,* edited by Jacques Maître and Guy Michelat, 59–72. Paris:
L'Harmattan.

CHAPTER 2

Deconstructing Archer's (Un)Critical Realism

Peter Doak

Introduction

This chapter responds to Margaret Archer's (2004) manifesto for admitting transcendence into theoretical "models of man."[1] It begins by situating Archer's insistence within the critical realist perspective (Archer, 1995), a central premise of which is that, contra the "epistemic fallacy" of positivism, not all that exists can be empirically observed. While realism avoids the erroneous reduction of the ontological to the empirically verifiable, it opens up a space for non-observable entities to exert causation, and it is this space that Archer (ab)uses to admit God by way of a philosophical "back door." While potentially philosophically sound, echoing the introductory analysis of this volume, I suggest that the model of man she proposes is not only non-sociological, but is, in fact, *anti-sociological* in that it posits causal dynamics which transcend the social. In Archer's terms, man is too often erroneously reduced to being solely "the gift of society," or a savvy and "opportunistic bargain hunter" (Archer, 2004: 64–65). She thus proposes to break with both hyper-constructionist and rational actor conceptualisations to depict a being who is neither an over-socialised cultural dope (Garfinkel, 1967; Archer, 1984: 100) nor *homo economicus*. While realism correctly draws attention to the deficiencies of such reductionist theorizing, it is difficult to see how the model of man proposed by way of tonic – the transcendental "Man of Faith" (Archer, 2004: 67), who derives his ultimate concerns from God – is anything more than, at best, a common-sense construct and, at worst, an obfuscation (or vindication) of the power structures which so often buttress such constructs. Specifically, because transcendental "man's" world *is* (potentially) "ongoingly penetrated by sacred beings and forces" (Berger, 1967), which presumably do not correspond to the normal dynamics of class, race, and ethnicity, his world seems beyond the scope or remit of sociological scholarship. This implies, theoretically, that social action is unchecked and unencumbered by normal sociological dynamics and is deeply suggestive that Archer's

---

1   Echoing Archer's acknowledgement, the usage of what was a current term does not imply authorial endorsement.

sociological imagination is subordinate to her situation in the religious field, illuminating her habitus, rather than casting light on the people she purports to theorise. The chapter moves on to suggest God's intervention in the world is profoundly socially determined. Because Archer's God is entirely situated and historically specific – contra the suggestion of ontological realism – the force described is ultimately and entirely a social construct. Because of a fundamental misrecognition of this situatedness, Archer's account falls short of satisfying the realist goal of providing "relatively better explanations" (Smith, 2010: 111) and fails to offer a sociological alternative to the assumption that religion, like all social phenomena, is socially constructed. Finally, the chapter considers the implications of Archer's intervention for sociology more generally.

Realist Ontology

Archer's call to admit transcendence into models of man draws heavily on established inferences of critical realism (Bhaskar, 1976; Archer, 1995). The purpose of this section is not to offer an exhaustive overview of critical realism but, rather, to draw attention to important strands of critical realist thought which inform the argument under consideration: emergence, ontological realism, anti-positivism, and truth.

Critical realism is "critical" in so far as it rejects the supposedly dominant paradigms of the natural and social sciences, positivist empiricism, and social constructionism respectively, and seeks to occupy a radical centre within this cleavage. The intertwined central assertions of critical realism concern the ontological reality of much of the world, which exists simultaneously outside of human consciousness, and, crucially for what follows, cannot be reduced to that which is empirically verifiable. Critical realism thus necessarily involves a "remorseless critique [of] empiricism" (Archer, 2004: 63), directed towards an inherent epistemic fallacy, namely, the positivist conflation of ontology (that which is) with empirical verification (that which is observable). Due to this collapse, positivism is charged with reducing reality to the level of the observable and therefore rendering the unobservable (but real) beyond scientific (empirical) enquiry. Crucially, this implies empiricist enquiry is doomed to neglect much of that which is real – and much of that which exerts causation, a negation realists deem fatal. Constructionism is critiqued on the grounds that it prioritises epistemology to the detriment of ontology and that it too is guilty of reductionism (with the social being generative). Critical realism objects to strong versions of constructionism which posit reality *per se* as socially constructed; instead, realists literally interpret Berger and Luckman's (1966) "treatise on the sociology of *knowledge*,"[2] to arrive at a reading whereby "people do not construct reality but only construct more or less well their meaningful beliefs about and interpretations and understandings of reality" (Smith, 2010: 94). Contra strong constructionism and postmodernism, then, critical realists argue for an ontological reality which cannot be deconstructed away.

For such thinkers, this reality emerges as part of an essentially irreducible process, which reductionist sciences, whether social or physical, struggle to grasp. Emergence refers to a complex process of becoming whereby ontologically existent entities come into being through the relationships between constituent parts, which are likewise ontologically existent, albeit at a "lower" level of reality. Reality thus consists, via emergence, of numerous overlapping levels of existence embedded or nested in the same position in space and time. Crucially, following emergence, the procedurally/analytically (as opposed to chronologically) new ontologically existent entities come to exert causal properties irreducible to constituent parts – the whole is greater than the sum of the parts. Examples include: water, which is irreducible to the causal properties of hydrogen and oxygen molecules; personhood, which is irreducible to biological or organic properties and is distinctive from other animals; and social structures, irreducible to collective actions. At lower levels of reality, emergence often seems driven by physical dynamics, at least in the first instance. At higher or more complex levels, the realist model acknowledges that "mechanisms of emergence [are] sometimes a mystery" (Smith, 2010: 60). Examples here include the Promethean spark which ignites the emergence of "life" from various chemical components. It is within this space for mystery and realism's (falsely) modest insistence on the fallibility of human knowledge *vis-à-vis* that which is not yet known, that potentially misleading terminology creeps in – an obvious example being the realist tendency to speak of "souls" when distinguishing "persons" from the colder analyses of empiricist "individuals." Within this space, metaphors designed to *signify* reality blur *with* ontological reality – the model of reality becomes conflated with the reality of the model – and this is something Archer deliberately capitalises upon, as will become apparent.

A second major assertion of critical realism concerns knowledge and truth. Critical realists argue that because of the ontological reality of much of the world, it can be known. Moreover, not only *can* the world be known, but the

---

2   Realists such as Smith (2010: 119) suggest many contemporary constructionists fatally misinterpret the constructedness of understandings of reality, treating it as synonymous with the constructedness of reality *per se*. In this sense, they say Berger and Luckman's (1966) work has been misread.

desirability imputed to the correct knowing of the world affords it a strange ontological status of "value," something positivist science cannot acknowledge.
The Enlightenment commitment to Truth, as something to be determined
through positivist empiricist verification is dismissed on the grounds outlined
above, namely positivism's inherent epistemic fallacy. Yet as noted above, critical realists hold that Truth has an ontological reality and is preferable to falsity
(a situated value judgement masquerading as ontology). Strong constructionists are criticised as misled (and misleading) to suggest that because all knowledge is situated, truth claims are arbitrary (Lyotard, 1984) or, worse still, a form
of terrorism (Baudrillard, 1986). Recall, there *is* an ontologically real world, and
that world *can* be known.

For critical realists, then, what *is* truth on one side of the Pyrenees is neither
synonymous with nor reducible to what is *thought* of as truth on that side.
Truth, which is absolute, irrespective of whether or not it is known, is ontologically separate from knowledge of truth (which is fallible on both sides of
the mountains). It follows, therefore, that "weak" constructionist positions are
more compatible with the realist conceptions of truth. The acknowledgement
that not only is knowledge situated, but that it is bound up with power structures and often serves to buttress inequalities – does not in and of itself dimin-
ish its ontological status (although this is where constructionists accuse realists
of uncritically accepting existing canons of knowledge). "Strong" constructionism, in particular, postmodernism, fares considerably worse in the critical realist appraisal. In a well-versed argument, postmodernism is critiqued for its
hypocrisy, including the paradoxical dismissal of truth claims via a truth claim
(Smith, 2010: 43), the rejection of metanarratives via the simultaneous espous-
al of the postmodern metanarrative itself, and the ironic illumination of the
historical specificity of all knowledge by an intellectual movement which is
remarkable for its historical specificity (emanating predominantly from late
20th-century Paris and Los Angeles!). For what follows, however, it is enough to
recall that critical realists assert the world has an ontological reality which cannot be deconstructed away, that it can be (fallibly) known, but that its ontological reality is irreducible to mere observables (epistemic fallacy). This trajectory
seems confined to an investigative paradox, namely the apparent impossibility
of ontological verification given the alleged inadequacies of empiricism.

This impasse is apparently traversed via the realist scientific method of retroduction, the admittance to models of "what has to be, whether visible or not,
in order to account for what we have reason to believe really is" (Smith, 2010:
113). Retroduction thus utilises not only positivistic analyses of the observable
but also "theoretically coherent" insertions of the unobservable to produce
relatively better explanations of the real. The admittance of the unobservable

into explanatory models does not exactly constitute a radical departure from conventional sociological methods. The subject matter of sociology is often necessarily unobservable, and most sociologists, including even the most committed sociological positivists, often stand accused of admitting unobservable entities into models on the basis of what Smith terms "trace effects" (2010: 94). For most sociologists, then, phenomena are admitted to theoretical models based on causal properties, whereby effects are held to betray existence. All that distinguishes critical realists in this regard is that they accord such phenomena an ontological and often essential status, something which sits uncomfortably with many constructionists and some sociologists. This aside notwithstanding, the not unreasonable realist possibilities of admitting the unobservable into theoretical models, coupled with the likewise not unreasonable rejection of the necessity of empiricist verification, provide the avenue which Archer manipulates to (unreasonably) admit transcendence into her model of man.

Archer's (Un)Critical Realism – Key Arguments

In her text on transcendence, Archer begins with a broad characterisation of the social sciences (elsewhere synonymous with sociology) as a body of enquiry which has "privileged atheism," presenting it as an "epistemologically neutral position" (Archer, 2004: 63). She assigns responsibility for this to sociology's founding fathers, the "masters of suspicion" Marx and Durkheim, and the "religiously unmusical" Weber (63). She implicitly suggests that atheism and the associated preclusion of transcendental relations constitute a disciplinary chauvinism. Specifically, by exorcising from the emerging sociology the possibility that the human subject's constitution is extra-social, the "unwanted modesty" (63) associated with this inconvenient acknowledgement can be avoided. Stated more simply, the greater the extent to which man is a demonstrably social product, the greater the scope, importance, and necessity of sociology. Linked to this, sociology's apparent "methodological endorsement" of empiricism, true to the established realist critique, is presented as a form of "physics envy" (Smith, 2010: 13) and is portrayed as necessarily incapable of capturing the unobservable reality of transcendental relations. In this inadvertently Bourdieusian portrait of the scientific battlefield, the formative sociologists, nay, the formative sociology, are characterised by shrewd and pragmatic epistemological and methodological preferences, which serve more to defend the discipline from allegations of being unscientific than to offer themselves as a reasoned and informed scientific method. Archer completes her portrait of sociology with the observation that the unjustified preclusion of transcendental relations has proven "defective for social science and for faith alike," a consequence of which is "believing [sociologists] can be counted on one's fingers" (Archer, 2004: 63).

This portrait is inherently problematic for (at least) three reasons. Firstly, while echoing existing characterisations (Stark, 2003; Smith, 2010), Archer's account of both the privileging of atheism and the associated small numbers of believing sociologists is a partially inaccurate characterisation of sociology. Religious sociology, entirely neglected in Archer's analysis, has existed alongside "secular sociology" since the discipline's inception, with particularly prominent schools in the United States (Blasi and Donahoe, 2002) concentrated within religious universities, such as Fordham and Notre Dame, and finding organisational expression through the American Catholic Sociological Society (Conway 2011: 38), the Religious Research Association, and the Society for the Scientific Study of Religion. Indeed, Blasi depicts American sociology of religion as a subfield erroneously characterised as "cryptoapologetic," perceived as an "enclave for sociologists personally sympathetic to religion," i.e. believers (Blasi, 2014: 11). Across the Atlantic, distinctive West European schools of religious sociology emerged rapidly during the post-war period (Dobbelaere, 2000: 433) in Ireland (Conway, 2011) and to a lesser extent in the UK (Brewer, 2007) and Germany. Even France, that most secular of states, boasted an indigenous religious Catholic sociology throughout the latter part of the 20th century which, following Le Bras's (1956) study of religious participation rates, incidentally, was heavily empiricist in orientation. Religious sociology refers to a sociology *for* religion, as opposed to the sociology *of* religion. It takes the form of detailed empirical analyses undertaken in the service of religious institutions (Luckman, 1967), including most notably the Catholic Church (e.g. Newman, 1962; Ryan, 1967, 1994), and/or attempts to introduce an ethical dimension into scientific practice, as well as into the conception of the human subject (Gill, 1974; Dobbelaere, 2000). At its most extreme, religious sociology denies religion's status as a social fact.

Religious sociology does not confine its enquiries to religious matters. Rather, a unifying feature of each of the distinctive "national schools" detailed above is a concern with "making sociology relevant and pertinent to the social world and on marshalling Catholic religious values and beliefs in realising this" (Conway, 2011: 38). In the context of Ireland, for example, enquiry was historically directed towards social change more generally, with a conservative emphasis on normatively constructed cultural decline. While this agenda was stoked by semi-colonial anthropologists seeking to "salvage" (Clifford, 1989) an "authentic" but disappearing culture from the Irish West (Arensberg and

Kimball, 1968), it was seized upon by clerical sociologists in service of church and state, who normatively chronicled the culturally and morally destructive consequences of urbanisation (McKevitt, 1952; Newman, 1957 and 1958; Ryan, 1994) and exposure to modern (secular and "foreign") cultural influences (Devane, 1942, cited in Bell 1990). Unsurprisingly, the Catholic Church, presented as the saviour from the moral decline associated with social change (McKevitt, 1944), casts a long shadow over this sociology. Indeed, in a comment that bears more than a fleeting resemblance to Archer's analyses, the priest-sociologist McKevitt succinctly summarises this: "Catholics have an important role in delivering science from the prejudices of those whose positivist outlook prevents their taking a comprehensive view of social development" (McKevitt, 1944: ix)'

Beyond Ireland, the clerical origins of many religious sociologists have not only guided the trajectory of enquiry within the subfield (Dobbelaere, 2000: 434) but have been implicated in the intellectual isolation of the sociology *of* religion from mainstream sociological debates (Beckford, 1989; Altglas, 2014; Bruce, 2014). Never internationally dominant, in certain national contexts, including Ireland, religious sociology has been more influential than its secular counterpart. In Ireland, this is attributable to the historically cosy relationship between clerical sociology and a clerically dominated state (Irish social policy was also largely clerically determined). Moreover, as the introductory analysis of this volume makes clear, well beyond the confines of quasi-theocracies, religious sociology is alive and well; indeed, it is arguably in ascendance within the subfield of the sociology *of* religion (Conway, 2011; Altglas, 2014; Bruce, 2014). In this sense, while it is true that secular sociology (as a distinctively more accurate depiction than Archer's "atheist" sociology) is and has been broadly dominant, it is simply wrong to suggest that *all* sociology privileges atheism, or that the number of believing sociologists is quantifiable on "one's fingers."

Secondly, Archer implicates the social sciences' methodological endorsement of empiricism in the preclusion of "authentic human relations with the divine" (2004: 63). Recall, the argument here is that positivistic empiricism is incapable of grasping that which is unobservable and is thus ill-equipped to investigate vast segments of ontological reality, hence the necessity of realism and retroduction. In this stylised portrait, the sociologist is indistinguishable from some caricatured natural scientist – clad in white laboratory coat as (s) he utilises specialist instruments and apparatuses to coldly observe the world, dismissing the unobservable as metaphysical speculation. As Archer doubtless knows, even the most apparently committed early positivist sociologists have long stood accused of admitting unobservables into their analyses. As Johnson et al., describing social theory more generally, note: "Structure is not accessible to direct observation. In fact what can be observed must, in turn, be explained by that underlying structure of material reality" (Johnson et al., 1984: 31).

Moreover, a glance in even the most elementary of contemporary sociology textbooks confirms sociology's canonical approach to be something other than strict positivist empiricism.[3] If once upon a time, "physics envy" genuinely motivated sociology's founding fathers, it is difficult to imagine contemporary sociologists bursting into tears at the misguided suggestion that their approach is "unscientific," let alone abandoning theoretical constructs premised on what Smith terms the "observable trace effects of the unobservable" (Smith, 2010: 94). To offer concrete examples, it is hard to imagine Bourdieu relinquishing the habitus from his theory of practice, Foucault the panoptican from his model of governmentality, or Butler the idea of patriarchy from her worldview, on the grounds that as unobservables, strict positivists would deny the ontological existence of such phenomena and relegate them to metaphysical constructs. Sociologists, whether realists or otherwise, rarely construct theoretical models comprising only empirically verifiable observables.

Thirdly, and perhaps the most alarming harbinger of what follows, is Archer's implication that sociology's "epistemological break: [wherein] the individual is, and cannot but be social" (Altglas, 2014: 8) is somehow a false premise. The citation of Alston's "man as capable of being addressed by God, capable of freely deciding whether or not to follow God's behests" (Alston, 1991: 240) foreshadows her proposed remedy to the preclusion of transcendence from social scientific models. While Archer implicitly postulates this remedial action as addressing the "defective" consequence of omission for "social science and faith alike" (Archer, 2004: 64), it remains unclear how this restoration benefits social science. The reason for the preclusion in the first instance stemmed, apparently, in part from empiricism, and in part from sociology's requirements of establishing the human subject as entirely social to chauvinistically buttress disciplinary prestige and power – one implication of which is that the divine was something sociologists simply *chose* to ignore for methodological, epistemological, and practical convenience.

To be sure, the proposed restoration benefits faith, faith-based enquiry, and, doubtlessly, Archer's own sensibilities, but it contradicts the central tenets of sociology and must, therefore, be resisted. As illustrated in reference to the ability to "freely decide," Archer's arguments regarding her "Man of Faith" (Archer, 2004: 67), coupled with her suspicion of, or outright attack on, the social (and sociological) origins of the human subject, are not only non-sociological – they

---

3   See, for example Browne (2015), Haralambos and Holborn (2013), Giddens (2013), or any other introductory text for confirmation.

are *anti-sociological*. If man is "free" from the established sociological confines of social structure (however non-deterministically conceived), to the extent that he can communicate with an extra-social world at his (or God's?) own pleasing, then he cannot be the centre of a sociological model; in fact, "man" here seems little more than a common sense protagonist. While realist interventions more generally begin from a premise that "things social are rarely, if ever as they seem" (Jenkins, 1996: 30), what appears here borders on an unchecked realism, whereby the casual designation of ontological reality to various unobservable phenomena risks regressing into common sense.

If the model refutes sociology's central premise that the individual is social, it is difficult to see how it can be thought of as a sociological model. Likewise, if rather than critically breaking with prenotions, it instead seeks to formalise, justify, or legitimise such common sense through incorporation into formal, codified scientific theory, this is not sociology (Mills, 1959; Durkheim, 1982). Archer's proposed model appears to fall short in both regards. If it is indeed the case that the model is not sociological, then it must be banished from beneath the canopy of scientific legitimacy that sociology bequeaths. Just as the atheist who, to use Archer's own terminology, demonstrates "a commitment to a belief in the absence of religious phenomena" (Archer, 2004: 63), should and taxonomically *could* not be considered a model "believer," so too the demonstration of such an *anti-sociological imagination* must not be promulgated under sociology's banner.

The Man of Faith: Archer's Model of Man

As should be evident from the above, the apparent deficiency of various models of man lies in their systematic preclusion of authentic relations with the divine. For Archer, this is epitomised by two distinctive and opposing models – "modernity's man" and "society's being." Of the former, she rightly critiques the "anchorman of microeconomics and the hero of neoliberalism" (Archer, 2004: 65) on the grounds of reductionism. With his actions reducible to instrumental rationality, this "opportunistic bargain hunter" stands "outside of history" (65). He is not constituted by historically determined relations, but is self-sufficient in his always conscious navigation of means-ends relationships. While *homo economicus* may be encroaching into American sociology (Becker, 1976; Elster, 1986), he has made precious few gains across the Atlantic, where rational actor theory remains a minority positon within the discipline's environs, confined, ironically, to occasional appearances via right *realist* criminology. The deficiencies of this impoverished imagining are too many to list here, and Archer needs no assistance to disarm this "colonial adventurer ... [in his] bid to conquer social science in general" (Archer, 2004: 65). Needless to say, this is achieved on the grounds of the reductionist impoverishment in terms of action, which, obviously, negates the apparently real emergent human capacity to "transcend rationality and to have ultimate concerns" (Archer, 2004: 65). In dismissing the reductive essentialism of "the modern self [as] universally pre-given" (64), Archer appears poised to mount a constructionist critique to finish off the now hapless rational actor, but instead turns her attention to the apparently equal deficiencies of the constructionist model itself. Ironically, as the following makes clear, Archer's attack of *homo economicus*' reductive essentialism is more applicable to the model of the transcendental self – the Man of Faith – she seeks to install as an alternative, than to that which she critiques.

Of "society's being," Archer depicts a socio-centric model, wherein "man is the product of society, as is his God" (Archer, 2004: 67). While this seems a not unreasonable starting point, this state of affairs is presented as the grand finale of an established realist critique, which centres on the model's apparent reductionism. Specifically, constructionists stand accused of reducing ontologically irreducible human powers of "selfhood, reflexivity, memory, emotionality and belief – to society's discourse" (Archer, 2004: 66). To dwell on emotion, evoking the assertions of a strong discursive psychology, society's being is as emotionally repressed as his rational cousin *homo economicus*. Moved to tears only when society has bequeathed the language and meaning of tears, his feelings are never his own: they are mere appropriations. In Archer's characterisation, society's being is an impoverished imagining, particularly in his postmodern variant, where he amounts to little more than "a grammatical fiction, a product of learning to master the first person pronoun system" (Archer, 2004: 66). In essence, and here we see the realist ontology coming to the fore, the objection is to constructionism's apparent inability to acknowledge the ontological reality of the self as existing separately from, and irreducible to, his organic molecular makeup, on the one hand, or his discursive construction – his pieced-togetherness out of pre-given discourses which are "society's gift" – on the other. Society's being, presented as such, is the enemy of the ontologically real emergent self, who, irreducible to biological or linguistic constituent parts, possesses emergent causal capacities to affect and interact with reality. Presented as such, society's being is a desperately impoverished imagining.

There remain, however, a number of impediments to the substitution of society's being for realism's self. Firstly, emphasis on the causal capacities of the "emergent self" echoes the "retreat of the social" diagnosed elsewhere (Kapferer, 2005; Altglas, 2014) and risks replacing a caricature of the overly socialised cultural dope (Garfinkel, 1967), with an equally problematic *agent unbounded* – free from the normal confines of structure. Here, again, we see *anti-sociological man*. Moreover, the critique targets not the intrinsically reductive essentialism of society's being *per se*, but Archer's deliberately reductionist *reading* of the constructionist model. Archer dismisses society's being as moveable only through "reasons appropriated from society" and suggests this "deflect[s] all real interest on to the forces of socialisation, as in every version of social constructionism" (Archer, 2004: 66). Not only is the appearance of "interest" here confusing, suggesting at once scholarly enquiry and the ideological interest of a super-organic society, but Archer casually corrals "every version of social constructionism" into the same conceptual enclosure.

This collapses the distinction between extreme versions of hyper-constructionism and less radical approaches, wherein few would deny that their agent is capable *in potentia* of emotionality, affectivity, or other obviously human motivations. For those who assert that the social is prior (a collective to which we might imagine most sociologists, not only constructionists, belong), this need not lead to the caricature advanced by Archer. All that is being asserted is that potential becomes actualised through the social.

We are capable of blushing with embarrassment, but as anthropology rightly notes, embarrassment is contingent upon historical specificity and cultural context. The argument here is more subtle than Archer acknowledges. Society's being is not the victim of social hydraulics but becomes relatively (dis)empowered through his interaction with collectively produced (as opposed to socially pre-given) and differentially available material, discursive, and symbolic resources. It is anti-sociological to imagine that the agent moved to bear arms in defence of his nation (or who refuses to), ostensibly a reasonable example of an "ultimate concern," does so outside human history – as if this ultimate concern is ontologically pre-given. Such an imagining not only de-historicises, reifies, and essentialises the (sociologically) obviously historically specific and socially constructed object of his motivations, but also implies the *agent unbounded* – the man who not only makes history, but does so under circumstances of his own pleasing. Here we find the primordial Braveheart whose unmediated and essential love of (ontological) nation moves him to ride into battle and cry freedom before the nation has been constructed (Said, 1978; Hobsbawm and Ranger, 1992).

Adopting a moderate constructionist approach, which necessitates historicising the episode, does not imply the agent is *incapable* of emotion. It merely acknowledges that that which awakens his emotion is situated rather than universal, contra Archer's realist actor who, equipped with essential causal properties, appears as outside human history as *homo economicus*. Moreover, there remains a suspicion that the purpose of the intervention is not to remedy the deficiencies and discontents of the constructionist model, but to forge a model which doesn't collapse when its protagonist transcends the fourth wall of the social to communicate with the extra social – in this case, the divine.[4] This is not assuaged when we find that, of all the causal capacities denied to society's being, his greatest failing is that he is "closed against revelation [except] in so far is it is mediated to him by society" (Archer, 2004: 67).

Whiskey: God's Gift, or Society's?

True to critical realism's central assertions, Archer posits an ontological reality that exists prior to language – a world of sometimes unobservable entities with causal properties (neatly encapsulated by gravity) – and positions the divine herein, claiming "God ... pertains to this space" (Archer, 2004: 74). Notwithstanding the rather unconvincing leap of faith required to move from gravity to God, straying beyond the usual realist remit, she argues that a direct and unmediated experience of reality (of which God has now become part) *is* a distinct possibility. "Imperialist empiricism's" epistemic fallacy, however, renders the positivist scientific method ill-equipped to adequately access reality (including the divine), as evidence of both is *experiential* and irreducible to sense perception. Returning to her original premise, Archer bemoans the fact that, unlike other unobservables, which are readily admitted into realist models, transcendence is "forced to stand before the bar of sense data" (2004: 70). Mimicking (but inverting) Bourdieusian *illusio*, she implicates "inconsistent realists" who conflate their "own lack of personal religious awareness" with evidence of the absence of the divine in this state of affairs. But how, if not through empiricism, do realists afford a given entity the status of ontological existence? Two linked propositions are advanced and swiftly dismissed, namely O'Hear's claim that ontologically existent entities will exert similar effects on similarly situated observers (O'Hear, 1984: 45) and Gaskin's assertion that "any other person rightly and properly situated with normally functioning *senses*, powers of attention, and a suitable conceptual understanding will have the same experience" (Gaskin, 1984: 80). Not only does Archer dismiss these on the grounds of a creeping empiricism (the italicisation of "senses" is her contribution), she argues they are philosophically flawed, countering with examples of her own: whisk(e)y and wine.

---

4 Or as it later transpires, a remarkably historically situated Christian understanding of the divine.

Conjuring the imagery of a tasting circle, the argument is that when the ontologically existing entities (wine and whiskey) fail to produce a similar effect
on similarly positioned observers (tasters), we do not cast the same suspicion
on the tasters' experience as we would on "believers" (Archer, 2004: 71). While
intoxicating, these examples belie either a gaping vacuum of understanding
pertaining to the construction of taste (Bourdieu, 1984), or a deliberately reductionist understanding of wine and whiskey as essential and pre-given – as
something other than cultural products (Beckert, Rossel, and Schenk, 2014). Of
the latter possibility, a good sociology of whiskey should be unconcerned with
adjudicating the intrinsic properties of the whiskey – the antithesis of sociological enquiry here is the question: which whiskey tastes best? Nor should a sociologist of religion concern herself with which religious practice, teaching, or
scripture offers the most accurate or authentic account of the divine. As Bourdieu (2010) cautions, theological debates are not sociological; these are tasks
for those with a stake in the religious field (or in this case, a quarrel between rival distillers!). Rather, the sociologist of whiskey must understand whiskey as a
cultural artefact – a social fact born not of essential quality (like gravity), but a
relational product, situated always within a field. Only by de-essentialising the
object (whether whiskey or religion) which, even though it may (or may not)
possess some ontologically real existence, is *always* mediated, can we begin
to understand why similarly positioned observers may experience it so differently and by doing so begin to arrive at an understanding of the construction
of taste (of whiskey as of religion). This requires an acceptance of the situatedness of the experiencer – meaning *sociological* analysis of the ways in which
an individual's experience of the cultural product is shaped by, amongst other
things, her ethnicity, class, gender. Given that globally, 50 percent of people do
not drink alcohol (WHO, 2011: xi), and that, as Archer is no doubt aware, a large
subset of this population practises abstinence for religious reasons, it is unsur-
prising that the experience of whiskey, including but not limited to the sensory
taste of the tipple, cannot but be social. That whiskey containing the letter "e"
sells (and tastes) better in Ireland than in Scotland should and must preclude
the possibility that taste is unmediated, strongly suggesting a constructionist
rather than realist explanation for Archer's example.

The same holds for Archer's apparently universal transcendental relations
between man and God which operate outside of human history. Drawing on
Merleau-Ponty and Piaget, she inverts strong constructionism, whereby "what
we experience reality to be will determine what we talk about in the public
medium, and not vice versa" (Archer, 2004: 68). Concretely, this implies the
direct experience of God sits outside God as mediated. In spite of this, it is
scarcely possible to imagine a *more* situated and historically peculiar God than

Archer's "God of Love" (Archer, 2004: 75). "He" (and it is a he) bears an uncanny resemblance to the transcendental power which moved the Irish priest-
sociologists (Devane, 1942; McKevitt, 1944; Newman, 1972) to social enquiry in
service of Church. To be sure, "he" is of Judeo-Christian extraction, evidenced
by the appearance of the bizarre citation from Luke's gospel, "Martha, you
worry and fret about so many things, and yet few are needed" (Luke 10: 41), and
the allusion to the "rich young man [who] chose love of Mammon over that
of God" (Archer, 2004: 77), from the gospel of Mark. Not only is the apparently
universal nature of God exposed here as highly historically specific, but despite
the appeals to religious experience, whereby man and God are apparently
united in a communion which is ontologically separate from the social, there
could be few more rigidly institutionalised and mediated religious experiences
than those of biblical scripture. Moreover, as Archer's argument unfolds, the
appearance of a highly peculiar discussion of sin (2004: 77), coupled with the
appearance of St. Ignatius (2004: 79), reveals that not only is the apparently
ontologically real God Christian, "he" is unmistakably Catholicism's God. The
problem, then, is that Archer's transcendence is an eloquently framed common sense construct, an emic discourse appropriated from the promulgations
of the Catholic Church and offered a degree of scientific legitimacy by being
disguised as realist ontology – and as sociology

The Implications of Transcendence

While the introductory analysis of this volume asserts that the sociology of
religion is besieged by the anti-sociological proposition that "religion cannot
be fully grasped as a social fact" (Altglas, this volume), Archer should not be
solely situated amidst these besieging forces. True, by asserting an authentic
and unmediated relationship with the divine, thus denying the forces of socialisation which lead to the formulation of a religious habitus (substituted in
her analysis as an extra-social "spiritual sensibility"), Archer is asserting that
religion can't be sociologically grasped. The idea that this sensibility is cultivated, not socially through embeddedness in a religious field composed of
religious institutions, wherein norms and values are incompletely inculcated,
but through extra-social communion with the divine, is anti-sociological. Undoubtedly, sociologists of religion would implicate Archer's *illusio* in her arguments, drawing attention to her (not unusual) positionality, whereby one
foot is planted in the scientific field and the other firmly in the religious field.
Like Archer, I am not a sociologist of religion and will leave it to more suitably

qualified colleagues to examine the implications of the encroachment of religion upon the sociology *of* religion as scientific practice, as well as to put forward the case for bringing the social back in. My objection to the admittance of transcendence concerns the implications not for the sociology of religion, but for sociology *per se*. Specifically, and as demonstrated below, the admittance of common sense constructs into scientific theory, coupled with what is tantamount to a denial of sociological understandings of identity, and worse, social practice, renders Archer's intervention something more than an assault on the sociology of religion.

The problem with the admittance of transcendence is akin to the problem with the admittance of any common sense construct into scientific theory – namely that an unchecked realism risks formalising and reifying such constructs (whether social, cultural, moral, or scientific) by according them a scientific legitimacy. Too often such constructs obfuscate, at best, or buttress, at worst, differential power relations, as is evident with Archer's highly peculiar, situated, and historically specific understanding of an apparently universal process. We can only presume that this authentic relation with (the unmistakably Christian understanding of) the divine is superior to inauthentic relations with multiple (or no) gods, which appear to be denied the ontological status of the Christian God in her account. As discussed above, a sociological understanding of the object (whiskey or transcendence) must not simply accept emic discourses and then regurgitate them, reified and essentialised, as scientific knowledge. In the case of religion, this is to descend into theology, while in the case of whiskey, it is to become a whiskey critic. Neither is an example of sociology.

Moreover, the charge of epistemic fallacy should not open the floodgates to the acceptance of all manner of common sense constructs. While the realist acknowledgement that much of the world consists of unobservables is both plausible and worthy, potentially remedying the privileged status that positivists afford to the observable, this should not gift the unobservable some equally privileged, unverifiable, or unquestionable ontological status. While not all that is real is observable, neither is all that is unobservable real – both must withstand scrutiny, whether empirical or otherwise. In Archer's case, the method, disguised as retroduction, seems to be an unquestioning acceptance of institutionalised Catholic teaching. We must guard against this realist entry via the backdoor. Such entry not only potentially affords the absurd, for example, magic, a place in scientific theory on the grounds that it can't be disproved without resorting to empiricism, but also risks reifying and essentialising profoundly social categories, such as gender, nationality, or religion, by affording them an ontological existence which necessarily limits alternatives (in much the same way as the word "natural" can close off alternative possibilities). Recall, a central weakness of religious sociology was and is the unquestioning assumption that (emic) religious values and beliefs provide a framework for a just and ethical society. While it is undoubtedly true that emic categories can become imbued with causal properties, they cannot be understood as "real," let alone pre-given. The purpose of sociology must be more than the reproduction of emic discourses and truth claims. Not to adopt such a position violates basic epistemological premises of sociology, demonstrating an *unwillingness* to dispense with prenotions and a reluctance to consider the ways in which social categories do not come to us (or emerge to acknowledge the realist contribution) as pre-givens. If emergence does occur, it is via construction and mediation.

Perhaps the greatest sociological abomination is the manner in which a spiritual sensibility apparently emerges and the types of action to which it gives rise. Archer is clear throughout; authentic transcendental relations are extra-social. They emerge from the cultivation of a spiritual sensibility that, by its very nature, is detached from any institutional anchor. Archer imputes a universalism to the interventions of the divine, in that everyone, apparently, has some experiential awareness of the divine (although she is arguably projecting her own experience onto those she claims to investigate) (Archer, 2004: 69). The key to cultivating an emerging spiritual sensibility is not to socially enmesh oneself in religious institutions, but more simply, not to "turn away" (73). A spiritual sensibility, defined thus, is the taxonomic other of a religious habitus (which is, and cannot but be, socially determined). Again, the sociological question here might pertain to *why* some turn away, while others don't – necessitating either an investigation of institutionalised religious identity formation, or an acceptance of a blind and un-socialised "faith." While this is a matter for sociologists of religion, a wider implication is that a spiritual sensibility is accorded causal properties, including the power to effect the emergence of identity (in the form of "ultimate concerns"), and, in turn, to influence (if not determine) social action. Here, Archer's account departs from merely asserting that religion cannot be grasped as a social fact – if both identity and action are extra-socially constituted, it follows that neither identity nor action can be sociologically understood. To accept this position is to emasculate the discipline. It posits, at the very least, a discrete category of identity formation and consequent action inaccessible to the sociological gaze, while permitting the possibility that other identities are likewise extra-socially constituted, giving rise to endless possibilities of action unmediated by the social. This is not sociology.

Conclusions

Archer posits that the preclusion of authentic relations with the divine has proved "defective for social science and faith alike" (Archer, 2004: 63). Yet beyond the confines of the subfield of the sociology of religion, the admittance to scientific theory of common sense constructs and emic discourses, legitimised by a (misguided) hyper-realist ontology, undermines sociological enquiry and risks legitimising the discourses of situated actors and interests. By proposing the existence of an emergent and extra-social spiritual sensibility, along with associated identities and action, Archer lapses into *anti-sociology* – effectively offering an essentialist model of identity which emerges outside the social and gives rise to an equally essentialist "agent unbounded" who acts outside human history.

In admitting common sense, (potentially) serving particular interests, and emasculating sociology through what is tantamount to a denial of the social (in terms of identity and action), Archer's supposedly "critical" realist model bears an uncanny resemblance to the (un)critical Catholic sociology of mid-20th-century Ireland, where one priest sociologist, likewise positioned simultaneously in the fields of religion and science, described sociology thus:

> Sociological instruments are at the service of the Church. Properly used they can be of immense practical value. But they are unable to provide complete explanations of human phenomena and they take no account of the mysterious workings of the grace of God.
>
> NEWMAN, 1962: 2

This is not a ground-breaking science at the limits of the social, but a retreat to a more reactionary position. By seeking to marry the religious and scientific fields by admitting transcendence, Archer has not addressed a defect in social science. Rather, through her *de facto* denial of the social, she has violated the discipline whose science she purports to practice.

References

Altglas, Véronique. 2014. *From yoga to kabbalah: religious exoticism and the logics of bricolage.* Oxford; New York: Oxford University Press.

Alston, William. 1991. *Perceiving God: the epistemology of religious experience.* Ithaca: Cornell University Press.

Archer, Margaret. 2004. "Models of man: the admission of transcendence." In *Transcendence: critical realism and God*, edited by Margaret Archer, 63–81. London: Routledge.

Archer, Margaret. 1995. *Realist social theory*. Cambridge: Cambridge University Press.

Archer, Margaret. 1984. *Realist social theory: the morphogenetic approach*. New York: Cambridge University Press.

Arensberg, Conrad M., and Solon T. Kimball. (1940) 1968. *Family and community in Ireland*, 2nd edition. Cambridge: Harvard University Press.

Baudrillard, Jean. 1986. *Simulations*. New York: Semiotext(e)/Foreign Agents.

Becker, Gary Stanley. 1976. *The economic approach to human behaviour*. Chicago: Chicago University Press.

Beckert, Jens, Jörg Rössel, and Patrick Schenk. 2014. "Wine as cultural product: symbolic capital and price formation in the wine field." MPIfG Discussion Paper 14/2. Cologne: Max Planck Institute for the Study of Societies.

Beckford, James. 1989. *Religion and advanced industrial society*. London: Routledge.

Bell, Desmond. 1990. *Acts of Union*. Basingstoke: Palgrave Macmillan.

Berger, Peter. (1967) 2011. *The sacred canopy: elements of a sociological theory of religion*. New York: Open Road.

Berger, Peter, and Thomas Luckman. 1966. *The social construction of reality: a treatise on the sociology of knowledge*. London: Allen Lane.

Bhaskar, Roy. 1976. *The possibility of naturalism*. Hemel Hempstead: Harvester.

Blasi, Anthony J. 2014. *Sociology of religion in America: a history of secular fascination with religion*. Leiden: Brill.

Blasi, Anthony J., and Bernard F. Donahoe. 2002. *A history of sociological research and teaching at Catholic Notre Dame University, Indiana*. Lewiston: Edwin Mellen Press.

Bourdieu, Pierre. (1987) 2010. "Sociologists of belief and beliefs of sociologists," *Nordic Journal of Religion and Society* 23(1): 1–7.

Bourdieu, Pierre. 1984. *Distinction: a social critique on the judgement of taste*. London: Routledge and Kegan Paul.

Brewer, John. 2007. "Sociology and theology reconsidered: religious sociology and the sociology of religion in Britain," *History of the Human Sciences* 20(2): 7–28.

Browne, Ken. 2015. *Sociology for AQA volume 1: AS and 1st year A-level*. Cambridge: Polity Press.

Bruce, Steve. 2014. "What sort of social theory would benefit the sociology of religion?" In *Sociological theory and the question of religion*, edited by Andrew McKinnon and Marta Trzebiatowska, 33–48. Aldershot: Ashgate.

Clifford, James. 1989. "The others: beyond the 'salvage paradigm,'" *Third Text* 3(6): 73–78.

Conway, Brian. 2011. "Catholic sociology in Ireland in comparative perspective," *The American Sociologist* 42: 34–55.

Devane, Richard F. 1942. *Challenge from youth: a documented study of youth in youth movements*. Dublin: Browne and Nolan.

Dobbelaere, Karel. 2000. "From religious sociology to sociology of religion: toward globalization?" *Journal for the Scientific Study of Religion* 39(4): 433–447.

Durkheim, Émile. 1982. *The rules of sociological method: and selected texts on sociology and its method*. London: Macmillan.

Elster, Jon, ed. 1986. *Rational choice*. New York: New York University Press.

Garfinkel, Howard. 1967. *Studies in ethnomethodology*. Englewood Cliffs: Prentice Hall.

Gaskin, John C.A. 1984. *The quest for eternity*. New York: Penguin.

Giddens, Anthony, and Philip Sutton. 2013. *Sociology*. Cambridge: Polity Press.

Gill, Robin. 1974. "The critique of religious sociology," *Social Studies* 3(2): 103–117.

Haralambos, Michael, and Martin Holborn. 2013. *Sociology: themes and perspectives*, 8th edition. London: Collins.

Hobsbawm, Eric, and Terrence Ranger. 1992. *The invention of tradition*. Cambridge: Cambridge University Press.

Jenkins, Richard. 1996. *Key sociologists: Pierre Bourdieu*, 2nd edition. London; New York: Routledge.

Johnson, Terry, Chris Dandeker, and Clive Ashworth. 1984. *The structure of social theory*. London: Macmillan.

Kapferer, Bruce. 2005. "Introduction: the social construction of reductionist thought and practice." In *The retreat of the social: the rise and rise of reductionism*, edited by Bruce Kaperer, 1–18. Oxford: Berghahn Books.

Le Bras, Gabriel. 1956. *Etudes de sociologie religieuse*, Volume 2. Paris: Presses Universitaires de France.

Luckman, Thomas. 1967. *The invisible religion: the problem of religion in modern society*. London: Macmillan.

Lyotard, Jean-François. 1984. *The postmodern condition*. Minneapolis: University of Minnesota Press.

McKevitt, Peter. 1952. "Sociological aspect of rural decline," *Christus Rex* 6: 52–62.

McKevitt, Peter. 1944. *The plan of society*. Dublin: Catholic Truth Society.

Mills, Charles Wright. 1959. *The sociological imagination*. Oxford: Oxford University Press.

Newman, Jeremiah. 1972. *Introduction to sociology*. Dublin: Talbot Press.

Newman, Jeremiah. 1962. "The priests of Ireland: a socio-religious survey," *Irish Ecclesiastical Record* 98: 1–27.

Newman, Jeremiah. 1958. "The future of rural Ireland," *Landmark* 47 (February): 402.

Newman, Jeremiah. 1957. "The sociology of rural Ireland," *Rural Ireland*, 75–80.

O'Hear, Anthony. 1984. *Experience, explanation and faith*. London: Routledge and Kegan Paul.

Ryan, Liam. 1994. "The changing Irish family," *The Furrow* 45(4): 212–220.

Ryan, Liam. 1967., "Social dynamite: a study of early school-leavers," *Christus Rex* 21(1): 7–44.

Said, Edward. 1978. *Orientalism*. Hammondsworth: Penguin Books.

Smith, Christian. 2010. *What is a person? Rethinking humanity, social life and moral good from the person up*. Chicago: University of Chicago Press.

Stark, Rodney. 2003., *One true God: historical consequences of monotheism*. Princeton: Princeton University Press.

World Health Organisation. 2011. *Global status report on alcohol and health*. Geneva: WHO, accessed 3 November 2016, from http://www.who.int/substance_abuse/publications/global_alcohol_report/msbgsruprofiles.pdf.

CHAPTER 3

Spirituality and Discipline: Not a Contradiction in Terms

Véronique Altglas

Introduction

This chapter develops a critique of one of contemporary sociology of religion's main paradigms, its distinction between spirituality and religion, based on a presupposed emancipation of individuals from social norms and constraints. It identifies the fundamental epistemological flaws in the origins of this paradigm, in particular the conflation of emic and etic discourses, leading scholars of religion to uncritically confuse social actors' beliefs with an analysis of the social world. Ultimately, the chapter argues that this epistemological flaw springs, in part, from intellectuals' ideological assumptions, suggesting the need for a more reflexive understanding of "freedom" as a socially situated ideal.

A common assumption in the study of religion is that religious traditions have lost their regulatory functions and, as a consequence, social actors have ceased to conform to social constraints and shared norms. Hervieu-Léger notes: "In the domain of religion like elsewhere, we have observed the capacity of the individual to elaborate his own universe of norms, and values from his own singular experience tend to impose themselves beyond the regulatory endeavours of institutions" (Hervieu-Léger, 1999: 69, author's translation). By and large, the figure of the autonomous believer who freely chooses religious practices and beliefs according to personal desires and needs to realise his or her self has become paradigmatic within the sociology of religion. "Spirituality,"[1] "New Age" or what Heelas calls "self religions" are often designated as the archetypes of such individualised forms of religiosity (Heelas, 1996). Hervieu-Léger, for instance, sees in New Age the "self-validation of belief," whereby individuals refer exclusively to their subjective experience in order to authenticate religious teachings (Hervieu-Léger, 1999: 180). Similarly, Heelas insists on the growing significance of a radical de-traditionalisation process resulting in

---

[1] "Spirituality" in this chapter refers to the use of the term by research participants and scholars.

"self-authority." In New Age, he says, individuals free themselves from institutions and collective beliefs in favour of a truth to be found "within," so that "authority lies with the self, or more broadly, the natural" (Heelas, 1996: 67).

This emancipation from the social dimension of religion has been said to constitute a societal shift: Heelas and Woodhead argue contemporary religious life is affected by "a turn away from life lived in terms of external or 'objective' roles, duties and obligations, and a turn towards life lived by reference to one's own subjective experiences" (Heelas and Woodhead, 2005: 2). According to them, this "subjective turn" expresses itself in a growing "subjective wellbeing culture" focusing on individual self-fulfilment which, in turn, fosters a "spiritual revolution" (2).

In the following passage, Wood discusses the epistemological and methodological weaknesses of what he calls the "paradigm of spirituality":

> In sum, by positing the existence of self-authority, the sociology of spirituality abnegates a properly sociological interpretation of the phenomena it addresses. Through its conceptual distinction between "religion" and "spirituality," this sociology lifts people out of their social contexts, with the result that it fails adequately to address social practice, social interaction, and the wider contexts of people's lives and biographies.
>
> WOOD, 2010: 267

Wood's (2007, 2009, 2010) work underscores the sociology of spirituality's lack of critical analysis of social actors' claims to self-authority, notably its focus on discourses to the detriment of the observation of social practices and interactions and its lack of consideration for the ways power and authority might be exerted in deregulated religious settings.

This chapter furthers this critique and invites the reader to a critical reflection on religious individualism by drawing on empirical research conducted on New Religious Movements (NRMs) over the past 15 years. The case studies are unconventional versions of Hinduism (Siddha Yoga, Sivananda Centres) and Judaism (Kabbalah Centre).[2] They combine pop psychology with yoga,

---

2   Muktananda, the founder of Siddha Yoga, started his own ashram near Bombay in 1961 and welcomed westerners before travelling worldwide in the 1970s. When he died in 1982, Siddha Yoga represented a transnational organisation said to attract 300,000 disciples and sympathisers who are overwhelmingly westerners. A woman, Gurumayi, is currently the leader of the movement. Siddha Yoga implies a strong devotional relationship between the disciple and the guru; the latter bestows the awakening of divine energy, called *shaktipat*. This experience, as well as meditation and chanting, is supposed to lead to the awareness of God

meditation or Jewish mysticism in teachings presented as "spiritual" – that is, understood as non-coercive, practical tools aiming at the realisation of the self. These movements characteristically attract individuals who are neither Hindu nor Jewish, who do not intend to convert to these religions but explore, successively or simultaneously, a range of teachings and alternative therapies. Despite being more circumscribed and organised than New Age's networks of individuals and events, these NRMs foster similar claims about individual freedom of choice and determination in "spirituality."

The chapter demonstrates why, even if we focus on social actors' discourses and representations, their assertions of their self-authority cannot be taken for granted as an accurate description of the social world but require critical analysis. It underscores that scholars' focus on self-authority is tremendously selective. It neglects the moral imperatives about personal growth and self-actualisation so pervasively expressed by "spiritual seekers" and their teachers. It also overlooks the recurrent references to transcendent authorities in discourses of spirituality which legitimate prescriptions and rules and promote certain attitudes and practices while discouraging others.

Overall, representations (and practices) show spirituality is envisaged – and enacted – by social actors as a discipline of the self that requires the awareness and control of one's emotions, behaviours, and thoughts. Spirituality, as a self-discipline, sheds light on the fact that, far from being "natural," the self, attitudes, and emotions are socially shaped and do not pre-exist the discourses and practices that constitute them. In fact, they are deeply political. The aim of realising a flexible, resourceful, and autonomous self resonates with strong social norms and imperatives, which clearly reflect contemporary Euro-American societies' political and economic structures. Although beyond

---

within, also understood as the realisation of the self. The name Sivananda is associated with one of the most well-known teachings of yoga, yet he never left Asia. His Indian and western disciples disseminated his teaching transnationally. One in particular, Vishnu-Devananda opened centres all over the world in his master's name. Their teaching training course is widely known in the world of yoga. The Kabbalah Centre was founded by a New Yorker, Philip Berg who started to teach Kabbalah in Tel Aviv in 1971 to reach out to young secularised Israelis with a non-coercive and spiritualised form of Judaism. Berg returned to the United States and, at the turn of the 1990s, his mission became the spiritual growth of humankind. Courses and literature were simplified and detached from their Jewish background; personal fulfilment and happiness became the central aim of the teaching. The Kabbalah Centre took off with the opening of a centre in California that attracted celebrities. It is claimed that 10 million have visited its centres, although the number of committed members probably amounts to a few thousand only. Today, the majority of members have no Jewish background (Altglas, 2014).

the scope of this chapter, it would be worth undertaking further research on initiatives and programmes offering spirituality to the poor, prison inmates, children, or the unemployed, as the attempts of religious movements to reach out to those who are the least in the position to freely choose spiritual teachings and practices sheds light on the normative and regulating potential of these disciplines of the self.

Analysing Discourses about Spirituality

Distinguishing Emic and Etic Discourses

> With a religion you've generally got a head and you've got someone telling you what you have to believe and what you shouldn't believe and Siddha Yoga isn't like that: they let you take on board what you're ready for. The thing about Siddha Yoga is you get the experiences to back up what the guru is explaining, you do get signs. It hasn't been my experience with Catholicism.
>
> ALISON, Siddha Yoga

> Sometimes in religion, it's a feeling that you have to do it. But in kabbalah and spirituality you don't have to do anything.
>
> NOA, Kabbalah Centre

Rejection of the authority of tradition and its rules is pervasive among those involved in New Age networks, holistic milieus, and NRMs and who identify with "spirituality." They recurrently depict "religion," especially the one they were born into, as "imposed from the outside," "out of touch with life," morally corrupted, normative, oppressive and prescriptive. By contrast, they identify their current practices and beliefs with "spirituality," which they present as coming "from within" and personally experienced, hence, authentic, free, personal, and fulfilling. These individuals are popularly called the SBNR – "Spiritual But Not Religious" (Erlandson, 2000). Their discourses reflect the trajectory of those socialised to religion in their youth, formally disaffiliated from familial religious institutions in early adulthood, and now looking for meaning and self-fulfilment in new settings that do not entail the obligations and commitments of their youth.[3]

---

3 Disaffiliated individuals do not always seek new forms of religiosity, as underscored by the increased number of people declaring no religion, but the great majority of "spiritual seekers" have had a religious socialisation of some sort (Wood, 2009: 245).

The SBNR emic discourse is transferred into academic understandings of contemporary religious life. Wuthnow (1998) contrasts "dwellers" whose beliefs and practices are stable and rooted in institutions with the growing number of itinerant "seekers" whose volatile spiritual journey follows personal experience and active choice. The former group is territorialised, stable, and suggestive of compulsory practices regulated by institutions, while the latter is characterised by fluidity of belief and practice, autonomy, and mobility. Similarly, Hervieu-Léger uses two ideal types to analyse religion in modernity: the "observant" and the "pilgrim" (Hervieu-Léger, 1999: 98, 109), while Fath divides contemporary religious life into those "inherited" and those "chosen" (Fath, 2010). These perspectives all suggest that the chosen religion grows – as does its eclecticism – at the expense of the inherited one, as individuals' lifestyle and identity become less and less affected by social norms and structures.

If we believe individuals are effectively emancipated from collective norms and structures, resulting in the personalisation of religiosity, we should be struck by the pervasiveness of social actors' discourses contrasting organised religion and spirituality and associate the latter with individual freedom of choice and self-realisation. The banality of claims to have a personal and freely chosen spiritual path is ironic but highly significant: as Bender writes, "One suspects that the similarities in seekers' narratives point to their participation in social networks where such language is cultivated" (Bender, 2003: 70). Indeed, the scholar should first recognise the existence of a social trend and then investigate the ways individuals may be socialised to such views about religion and spirituality. We do not have to investigate at length to observe that claims about spirituality as freely chosen and beyond conformity to social norms are recurrently made by all sorts of "spiritual" leaders and teachers, within the loosest spiritual networks (see, for instance, Champion, 1990) or in more circumscribed settings, from NRMs to historical congregations.

In addition, these claims have a long history. For example, Vivekananda, who introduced Hinduism on the international scene at the World Parliament of Religions in Chicago in 1893, presented Vedanta as a "practical spirituality":

While some people devote their whole lives to their idol of a church and never rise higher, because with them religion means an intellectual assent to certain doctrines and doing good to their fellows, the whole religion of Hindu is centred in realization. (Vivekananda, 1965: 16)

Throughout the 20th century, Indian gurus frequently used this rhetoric to appeal to a Euro-American audience. They evoked "spirituality," relating it to personal fulfilment and subjective experience, presenting Vedanta, yoga, or meditation as the ultimate means to reach these goals. By contrast, they sometimes reproved the doctrinal and ritualistic character of religion – which initially implicitly meant Christianity (Halbfass, 1988: 380–381, 395–398). This rhetoric sprang from an affirmation of Hinduism in response to European imperialism and Christian missions in India, but it was also an efficient rhetorical means to spread their teaching abroad. Indeed, it resonated with Americans' and Europeans' sense of disenchantment and their desire to find in the Mystical East the virtues they believed the West had lost.

This discourse has certainly not faded. Chidananda, one of the leaders of the Divine Life Society founded by Indian guru Sivananda, defines yoga in the following way:

> Yoga is the practical aspect of the inner side of man's religion. The outer side of religion in its institutionalized and organized social aspect is its traditional form, made up of the periodical common or collective worship, be it in church, synagogue, mosque, temple or prayer house; its sacraments, ceremonial, ritual, etc. Whereas the inner side of religion in its deeply personal aspect of the individual's effort to spiritually progress towards God and obtain vital religious experience is termed yoga.
>
> CHIDANANDA, 2000

The rhetorical opposition of religion and spirituality is far from specific to neo-Hindu movements. Drawing on another religious tradition, the Kabbalah Centre's teachers, for example, associate religion with dogma, constraint, obedience, mindless ritual, lack of consciousness, and lack of fulfilment, opposing this to kabbalah and its spiritual nature. Through this approach, Kabbalah Centre teachers distinguish themselves from mainstream Judaism, with which they have had conflicting relationships: they often argue that Orthodox Jews observe rituals out of fear and obedience, ignoring their true meaning and purpose. In other words, some observe religion because they have inherited it as a tradition, while others choose voluntarily and consciously to undertake personal growth. This discourse has also been used by secularising Jews who, indeed, sometimes find in kabbalah a vibrant, mysterious – but Jewish – alternative to the mainstream religious institutions from which they have disenfranchised themselves. When the Kabbalah Centre started to reach out to non-Jews at the end of the 1990s, the rhetoric appealed to those eager to discover kabbalistic mysteries, yet unwilling to convert or even get close to Judaism.

In short, kabbalah is constantly claimed to be a universal wisdom for all humanity which has nothing to do with religion – including Judaism. I have repeatedly observed that these rhetorical discourses coming from a wide range of leaders and teachers of various organisations and networks are shared and reasserted by students and sympathisers alike. This certainly underlines their significance but obviously does not suggest their relationship to spirituality precludes collectively shared ideas and norms.

In other words, by uncritically embracing the beliefs of the religious field itself (i.e. being "spiritual" is being "not religious," so relations to transcendence and meaning have two different expressions, one individual and one social), scholars prevent themselves from developing a proper understanding of the notion of "spirituality." As already noted in Wood's work, taking for granted the representations of social actors as an accurate description of the social world is an important epistemological mistake. It obliterates the analytical work social scientists are supposed to produce about the data they collect and, hence, reproduces common sense assumptions – here, the ideological biases that underlie the notion of freely chosen spirituality.

Tracing its philosophical and theological origins, Martin shows how the notion of spirituality, deriving from William James' distinction between "religious experience" and "religious institutions," entails the assumption that there exists a universal and authentic life of the spirit, subsequently formalised in institutions and corrupted by human quests of power (Martin, 2014: 53–68). Indeed, contemporary theologians often contrast the institutional and collective dimension of religion with an inner and experiential dimension of human life, termed spirituality. For instance, Schneiders describes religions as "cultural systems" (Schneiders, 2003: 169–170) that carry the ultimate values of a given society, while spirituality is a universal anthropological constant:

> (S)pirituality, like personality, is a characteristic of the human being as such. It is the capacity of persons to transcend themselves through knowledge and love, that is, to reach beyond themselves in relationship to others and thus become more than self-enclosed material monads. In this sense, even the newborn child is spiritual while the most ancient rock is not.
>
> SCHNEIDERS, 2003: 165

Similarly, Habermacher presents spirituality as a "fundamental anthropological structure" which, before having a content,

> relates to the human condition, to the experience we have of our ways of being in the world. It designates the concrete quest of meaning, the

capacity to respond to life's daily challenges. Such quests and requests, attitudes and behaviours, go well beyond the frame of institutionalised religions.

HABERMACHER, 2012: 152; author's translation

Like Schneiders, Habermacher associates spirituality with experience of transcendence, expressed through needs for wisdom, unity, freedom, and fulfilment, while religion is understood as the (social, historical, cultural) ways in which this experience takes place. Therefore, while beliefs may change over time, the propensity to search for meaning remains (Habermacher, 2012: 157).[4]

The polar opposition of religion and spirituality used by sociologists of religion (for a discussion of examples in the academic literature, see Wood, 2010) is, therefore, a fundamentally religious representation. In addition, as Martin rightly observes, the ontologisation of "spirituality" as a human universal unavoidably prevents one from considering it as a social and cultural construction (Martin, 2014: 61). It is utterly problematic that academics reiterate uncritically such views of spirituality, not least because there is no scientific basis for the universality of such needs and dispositions outside the socio-cultural context. In fact, distinguishing a personal and untouched life of the spirit from "organised religion" is sociologically flawed since the individual is a product of society. It makes no sense to oppose the individual with the social expressions of religiosity, or to see subjectivity as innate and unaffected by culture (Wood, 2007). In fact, Foucault (1991) has shown there is nothing natural in the self, and power is exerted through subjectivity – something the case studies of this chapter will illustrate.

Spirituality, Moral Imperative and Individual Responsibility

Spirituality is about being able to see what's wrong with ourselves, accepting the idea that we can change, and then showing a willingness to actually transform ourselves. Rather than relying on an ego that says, "I'm okay and the rest of the world is a problem," it's the capacity to say, "I'm willing to see that I need to improve myself and I'm willing to give before I take."

BERG, 2005: 80

---

4 See also Martin's discussion of Sheldrake's understanding of "spirituality" which shares certain features with those of his fellow theologians (Martin, 2014: 54–55).

In this citation, Kabbalah Centre's leader Karen Berg illustrates Wood's argument according to which by taking for granted social actors' claims of self-determination, the paradigm of spirituality overlooks discourses about "duty, obedience, and submittance" (see Wood, 2010: 272). Spirituality is also understood as accepting the *necessity* for the individual to commit to a process of change, learning, and progress – what "spiritual seekers" and their teachers call "working on oneself." Susan, who practices yoga at the Sivananda Centre in London, explained to me that it was her "duty to progress on (her) spiritual path." The "spiritual path" is as much desired as it is imperative: social actors often claim that "we must work on ourselves again and again"; they say they "really work hard," "really, sincerely and constantly." Accordingly, they are driven to attend classes, workshops, and retreats, read books they associate with spirituality and personal growth, practice yoga or meditation, visit Buddhist temples, study Kabbalah and so forth. The imperative nature of this work on oneself is reflected in the expressions of guilt I frequently heard in my field-work – about not working enough or consistently on oneself, or breaking a "spiritual" lifestyle by drinking alcohol, smoking, partying etc.

Correspondingly, leaders and teachers such as Karen Berg encourage individual autonomy and choice all the while being prescriptive about the dedication and seriousness spirituality requires. Responding to a disciple who was having difficulty finding time to practice meditation, Muktananda, the guru who founded and popularised Siddha Yoga, said, "If you don't make time to work for your spiritual growth, what is the point of your human birth?" (Muktananda, 1994: 5). By the same token, Muktananda's successor, Gurumayi emphasises the vital importance of "discipline" as the "mainstay of purification" and "as regular as a heartbeat" (Gurumayi, 1996: 18). And Vishnu-Devananda, founder of the Sivananda Centres in the name of his master Sivananda, warns, "Cessation of practice is a grave mistake; sadhana, spiritual practice, should never been given up under any circumstances" (Vishnu-Devananda, 1978: 209).

Unsurprisingly, yoga and sadhana (the aim of realising the divine self) are defined as "self discipline" (London Sivananda Centre, n.d.; Vishnu-Devananda, 1988). This seemingly paradoxical discourse celebrating individual freedom and discipline can be understood as an attempt to adapt to secularising individuals who perceive religion as constraining and coercive, but who are nonetheless eager to undertake a form of personal development. In a fascinating encounter between swami Muktananda and Zalman Schachter-Shalomi, founder of the 1960s American Jewish Renewal movement, the latter evokes the necessity for religion to adapt to new generations, and Muktananda concurs:

We have to be realistic. What has become outmoded and mere empty ritual should not be imposed on the new generation. We have to see what will be conducive to young people's growth and then apply only those aspects of religion which will help them grow.

MUKTANANDA, 1978: 142–143

Nonetheless, adds Muktananda, "strict religious discipline is essential for spiritual growth," so "if you dilute the discipline, realisation is also diluted." Schachter-Shalomi agrees, and Muktananda criticises those who want an easy spiritual discipline:

You can make certain external aspects easier, but as far as the inner truth of religion is concerned, you can't do anything about it. It is what it is. Ironically, you find young people all over the world wanting religious discipline made very, very easy, while their worldly life is becoming more and more complex.

MUKTANANDA, 1978: 142–143

This citation emphasises "spiritual" leaders' ambivalence toward the compromise their followers seem to make.

One of the Kabbalah Centre's teachers, Yehuda Berg, rejects the "state of mind that a lot of people have when it comes to spirituality called free thinker mentality":

"Oh, you know what, I'm a spiritual person, I'm into freedom, I do what I want, when I want it, that's so spiritual." People think that spirituality is going to yoga class when you feel like it, you buy an occasional crystal and you wear it, or you put it by your TV, "oh you're so spiritual." That's not necessarily spiritual.

KABBALAH CENTRE, 2007

Once again, spirituality is closely associated with dedication, effort and discipline. As he goes on, Yehuda Berg places great emphasis on individual responsibility and effort for personal change through the notion of "free choice":

The idea is, if we don't apply a strong structure and a discipline to our journey, we never gonna get anywhere. Are you willing to buckle down, and say "I'm gonna commit to these tools, these techniques, the K-tools" (the tools of Kabbalah) and say, "I want to see specific results in my life?"

KABBALAH CENTRE, 2007

Yehuda's exhortation illustrates the fact that, by and large, individual responsibility is core to the ways teachers and students envisage "spirituality."

All of the students of neo-Hindu movements and the Kabbalah Centre whom I interviewed shared the idea that the self-realisation they so highly desire solely depends on self-improvement. In fact, spirituality is as much associated with freedom as it is with the responsibility and moral duty to work on oneself. For example, during a Shabbat service I was observing for fieldwork, a Kabbalah Centre teacher intervened because the audience was starting to chat loudly. He explained the blessing was not given only to the person reading the Torah, but to everyone present: "So if you're talking, you're not paying attention." And he added, "Now you have free choice." In other words, once students are informed, they are "free" to decide to be quiet and receive the blessing or to decide not to. The room fell silent: the desirable "choice" was made clear to everyone in the room.

Here, I depart from Martin's argument that spirituality does not make demands (Martin, 2014: 72). It does make demands, but in a peculiar way: in discourses on spirituality, "free choice" often means the personal responsibility for making the "right" choice. And "right choices" are rarely solely defined by individuals, for value is collectively granted to these choices, as the example above shows. Thus, "we are free to choose, but freedom does not mean that we can do whatever we like to do," according to swami Durgananda (2008: 13), one of the Sivananda Centre's current leaders. In other words, as a rabbi encapsulated it in a recent talk during fieldwork in a synagogue, the meaning of freedom is "I am free to choose the right path" – this should also question the distinction often made between so-called spirituality and mainstream religion.

Discursive Expressions of Authorities

> Our destiny is in our thought. This is not a religious teaching but the cosmic law of cause and effect. If we accept this cosmic law with love, patience and purity, our life will be filled with Divine Grace.
>
> DURGANANDA, 2006: 24

While analysing discourses about "spirituality," we should pay attention to references to transcendent authorities. Indeed, the choices a person is expected to make in his or her spiritual life are often (if not always?) explained in relation to transcendent principles. One of the first ideas to which students of the Kabbalah Centre are introduced, for instance, is that spiritual laws govern the universe. Spiritual laws of the universe are described as no less inescapable and consistent than the laws of physics; their main principle is one of "cause and effect" (unsurprisingly, the law of karma is sometimes depicted in similar terms). Thus, living in accordance with these laws allows and maintains a connection with the Light of the Creator which, in turn, helps remove chaos in a person's life and, more largely, in the world. Often compared to gravity and electricity, the works on these spiritual laws suggest they should be observed for practical reasons, not out of fear or obedience. Yitzhak, an Israeli student of the Kabbalah Centre, explains that "mitzvot" have often wrongly been presented as "commandments"; rather, he says, they are "recommendations," like avoiding "jumping off the roof":

> There is no law against jumping off the roof. But you know what happens for physical reasons if you jump off the roof (…). The same thing about mitzvot. You'd better follow them because sooner or later you're going to face the consequences of not following them.

Yet God does not reward or chastise, just as "no one is punished by electricity when electrocuted by putting their fingers in the socket" (Berg, 2001: 26). Consequently, it seems that at first sight, through their understanding of these laws, adherents accept, of their free will, to respect these higher principles, as explained by Amira, a student from Tel Aviv:

> You need to learn why and then you will want to do it (…), because if you don't do it there is cause and effect on something. But not because something is punishing you, because there's just, you know … if you put your hand in the fire, you will burn your hand – it's just cause and effect.

This rationalisation of religious rules may underline a transformation of a social actor's relationship to transcendent authorities, but it does not suggest the disappearance of these authorities. These spiritual laws are seen as transcending human influence and as inescapably requiring and justifying particular actions and behaviours from individuals. In the transcript of a meditation class in the Sivananda Centres that follows, Durgananda provides advice about postures, gestures, and when and where meditating is best. Although she concludes by asserting that "all this is very individual, you do not have to do it this way," her advice is actually much more prescriptive, as she commandingly interrogates students about their practice of meditation:

> Who else meditates? You do? You look like somebody who is meditating. You like it, isn't it?
> – I meditated up to some years ago.
> Are you still practicing meditation at present?

– Sometimes.

Are (you) meditating at present, yes or no?

– I meditated this morning

Very good, what did you do?

– I set down behind my paravent, on the *Yellow Pages*…

Excuse me, did you say *Yellow Pages*? Up to now everything was good, but I don't agree with the *Yellow Pages*. There are so many names in the *Yellow Pages*, each name has its own vibration, so you are sitting on the whole city…

– No, actually it is not the *Yellow Pages*, it is a fashion catalogue.

Don't you think that it also contains the vibration of other people? Better not sit on the catalogue. And this does not mean that you should sit on a spiritual book instead. One should never sit on any book. This is a cosmic law.

DURGANANDA, n.d.

Swami Durgananda's reference to the "cosmic law" reminds students of a transcendent principle that demands a particular behaviour – here, not to sit on a book while meditating. To reiterate, then, concentrating exclusively on references to freedom and freewill in relation to spirituality constitutes a very partial approach to empirical data.

Representations of Spirituality as Discipline

The example above suggests that another way to take discourses seriously in relation to "spirituality" is to explore the ways they may encourage particular types of attitudes and practices. We could, for instance, ponder what this "discipline," as described by "spiritual seekers" and teachers, entails. In a large array of teachings, "spirituality" involves constant observation, assessment, and regulation of the self. The work on oneself includes monitoring and assessing emotions, behaviours, and thoughts, controlling or eliminating "negative" attitudes, and adopting "positive" ones, in other words, being resilient, open to others, expressing love, and accepting difficulties, while repressing anger, selfishness, fear, etc. For example, Indian gurus tend to stress the control of the "mind" to preclude "negative" thoughts through the practice of yoga and meditation, with the latter often described as a way to become a "witness" to one's thoughts.

Not reacting emotionally to the external world is a central principle of the Kabbalah Centre's teaching, expressed in the distinction between "reactive" and "proactive" behaviours. Being reactive is about unrestrained and undesirable attitudes that require no discipline or effort and will engender suffering, including impatience, over-confidence, low self-esteem, vindictiveness, animosity, greed, selfishness, self-indulgence. By contrast, being proactive is to "resist" impulses, to pause and to think about what to do in a given situation; it is to willingly and actively control attitudes to bring happiness. Freedom of choice is asserted, but the "right" thing to do is clearly set as well – and it implies individual responsibility, accompanied by self-examination, knowledge, and control.

By and large, spirituality is presented and perceived as a "self-discipline" through which individuals can become the active and autonomous agents of the regulation of their thoughts, emotions, and attitudes. This is the reason why the distinction between the centrality of conformity to social norms and individual subjectivity made by some scholars makes little sociological sense. As suggested by Foucault, subjectivity is the object of normative discourses that encourage its constant observation and regulation (Foucault, 1991), not the locus of the "natural" untouched by the social, as Heelas (1996: 67) claims. The representations of the ego in New Age milieus and NRMS are particularly illustrative in this regard. The ego is commonly understood as the "enemy within" that one has to tame in order to grow. My research participants variously described it as the "wild" part of us that stimulates undesirable emotions and attitudes, manifesting itself in "personal wants," a "kind of gimme gimme gimme" attitude, or "everything that is impulsive," the "primal reaction" and, strikingly, "what has not been worked on." As such, the ego is the source of personal difficulties and an obstacle to personal fulfilment. This, again, suggests the self is the main source of personal difficulties, and solutions are to be found in oneself, in particular in the control of oneself, reflecting the centrality of individual responsibility in discourses about "spirituality."

It is ironic that scholars of New Age and spirituality do not see the normative aspects of the spirituality of discipline, since "spiritual seekers" certainly do. As a yoga student at the Sivananda Centre put it, "We always talk about spirituality, yeah, that's convenient, you're made to swallow lots of bitter pills with it." Indeed, in practice, these teachings are used to evaluate and regulate the behaviours of others: during fieldwork in a variety of settings, I have heard individuals criticising others for their "ego behaviours" countless times.

Observing Spirituality in Practice

> The measure of a narrative's force cannot be found through interviews alone but must be coupled with observation of the various contexts where we might understand how such self-descriptions shape individuals' activities, approaches, and values.
>
> BENDER, 2003:70

As underscored by Bender above, as well as Wood (2009, 2010) and Wood and Bunn (2009), one of the main weaknesses of the paradigm of spirituality is that it tends to concentrate on discourses and, based on what people say, to infer what they actually do. I would like to illustrate this epistemological point using an example from my fieldwork. During an interview, Hélène, a regular member of the Kabbalah Centre in Tel Aviv, emphasised the importance of individual freedom of choice and responsibility. She explained to me that the teacher's duty is to provide students with tools: "[However] after this, it's up to you to do whatever you want with them. They are not behind you to check what you do, it's you, it's your work with yourself, and God, that's all. Either you know how to use them or you don't." This comment was somewhat surprising, as I had met Hélène at one of my first Shabbats in Tel Aviv. When I asked for her phone number, she told me to be quick because the teachers are "not very paper-pen here," referring to the prohibition of working (hence, for some, of writing) on Shabbat. As I was writing down her number, she was covering my bag and my notebook with her shirt, looking around, hoping no one would notice and at-tempting to avoid reprimand from the teachers who, she said later in the inter-view cited above, "are not behind your back checking what you do."

In fact, participant observation in various settings placed me in situations where I was taught what to do, socialised to the "right" ways of doing things, (gently) told off for not doing so, told how to interpret my personal life, had the features of my personality explained to me, and so on. This method of enquiry allowed me to see that even the shortest and least committal contexts foster individuals' socialisation to practices, values, and beliefs. The majority of those frequenting Siddha Yoga, the Sivananda Centres, or the Kabbalah Centre are sympathisers who, on a short-term basis and often in conjunction with other "spiritual" teachings, attend workshops, classes, and retreats and, less often, these movements' rituals and festivals.[5] The involvement of the majority is, therefore, superficial, short-term, and plural. Through seminars, courses, and workshops, these "spiritual seekers" are nonetheless socialised into the require-ments of self-discipline: indeed, adopting a new outlook on life and finding efficient practices for the realisation of the self is the whole point of attend-ing these events. Through classes and structured interactions such as "shar-ing," individuals are taught to re-interpret their life events and experiences; they are socialised in collective norms about the self, the necessity to work on

---

5 Obviously, some exclusive religious organisations demand a high level of observance and compliance with the teaching by all members; these are beyond the remit of this chapter on "spirituality" as free-floating, non-institutionalised religiosity, although I would not be surprised if some of the most conservative forms of religion use the term and also refer to individual responsibility.

themselves, the efficiency of certain practices and virtuous attitudes, and the precise ways in which these practices should be undertaken. The fact that this "learning environment" is paid for and may involve a very short-term commitment does not prevent it from being a formidable locus of learning new ideas and practices – and this is best observed through practices and interactions.

In the Kabbalah Centre's cycle of ten courses, Kabbalah One, participants are introduced to the spiritual laws of the universe and the necessity to transform themselves and told how to do so by resisting to reactive impulses, being proactive, and sharing. As in other classes I attended in the Kabbalah Centre, the transformation of the self is an imperative, not an offer: those who think everything is going well in their lives are in a very bad situation, asserted my teacher for Kabbalah One. This imperative was repeatedly reasserted by the teacher's demand for students to "share" "transformation stories" that had occurred since the previous class. Observing our own behaviours, changing them according to learnt kabbalistic principles, and noting their positive outcomes in our life constituted the "coursework" we had to complete every week. These transformation stories were then discussed among students sitting around a table, or narrated in front of all the attendants and commented upon by the teacher. In addition, during moments of questions and answers, students would tell of a recent difficulty they encountered, a conflicting interaction with someone else; they would explain how they responded to the situation and ask the teacher whether he thought their behaviour was reactive or proactive. Other students told how, in applying the newly taught principles, they were rewarded by positive outcomes, thus encouraging others to follow their example.

In various courses of the Kabbalah Centre, I observed students asking the teacher why they had such and such behaviours or why a particular event occurred in their lives. For the most part, the teacher would provide an interpretation relating to the spiritual laws of the universe and suggest the need to improve themselves by applying the teaching to their lives. In all the different forms of interactions, personal stories and experiences are given a new meaning according to the course content, through interactions with a teacher and/or other attendants. Simply stated, new meanings do not spring from self-authority – if such a thing exists – and the significance of interactions with leaders and teachers should not be underestimated.

Kohn criticises Heelas' claim that individuals are empowered to exert "self-authority" in what he calls "self religions." Exploring three of these so-called self religions (Da free John, Scientology, and Est), Kohn shows that the celebration of the self is undermined by the assumption, in these movements, that their leaders have reached a higher level of empowerment, knowledge and fulfilment. In other words, the ideology of free choice and freedom "did not occur at the expense of the leader's authority" (Kohn, 1991: 149). This remark is equally true for the chapter's three case studies.

Contextualising Religious Discourses

The Politics of Self-Realisation

Ultimately, religious narratives do not have an independent life of their own: discourses (and practices, for that matter) need to be referenced in their wider economic, political, and cultural contexts. Spirituality as self-discipline and the kind of self it celebrates can be understood in the larger context of the "psychologisation of social life" (Rose, 1989, 1998, 1999). The psychologisation of social life constitutes a particular way to exert power in affinity with neoliberalism's political and economic mechanisms of privatisation. Based on the moral principle of freedom, neoliberalism aims to regulate individuals conceived as subjects of freedom. The American and British New Right, in particular, developed policies promoting individuals' and civil society's initiatives, under the assumption that the moral and economic regeneration of the nation requires the destruction of a dependency culture and its replacement by a culture of enterprise (Du Gay, 1995: 64). Individuals, "communities," families, charities, or religious organisations have been increasingly perceived as the "empowered" partners of the state and, therefore, in charge of their own wellbeing. Individuals are expected to be adaptive and proactively seeking self-actualisation: in a flexible accumulation economy, they are less defined by their present post or the skills they have acquired and more by their capacity to develop new dispositions in order to adapt to tomorrow's challenges. Thus, the neoliberal social model rewards "enterprising selves," individuals who are willing to actualise themselves, who know how to control and manage their attitudes, to develop new skills when the situation demands it, and to adapt to their environment rather than attempting to change it.

Students of kabbalah, yoga or meditation are not mistaken when they describe self-improvement as an imperative: by and large, Europeans and Americans increasingly seek the techniques to become this autonomous and realised self, believed to be the source of every success if actualised through counselling, therapies, self-help, personal growth, and coaching, but also through so-called spiritual and holistic milieus which contribute to these therapies of normality. Indeed, spirituality presents itself as an inner-worldly quest of fulfilment, which requires individual autonomy: by taking responsibility for their fate and accepting to change, "spiritual seekers" are encouraged to control their emotions and thoughts, to be proactive instead of reactive, to be sharing, open, "positive," etc. In this regard, the "spiritual" fully converges with the wide range of existing therapeutic methods, in the aim of enabling individuals to be in charge of their professional success, the harmony of their family life, and their good health. In other words, individuals' commitment to their "spiritual path" epitomises the imperatives and constraints exerted on them in Euro-American societies today – to be "enterprising selves" who have understood that only by "working" on themselves can they become realised and fulfilled in this world.

The fact that self-realisation is desired and voluntarily pursued by social actors does not exclude the fact that it is a socially constructed incentive with increasing political and economic significance. Accordingly, the project of self-realisation that social actors consider they undertake freely does not demonstrate the authority of the self, but conformity to social imperatives to be adaptable, control emotions, and cultivate particular moral dispositions. The claim that spirituality today contributes to a more "effective" and "subtle" "counter-culture" (Heelas, 2008: 14) seems preposterous.

Spirituality in Educating and Reforming Projects

Finally, these norms and practices about the regulation of the self are not only offered to non-committed "spiritual seekers" in consumerist settings. Like mainstream religions, when they have the opportunities to do so, NRMS develop charitable activities for deprived populations, educational programmes for schools, and prison projects for inmates.

Like many other NRMS, neo-Hindu movements invest substantial amounts of financial and human resources in outreach and charitable projects, referring to values such as world peace or universal love. This is in continuity with 19th-century Hindu movements of socio-religious reform, which responded to Christian missions and their philanthropic activities by developing their own activities, as well as with Vivekananda's ethics of social service. In the Indian context, these activities celebrate a Hindu progressive and humanist attitude and combat obscurantism; therefore, they can contribute to nationalist identity-claims, as suggested by Lépinasse (2007) in a discussion of the Art of Living and the Brahma Kumaris. Beyond the realm of the Indian political scene, neo-Hindu movements use their charitable initiatives to build up legitimacy – by insisting on their NGO status, for example. During the counter-culture, neo-Hindu movements mirrored Christian missions in India by developing activities of social service to popularise their teachings. They developed, for instance, programmes for drug users during the 1960s psychedelic wave (Anthony and Robbins, 1969). Poverty relief has, nonetheless, taken precedence. In the 1980s, Gurumayi founded Prasad, defined as a volunteer and humanitarian organisation aiming to support the development of the valley of Tansa, the region where Muktananda founded his ashram. This organisation supports a hospital and an itinerant medical service staffed by voluntary doctors (Brooks et al., 1997: 152). In 1992, Prasad developed new initiatives in the United States and Mexico.

The Kabbalah Centre directs its peace promoting activities in the Israeli-Palestinian context by distributing kabbalistic books, for instance, but it also founded "Raising Malawi" in 2006 "to bring an end to the extreme poverty and hardship endured by Malawi's 1.4 million orphans and vulnerable children" (Raising Malawi, 2013). Supported by Madonna, who adopted two children in Malawi, Raising Malawi's major projects include building schools and supporting girls' education.

To what extent these initiatives socialise deprived populations into a form of spiritual discipline is unclear and requires further investigation. The linkage is more obvious when it comes to educational projects. The values of educational programmes of the Brahma Kumaris and Sai Baba, respectively, "Living Values: An Educational Program" and "Sathya Sai Education in Human Values," have been extensively studied in the British context (Arweck and Nesbitt, 2007, 2008; Arweck, Nesbitt, and Jackson, 2006). Under the category of the spiritual, moral, social, and cultural (SMSC) development of pupils in the British curriculum, various religious movements attempt to provide programmes ready to use in schools. To be successful, they need to teach values felt to be universally applicable, detached from their original religious context. In fact, the law forbids promoting the teachings of a particular religious tradition in publicly funded schools. The Brahma Kumaris programme insists on peace, respect, love, tolerance, honesty, humility, cooperation, responsibility, happiness, freedom, simplicity, and unity. The Sathia Sai Baba programme refers to the guru, and the Indian roots of the values it promotes are obvious: love, truth, peace, right conduct as dharma, non-violence (*ahimsa*). These two educational projects entail a holistic perspective of the individual. Addressing children's "spiritual" and emotional forms of intelligence, they encourage self-knowledge and reflexivity – one even defines itself as a "self-development programme" (Arweck, Nesbitt, and Jackson, 2006: 331). They convey very specific ideas about the self, if not its enhancement. Indeed, Arweck, Nesbitt and Jackson argue these programmes are "in tune with current ideas promoted by life coaches, personal trainers, creative management and self-help programmes based on 'spiritual' principles" (2006: 338).

Similarly, Spirituality for Kids (SFK), the Kabbalah Centre's educational programme founded by Karen Berg, has been implemented in a small number of schools in London. Volunteers and teachers all insist SFK, as a registered educational charity, is fully independent from the Kabbalah Centre; its programme, they say, does not teach kabbalah, but universal values and "spiritually based, non-denominational life-skills." "Spirituality" may be non-denominational but it is far from being neutral, as this chapter has shown. Furthermore, the Spirituality for Kids course content (2006) clearly derives from the key principles of the Kabbalah Centre's teaching. Like Kabbalah One, the first level of Spirituality for Kids teaches "the game of life," – in other words, the spiritual laws of the universe. It presents challenges as a source of happiness; it addresses free choice and responsibility and it values effort-making, teamwork, caring, and sharing attitudes. It also teaches the principle of cause and effect – everything we do has consequences, so we need to take responsibility.

Prisons are also places where NRMs spread their teaching. The assumption is such programmes can support those who are incarcerated and contribute to reforming their attitude. For example, the Sivananda Prison Outreach Program aims to teach prisoners "a new way of thinking that empowers them to lead cleaner, more peaceful lives through yoga in its many forms" (Sivananda Yoga Vedanta Center, n.d.). The programme involves correspondence and personal visits to inmates, sending them books on yoga, as well as teaching them hatha yoga, yoga philosophy and meditation. In 1979, Muktananda founded a programme called the "prison project" to provide correspondence courses and meditation classes to inmates. The Sivananda Centres have been teaching in prisons since the 1960s (Sivananda Yoga Europe, n.d.). The Art of Living Foundation and Transcendental Meditation has also developed activities in prisons.

"Correctional Outreach Initiative" is a Kabbalah Centre programme, but it is "not a religious program," according to the website. It doesn't "preach in any way" but still improves lives (Kabbalah Centre Correctional Outreach Initiative, "Welcome"). "We feel that we can be a part there, because Kabbalah is all about taking responsibility for yourself, being the best you can be," a student of the London Kabbalah Centre explained to me, stressing individual responsibility *with* the imperative of self-improvement as justification for the programme in prison. Indeed, the Correctional Outreach Initiative teaches prisoners that "none of us are actually 'victims' of the world around us and that our choices and actions directly impact ourselves and others," and they will "truly benefit from behavioral transformation" (Kabbalah Centre Correctional Outreach Initiative, "Key Concepts," "About"). To this end, the programme socialises inmates to the spiritual laws of the universe and differentiates between reactive and proactive behaviours:

> No matter how successful incarcerated people may be within the walls of a correctional facility, they are often unable to recognize and resolve their

problems successfully once they are released. Consequently, when challenges arise and addictive substances are readily available, the individual
is more likely to act out blindly, often in a criminal manner. (...) By changing defeatist belief systems, the program gets to the positive core of the
individual.

> Kabbalah Centre Correctional Outreach Initiative, "About"

In other words, prisoners are defined by flawed attitudes; this, in turn, justifies,
even demands, transformative interventions. The locus of these transformative interventions is subjectivity. This approach is not different from the rest
of the Kabbalah Centre's teaching; what is striking is its application as a mode
of regulating an incarcerated population believed to be flawed.

Again, these sorts of initiatives need to be contextualised: neoliberal forms
of governance entail an increasing popularity and legitimacy of psychothera-
peutic modes of intervention to regulate social problems generated precisely
by this new context of social vulnerability. Learning issues, drug use, delin-
quency, unemployment, illness, or lack of efficiency at work are increasingly
identified as problems of selfhood. Consequently, they are addressed by psychological interventions in order to generate "adapted," desirable behaviours
from "self-regulated" individuals (Otero, 2003: 3). In other words, the subjectivisation of social life can be seen as a contemporary form of "risk management"
(Castel, 1981). This contrasts with post-war assistantialist welfare practice and
with various forms of repression and punishment in that it represents a flexible way to regulate populations by extending individual responsibility. In
fact, responsibility has become a core feature of the contemporary individual
(Ehrenberg, 1995: 14).

In this regard, it is not irrelevant that the Kabbalah Centre in London,
through a venture called Business Gym Global, has developed a project to address the problems of the workplace (absenteeism, sick days, low individual
performance). The general aim of this network is to teach Kabbalah to "members at any business level" through "monthly seminars, transformational
courses, and interactive workshops," so they can "learn, exchange ideas and
forge new business relationships" (London Kabbalah Centre, 2011). Since work
issues are believed to be the result of personal issues, the solution offered is,
unsurprisingly, to change employees' attitudes through courses teaching them
to identify the source of their problems – in their self and attitudes – and to apply the Kabbalah Centre's teaching that encourages individuals to take responsibility, act proactively, and work on themselves rather than blaming external
factors for their difficulties. Business Gym Global has to be understood in the
context of a wider "corporate spiritualism" that is now part of the training in-
dustry, a main principle of which is that "a spiritually therapeutic environment

enhances productivity by facilitating employees' commitments to organ-isational goals, which are seen as the route for individual self-actualization" (Nadesan, 1999: 14).[6] In fact, the Kabbalah Centre's values and practices could not be more in tune with the requirements of neoliberal governance and its psychologisation of social life. One of Business Gym Global's projects aiming at "solving youth unemployment" by "awakening the power of engagement and entrepreneurship within" illustrates perfectly the idea of reforming the "flawed self" in response to a "social problem":

> (W)e crafted very unique, 3-month, intensive courses to help create a new generation of positive leaders and empower this "lost generation." Our target-driven educational format gets under the skin to tackle the emotional wellbeing, family life, mental and physical health issues, too often misunderstood and neglected by society. We ignite the values of as-piration, resilience, sustainable wealth creation, individual responsibility and community consciousness. Our involvement results in positive and life-changing solutions to youth disengagement, proving that sustainable employment, happiness, passion and purpose are effects of our "inside-out" curriculum.
>
> LONDON KABBALAH CENTRE, 2011

These initiatives to regulate, reform, and educate are very small-scale, and their impact is probably minimal. More studies are needed to explore them in practice. Nonetheless, they clearly indicate the normative character and dis-ciplining ambitions of teachings called "spiritual," once we look beyond the leaders' and disciples' discourse. Indicatively, they offer their teaching to those who are least able to freely "choose" it – children, prison inmates, deprived populations in developing countries, workers, and the unemployed.

Conclusion

> Luther, we grant, overcame bondage out of devotion by replacing it by bondage out of conviction. He shattered faith in authority because he restored the authority of faith. He turned priests into laymen because he turned laymen into priests. He freed man from outer religiosity because

---

6 Bovbjerg (2010) develops similar arguments in her research on the ways in which Neuro-Linguistic Programming is applied in Danish workplaces.

he made religiosity the inner man. He freed the body from chains because he enchained the heart. But, if Protestantism was not the true solution of the problem, it was at least the true setting of it. It was no longer a case of the layman's struggle against the priest outside himself but of his struggle against his own priest inside himself, his priestly nature.

MARX, 2008: 51

Religion in modernity is increasingly thought of as the object of a free and voluntary individual choice. In this perspective, contemporary religious life does not spring from social structures but is individual-centred and shaped by self-authority. This, subsequently, explains the decline of – constraining, coercive – organised and inherited religions and the ascendance of "spirituality," based on subjective experience and responding to universal human needs for meaning and fulfilment.

However, understanding the expressions of this religious individualism as evidence of individuals' ability to exert absolute freedom in "spirituality" is highly problematic: it conflates emic and etic discourses and reiterates common sense assumptions. This chapter underlines that "spiritual seekers'" expressions of religious individualism are (necessarily) socially constructed; they reflect conformity to a collective discourse which is encouraged and shaped by leaders and teachers in alternative religious circles. Overall, the meaning of religious individualism is less about freedom than it is about taking personal responsibility for fulfilment, by making the right "choices" (accepting the need to change, practicing yoga regularly, controlling reactive behaviours etc.). And these "right choices" are not defined by students but by "spiritual" leaders, who justify them by referring to transcendent authorities (God, the Light, the cosmic law of the universe etc.) and their own legitimacy (as an example of self-realisation, as having a different soul, as being initiated by this or that master etc.). In this regard, "spirituality" makes the self the locus of discipline and conformity to collective values and incentives.

According to teachers *and* students, spirituality is about accepting the imperative to improve oneself, evaluating and controlling one's thoughts, emotions, and behaviours, using the appropriate techniques (yoga, meditation etc.) to do so, and cultivating moral virtues. This does not reflect a form of "self-authority," but results from individuals' socialisation to shared values and practices, especially during seminars, courses, and workshops. Ultimately, the desired selfhood (proactive, self-reliant, flexible, resilient, endlessly actualising itself) is congruent with the "enterprising self" required by a highly flexibilised economy combined with the undermining of state welfare provision. These imperatives pre-exist and drive quests for therapeutic and religious resources.

Achieving selfhood is not a "raw" subjective experience independent from the social and the cultural. In other words, there is no sociological reason for distinguishing between religion as socially shaped and spirituality as transcending institutional, cultural, and shared norms.

In short, bringing the social back into the sociology of deregulated forms of religion entails reclaiming sociology's epistemological foundations. It involves the understanding of individuals' discourses and action, including claims of self-authority and heterodox religious choices, as manifestations of social trends. In this instance, it encourages us to reflect on the meaning of contemporary religious individualism. Despite claims to the contrary, "spiritual seekers" are firmly anchored to the social ground and its requirements. Individualism and subjectivism actually contribute to a new way of regulating social actors through individual responsibility and self-discipline, which is what Marx writes in relation to Protestantism. Thus, analyses of such sociocultural trends should start with the principle that the self, subjectivity, and experiences are not raw or natural and, hence, opposed to the social, but are shaped by the social.

Students of religious individualism need to remember that social structures manifest themselves precisely through agency. Social determinism entails active and personal involvement from social actors, not passivity. As Lahire puts it, "To be resolutely *determined* to commit this or that action is a common way of feeling and living the social determinisms of which we are the product" (Lahire, 2011: 206). Conversely, the assumption that choice demonstrates individuals' empowerment is problematic and must be questioned, not least because they are expected to make the "right" choices (with unequal competence and means to do so) and to take personal responsibility for the outcomes of these choices (Ehrenberg, 1995, 2010).

Bourdieu notes that "the illusion of freedom from social determinants' precisely characterizes intellectuals," but ironically, through this illusion "social determinations win the freedom to exercise their full power" (1990: 14–15). Bourdieu's reference to intellectuals' social positioning resonates with Skeggs' critique of sociologists of de-traditionalisation and mobility, such as Giddens, Beck and Urry, for the ways their social theories translate their specific experience (as white, male, and privileged academics) into general explanations of the social world, leading them to generalise – and inflate – their own emancipation (Skeggs, 2004: 49). This lack of reflexivity also concerns scholars of religion who claim social actors are emancipated from social norms and craft their religious beliefs and identities according to their personal experience. Exactly whose experience is generalised and authenticated?

Therefore, we need to ponder the "naturalization of freedom as a social ideal" (Mahmood, 2005: 10), or in other words, query the assumption that individuals inherently seek emancipation from social norms. Drawing on a very different case study, Mahmood criticises "liberal assumptions" of human beings' innate desire for autonomy. These, she says, make scholars of Muslim fundamentalism prone to look for expressions of resistance to authority and domination, rather than trying to understand how power works (Mahmood, 2005: 5) – and, of course, this is exactly what scholars of spirituality do as well. Indeed, the points she makes about women's involvement in the Islamic revival in Egypt apply to my arguments more generally: she argues that ideas about resistance and the quest for autonomy and self-fulfilment "impose a teleology of progressive politics on the analytics of power" which "makes it hard for us to see and understand forms of being and action that are not necessarily encapsulated by the narrative of subversion and reinscription of norms" (Mahmood, 2005: 9). Mahmood invites us to explore agency, not only as a way of resisting norms but also as a way of "inhabiting" them (2005: 14).

These progressive liberal ideals criticised by Mahmood underlie the polar distinction religion / spirituality and confer the consequent normative and ethnocentric implications. Indeed, the celebration of an empowering freedom in spirituality, as distinguished from imposed, organised religion, sometimes amounts to distinguishing the good guys (the spiritual, liberal, pluralistic, and emancipated middle-class) from the bad guys (religious, fanatical intolerants, and those who cannot have chosen), with "fundamentalist Islam" often epitomising the latter (Martin, 2014). Hence the authentication of scholars' own experience. The argument is not farfetched: Martin supports it by referring to Heelas' description of "holistic spiritualities" (Heelas, 2008: 6) as fostering humanistic principles, thereby representing a "worthy successor to Christianity in western settings; and, in the longer term, to exclusivistic, iron-cage forms of Islam (for example) in countries like Pakistan" (Martin, 2014: 29).[7] Ultimately, rethinking religious individualism demands a reflexive turn from students of "spirituality" in relation to their personal beliefs about freedom, which might have more to do with their positioning as social actors than with their sociological analysis of the human world.

---

7   In my view, this citation also suggests these mainstream liberal ideals may lead to understanding choices as "wrong," not as "choices" social actors could have made; hence, the pervasive and enduring references in common sense to so-called cults' "brain-washing techniques" or "radicalisation" in Islam to make sense of processes through which people may join these religious settings.

References

Altglas, Véronique. 2014. *From yoga to kabbalah: religious exoticism and the logics of bricolage*. Oxford; New York: Oxford University Press.

Anthony, Dick, and Thomas Robbins. 1969. "Eastern mysticism and the resocialization of drug users: the Meher Baba cult," *Journal for the Scientific Study of Religion* 8(2): 308–317.

Arweck, Elisabeth, and Eleanor Nesbitt. 2008. "Peace and non-violence: Sathya Sai education in human values in British schools," *Journal of Peace Education* 5(1): 17–32.

Arweck, Elisabeth, and Eleanor Nesbitt. 2007. "Spirituality in education: promoting children's spiritual development through values," *Journal of Contemporary Religion* 22(3): 311–326.

Arweck, Elisabeth, Eleanor Nesbitt, and Robert Jackson. 2006. "Common values for the common school? Using two values education programmes to promote 'spiritual and moral development,'" *Journal of Moral Education* 34(3): 325–342.

Bender, Courtney. 2003. *Heaven's kitchen: living religion at god's love we deliver*. Chicago: University of Chicago Press.

Berg, Karen. 2005. *God wears lipstick: Kabbalah for women*. Canada: Research Centre of Kabbalah.

Berg, Michael. 2001. *The way: using the wisdom of Kabbalah for spiritual transformation and fulfilment*. Hoboken: John Wiley & Sons.

Bourdieu, Pierre. 1990. *In other words: essays in reflexive sociology*. Cambridge: Polity.

Bovbjerg, Kirsten Marie. 2010. "Ethic of sensitivity: towards a new work ethic." In *Religions of modernity: relocating the sacred to the self and the digital*, edited by Stef Aupers and Dick Houtman, 115–133. Leiden; Boston: Brill.

Brooks, Douglas R. et al. 1997. *Meditation revolution: a history and theology of the Siddha yoga lineage*. New York: Agama Press.

Castel, Robert. 1981. *La gestion des risques: de l'anti-psychiatrie à l'après-psychanalyse*. Paris: Éditions de Minuit.

Champion, Françoise. 1990. "La nébuleuse mystique-ésotérique: orientation psycho-religieuse des courants mystiques et ésotériques contemporains." In *De l'émotion en religion*, edited by Françoise Champion and Danièle Hervieu-Léger, 17–69. Paris: Centurion.

Chidananda. 2000. "What is yoga?" accessed 22 August 2013, from http://www.dlshq.org/discourse/apr2000.htm.

du Gay, Paul. 1995. *Consumption and identity at work*. London: Sage.

Durgananda. 2008. "Be up and doing: the yoga of action," *YOGALife* (Summer): 13–16.

Durgananda. 2006. "Practice with understanding." *YOGALife* (Spring/Summer): 22–24.

Durgananda. n.d. "Meditation and modern city life," accessed 22 August 2013, from http://www.sivananda.eu/fileadmin/user_upload/inspiration/swami_durgananda/Meditation_and_Modern_City_Life.pdf.

Ehrenberg, Alain. 1995. *L'individu incertain*. Paris: Calmann-Levy.

Ehrenberg, Alain. 2010. *La société du malaise*. Paris: Odile Jacob.

Erlandson, Sven. 2000. *Spiritual but not religious: a call to religious revolution in America*. Bloomington: iUniverse.

Fath, Sébastien. 2010. "Héritage/choix." In *Dictionnaire des faits religieux*, edited by Régine Azira and Danièle Hervieu-Léger, 476–480. Paris: Presses Universitaires de France.

Foucault, Michel. 1991. *Discipline and punish: the birth of the prison*. London: Penguin.

Gurumayi. 1996. *Magic of the heart: reflections on divine love*. South Fallsburg: SYDA Foundation.

Habermacher, Jean- François. 2012. "Pertinence théologique et inscription en église." In *Penser le religieux, le théologique et le social avec Pierre Gisel*, edited by Philippe Gonzalez and Christophe Monnot, 151–169. Geneva: Labor et Fidès.

Halbfass, Wilhelm. 1988. *India and Europe: an essay in understanding*. Albany: SUNY Press.

Heelas, Paul. 2008. *Spiritualities of life: new age romanticism and consumptive capitalism*. Oxford: Blackwell.

Heelas, Paul. 1996. "De-traditionalisation of religion and self: the new age and postmodernity." In *Postmodernity, sociology and religion*, edited by Peter C. Jupp and Kieran Flanagan, 64–82. London: Macmillan.

Heelas, Paul, and Linda Woodhead. 2005. *The spiritual revolution: why religion is giving way to spirituality*. London: Blackwell.

Hervieu-Léger, Danièle. 1999. *Le pèlerin et le converti*. Paris: Flammarion.

Kabbalah Centre. 2007. *The living Kabbalah system level 2: into the light* (Learning Package). USA: Kabbalah Centre International, Booklet p. 37.

Kabbalah Centre Correctional Outreach Initiative. n.d. "Welcome," accessed 27 November 2007, from http://coi.kabbalah.com/index.html.

Kabbalah Centre Correctional Outreach Initiative. n.d. "Key concepts," accessed 27 November 2007, from http://coi.kabbalah.com/concepts.html.

Kabbalah Centre Correctional Outreach Initiative. n.d. "About," accessed 27 November 2007, from http://coi.kabbalah.com/about.html.

Kohn, Rachel. 1991. "Radical subjectivity in 'self religions' and the problem of authority." In *Religion in Australia: sociological perspectives*, edited by Alan W. Black, 133–150. Sidney: Allen & Unwin.

Lahire, Bernard. 2011. *The plural actor*. Cambridge: Polity Press.

Lépinasse, Pascale. 2007. "L'humanitarisme hindou ou la dévotion civile," *Archives de Sciences Sociales des Religions* 137: 85–105.

London Kabbalah Centre. 2011. "Business gym network," accessed 24 August 2011, from http://www.businessgymglobal.org/.

London Sivananda Centre. n.d. "Certificate courses," accessed 11 March 2013, from http://www.sivananda.org/london/residential_courses.html.

Mahmood, Saba. 2005. *Politics of piety: the Islamic revival and the feminist subject*. Princeton: Princeton University Press.

Martin, Craig. 2014. *Capitalizing religion: ideology and the opiate of the bourgeoisie*. London; New York: Bloomsbury.

Marx, Karl. (1844) 2008. "Introduction to a contribution to the critique of Hegel's philosophy of right." In *On religion*, by Karl Marx and Friedrich Engels. Mineola: Dover.

Muktananda. 1994. *From the finite to the infinite*. South Fallsburg: SYDA Foundation.

Muktananda. 1978. *In company of a Siddha: interviews and conversations with swami Muktananda*. Oakland: SYDA Foundation.

Nadesan, Majia Holmer. 1999. "The discourses of corporate spiritualism and evangelical capitalism," *Management Communication Quarterly* 13(1): 3–42.

Otero, Marcelo. 2003. *Les règles de l'individualité contemporaine: santé mentale et société*. Montréal: Presses de l'Université Laval.

Raising Malawi. 2013. "About raising Malawi," accessed 10 April 2013, from www.raisingmalawi.org/pages/about.

Rose, Nikolas. 1999. *Powers of freedom: reframing political thought*. Cambridge: Cambridge University Press.

Rose, Nikolas. 1998. *Inventing our selves: psychology, power, and personhood*. Cambridge: Cambridge University Press.

Rose, Nikolas. 1989. *Governing the soul: the shaping of the private self*. London: Routledge.

Schneiders, Sandra M. 2003. "Religion vs. spirituality: a contemporary conundrum," *Spiritus: A Journal of Christian Spirituality* 3(2): 163–185.

Sivananda Yoga Europe. n.d. "Ways you can help," accessed 11 March 2013, from http://www.sivananda.eu/en/sivananda-yoga/about-us/ways-you-can-help.html.

Sivananda Yoga Vedanta Center San Francisco. n.d. "Sivananda prison outreach program," accessed 11 March 2013, from http://sfyoga.com/pages/prisonproject.shtml.

Skeggs, Beverley. 2004. *Class, self, culture*. London: Routledge.

Spirituality for Kids. 2006. "Curriculum," accessed 27 November 2007, from https://spiritualityforkids.org/qa.htm.

Vishnu-Devananda. (1960) 1988. *The complete illustrated book of yoga*. New York: Harmony Books.

Vishnu-Devananda. 1978. *Meditation and mantras*. New York: OM Lotus Publishing Company.

Vivekananda. 1965. *The complete works of Swami Vivekananda*, Volume 1. Calcutta: Advaita Ashrama.

Wood, Matthew. 2010. "The sociology of spirituality: reflections on a problematic endeavour." In *The new Blackwell companion to the sociology of religion*, edited by Bryan S. Turner, 267–285. Oxford: Blackwell.

Wood, Matthew. 2009. "The nonformative elements of religious life: questioning the 'sociology of spirituality' paradigm," *Social Compass* 56(2): 237–248.

Wood, Matthew. 2007. *Power and the new age: ambiguities of authority in neoliberal societies*. Aldershot: Ashgate.

Wood, Matthew, and Christopher Bunn. 2009. "Strategy in a religious network: a Bourdieuian critique of the sociology of spirituality," *Sociology* 43(2): 286–303.

Wuthnow, Robert. 1998. *After heaven: spirituality in America since the 1950s*. Berkeley: University of California Press.

CHAPTER 4

Congregational Studies, Worship and Region Behaviour

Matthew Wood

Editor's Preface

Matthew Wood passed away before being able to turn his 2014 symposium paper into a chapter, so a brief introduction to his work is in order. The introduction combines editorial commentary with large portions of text that Wood meant to publish in a monograph. The proposed monograph draws on Wood's extensive research[1] on Methodist congregations in London. British Methodism is the third fastest declining Christian denomination in Britain, yet it remains the largest nonconformist denomination by far (and the third largest Christian denomination). In London, the situation is somewhat different. With successive waves of immigration since the late 1940s, first from the Caribbean and then from West Africa, with South Asia thrown into the more recent mix, many churches have either maintained or increased their numbers.

At the time of Wood's initial research, from 2000 to 2002, a unique situation had arisen that can be characterised as "stalwarts in transition." Most churches boasted "stalwarts" who, in theory, represented a link to a vibrant local religious culture, but this had all but disappeared, leaving a small number of older white British who sought to maintain the status quo. Early migrants seeking to worship in these churches found British Methodism lacking in religious culture; worse yet, they encountered racial discrimination and prejudice. Africans arriving during the 1980s and 1990s began attempts to renew the local religious culture by re-establishing or inventing small group fellowships. These efforts were led by those from similarly "stalwart" Methodist families "back home" and were resourced through transnational experiences and connections. Perhaps unsurprisingly, their initiatives had a mixed reception from ministers, white stalwarts, and even other migrants. This period of contested renewal

---

*   Edited by Véronique Altglas.

1   Wood examined Methodism across London as a whole, conducting ethnographic research at five different churches, gathering original survey data for all churches, and setting the results within the framework of a major "global city" and its recent history.

in London Methodism was offset by the lack of second and third generation migrants staying in the Church, so that the promise of its recovery through immigration was being lost precisely when its renewal appeared by many to be assured. Data from the English Church Attendance Surveys show British Methodism lost 18 percent of its ethnic minority attendance from 1998 to 2005. Wood's period of research, therefore, coincided with a highpoint of first generation migration-induced London Methodist renewal and provides a unique position from which to understand its subsequent decline.

Around this time, two other related social changes were under way. Firstly, Britain was entering a new phase in the treatment of ethnic diversity, with multiculturalism emerging as an explicit policy of the New Labour government that had swept into power in 1997. The Methodist Church, at national and local levels, reflected this shift, providing a valuable discourse for ministers to manage their local churches and for some lay members to contest their position within them. "Race relations" and the management of diversity became central topics that had to be addressed. Secondly, London itself was changing, having become in the 1990s one of a few truly "global cities" across the world. This provided Methodist churches with not only new members, adherents, and related "communities" for their religious activities, but also with the potential for new clients for their public and welfare services. Such service provisions had been encouraged within Britain since the 1980s, with churches and other "faith" groups positioned as appropriate providers of some forms of welfare, through their supposedly unique access to inner-city "communities." Of course, this raises important issues of secularisation and post-secularisation, a topic not tackled in this particular chapter.[2]

Briefly stated, Wood investigated the reception of Methodist migrants and set their attempts to belong to their new local churches in the context of the roles played by ministers and white British members (2006, 2010a, 2014). He sought to understand how status is achieved and contested amongst lay leaders in highly diverse congregations, how ministers seek to manage diversity in their congregations, migrants' experiences of racism and anti-racism, the limits to strategies drawing on migrants' transnational experiences and resources, and how these issues relate to the public and private roles of religion in the contemporary city.

This chapter has to be read in the context of Wood's observation that congregations represent a topic now receiving considerable attention in sociological studies of religion, particularly in the United States. In Wood's view, this attention, whilst welcome in many ways, tends to focus on growing, often

---

2   On these issues, the editor refers the reader to Wood (2015).

independent, churches rather than mainstream or historic denominations that may be experiencing overall decline. What equally requires attention is the way these sorts of denominations respond to internal and unprecedented social and cultural diversity in the context of migration flows. This topic is particularly significant because national governments increasingly consider religious organisations as providing connections to ethnic and migrant communities. This is often articulated by a political discourse of multiculturalism, which denominations and local churches, in turn, promote and celebrate. But according to Wood, what diversity and multiculturalism mean in practice and their significance for the future of these religious groups requires close examination.

In the following, Wood provides a critical reflection on the study of congregations within the sociology of religion, notably the focus on worship as an individual activity. He argues this perspective derives from a theological presupposition that ignores or downplays other central organisational features of congregations – in particular, what goes on in committees. Indeed, the structuring and limiting of the acknowledgement, promotion, and management of diversity is forged and revealed in behind-the-scenes discussions and committees in local churches, such as those addressing circuit changes, welfare and services, worship, and finance and property. Committees develop a life of their own that is usually hidden (including from many social scientists studying churches). This independent life owes much to their regular usage. Moreover, it is very often the same people who attend and/or are active in them; there is seldom a sense of new inclusion or regular turnover of membership. Ultimately, they represent an important way local churches become institutionalised. More specifically, new practices and discourses are incorporated into a church by its committees; these, in turn, have origins in the denomination, the wider religious field, or other fields of power with which a church engages.

The central role of ministers in committees and the manner in which decisions are made in them are foundational sources of ministerial authority and separate ministers from even the most respected and involved lay leaders. This is heightened by ministers' mediating role between committees and outside bodies or professionals, such as local government, charities, accountants, or architects. This displaces authority from the white stalwarts, who otherwise are the most active speakers in committees; they are a ready repository of knowledge about "how things are done" in the local church. Their position is sometimes further undermined by ministers striking up friendships with younger professionals and involving them in committees or by their dealings with outsiders. By contrast, the lack of engagement by most migrants in these committees, including those who are otherwise actively involved in the local church, is both striking and dissonant. Together and in private, migrants readily talked to Wood about their exclusion from meaningful participation in committees (and, indeed, in church life more generally) and the exclusion of topics relevant to their racialised lives. Ministers' pursuit of "faith" community projects actually intensifies racial divisions in local churches, as these involve lay members only tangentially and position white ministers as public representatives of majority black churches. Thus, whilst migrants are not reducible to racial, ethnic, or national identifications, their perceptions and practices cannot be understood without reference to those. In short, committees offer migrants little scope for the development of authority, not least because this is the locus within which ministerial authority is most fully manifested in relation to laity in general.

As these observations suggest, whilst Wood connected religion and ethnicity, he always sought to think about power and authority in relation to religion – i.e. bringing the social back into the study of religion. Strategies for the attainment of authority are more clearly sought and manifested in an area of Methodist life that is largely derelict in Britain, an area where migrants have considerable experience: small group fellowships. Such groups become the principal arena in which migrant stalwarts and those from stalwart families "back home" seek to reproduce their stalwart status in Britain. The reinvigoration and invention of small groups, institutionally accepted as part of the Methodist heritage, provides an opportunity for migrants to reproduce their cultural and social capitals in Britain and, thus, earn and wield symbolic power in contradistinction to the symbolic violence they face in and outside the church.

Introduction

Joseph appeared to be an important member of his Methodist church in East London. Having arrived in England from Ghana in the mid-1980s when he was in his thirties, he had been elected a steward of his church and a steward of the grouping of local Methodist churches (what Methodists call a "circuit"). At church services, Joseph played a prominent role, such as reading the notices or taking up the collection. In many ways, he was the British stereotype of West African men – standing over six feet tall and with a physique to match, he was ebullient, loud-spoken, even flamboyant. When I arrived at a meeting of the circuit stewards one evening, Joseph was behaving in his usual manner, holding forth on a number of issues concerning Methodism and religion as he conversed with the senior minister in the circuit. This continued as the minister from his own church arrived, along with the senior circuit steward. The British government, Joseph told us with expressive hand gestures, has a "moral duty" to fund churches because this is a Christian country. Responding to the sceptical views of the others, Joseph concluded in a jovial, self-derisory fashion by apologising for what he called his "extreme ideological views." I was, therefore, taken aback when, as the meeting formally began, Joseph subsequently said barely one word and visibly shrank into the background. At most, he murmured his assent to the opinions voiced and the decisions made by the others.

Of course, there could have been many reasons for Joseph's change in behaviour. Perhaps he suddenly felt unwell or did not feel comfortable in an official setting. However, his behaviour fitted a pattern I have observed amongst migrants in different sorts of meetings in a number of Methodist churches where I have conducted participant observation. Whilst migrants from West Africa and the Caribbean are often highly visible in leading church services, when it comes to committee meetings, a small number of white British lay leaders, alongside the ministers who are nearly all white British, dominate discussions and decision-making – even though most of the migrant lay leaders have a strong Methodist background in their countries of origin and are quite familiar with Methodist rules and procedures.

I open my chapter with this example because it illustrates the problem of focusing on just one area of behaviour within an institution. Yet that is precisely what is done by many recent sociological studies of congregations. By exposing this problem, I can highlight some of the methodological and theoretical weaknesses that are increasingly apparent in the sociology of religion, many of which are explored in other chapters of this volume.

Congregational Studies

Congregational studies only emerged as a distinct area of sociological research in the late 1980s, with ethnographic case studies in America published by Nancy Ammerman, *Bible Believers* (1987), and Stephen Warner, *New Wine in Old Wineskins* (1988). These studies view congregations as multifaceted institutions in which worship services, fellowship meetings, committee structures and leadership selection are related to each other. This holistic approach was extended in later multi-sited studies by these same sociologists, as they sought to relate congregations to their wider environments. The communities in which migrants are located and how these change over time are explored in *Congregation and Community* (1997) by Ammerman, for example, and the effects of new American immigration are examined in *Gatherings in Diaspora* (1998) by Warner and Judith Wittner.

These developments in American sociology have not been matched in the United Kingdom, where congregational studies remain rare. There have been some anthropological studies of congregations formed by immigrants to Britain, such as those from Jamaica in Nicole Toulis' *Believing Identity* (1997) and from Nigeria in Hermione Harris' *Yoruba in Diaspora* (2006), as well as ethnographic studies of migrants belonging to other religious traditions, such as Kim Knott's study of a Hindu temple composed of East African migrants, *Hinduism in Leeds* (1986). But there are very few studies of long-established Christian congregations in the UK. Notably, those few tend not to pursue the holistic approach taken by studies in the US, focusing instead on worship, as in Mathew Guest's (2007) study of an evangelical Anglican church in York and Martin Stringer's (1999) study of four Christian congregations in Manchester.

A preference for a non-holistic approach is now emerging in American congregational studies, with many focusing on ethnic and national diversity. For example, Gerardo Marti's study of how a large multiethnic Baptist church in Los Angeles enables the construction of what he calls "a new corporate identity that transcends ethnicity" explicitly excludes research into "mechanisms for decision making, church discipline, and negotiation of competing visions for the church" (Marti, 2005: 190–191). Instead, it focuses on worship, within the congregation as a whole and within small groups.

It is interesting to consider how worship is viewed in this and other recent studies. Firstly, worship is seen as the most important feature of congregations. For example, Guest says worship was his initial concern in the congregation he studied; this led him to attend Sunday and mid-week services, as well as an Alpha course and home group meetings (Guest, 2007: 231). Similarly, Korie Edwards writes of what she calls an "interracial" conservative Protestant congregation in America. Worship services, she says, are the "most central" activities in churches:

> People are proclaiming who they are, not only to themselves, but also to others. They tell us what the people who participate in these rituals and practices are about. They tell us who belongs and who does not. They tell us what is allowed, what is praiseworthy, and what is unacceptable.
> EDWARDS, 2008: 20–21

I will return later to the issue of belonging. Secondly, worship is seen as an individual activity – that is, as involving the "faith" of the individual congregant. Scholars of religion pay little attention to the interactions amongst congregants during worship, even though the studies in question are based on participant observational research. As a result, the individual worshipper's "subjectivity" is highlighted, and this is often linked theoretically to a "subjectivisation" thesis. Thirdly, worship is understood to be determined by theology; put otherwise, the theology understood to animate the individual's faith is expressed in worship. Because worship is seen as explaining congregational change, this means, fourthly, changes in theology are the real reason for congregational change.

These assumptions about worship reveal how this area of study has become strongly linked to theology and religious studies, reducing sociological explanation to the views about religion that are dominant in those disciplines. It is telling that British scholars who present their congregational studies as sociological tend to work in theology or religious studies departments and, more significantly, rarely publish in sociology journals.

Contextualising Worship

If worship is to be adequately understood sociologically, two things must be done: firstly, attention must be paid to the social interactions and authorities that exist during times of worship, and, secondly, worship must be contextualised within wider congregational life. Erving Goffman's ideas about "region behaviour" are helpful here, as worship is both very public and intimately related to what goes on out of the public eye. In Goffman's terms, worship, especially in church services, is "front region" behaviour (1990: 110). The congregation is appearing in public and, as Goffman explains, there is an effort to maintain and embody "certain standards" relating to politeness and decorum. To focus wholly or primarily on front region behaviour, however, is to miss how it is shaped by "back region behaviour." To cite one of Goffman's examples, what goes on in the dining area of a restaurant can barely be understood without paying attention to what goes on in the kitchen, where the food is chosen and prepared and where the structural roles of the staff are most evident. It is in the back region where, to use another of Goffman's terms, the "impression management" of the organisation is produced (1990: 110). In the case of congregations, a variety of back regions shape worship and frequently change it – most notably committees of the local church and wider denomination, but also training sessions for leadership roles, the organisation of church-based activities, and the preparation of youths and new members.

Whilst in many contemporary religious traditions, the front region behaviour of worship promotes an ideology of egalitarianism and subjectivisation, back region behaviour consists of highly structured roles and relations that are formative of congregational life. To study congregations without paying attention to these is to exclude from analysis issues of power, authority, and contestation that are necessary for a sociological understanding. Those who exclude them often claim they are overturning the reductionist focus of sociology which, they say, is unhelpfully focused on the role of power. But the reverse is clearly the case, as it is they who are reducing congregations to a single aspect of their behavioural lives. Indeed, to accuse sociology of reductionism – a tediously common refrain – is to miss the point. Like all science, good sociology is necessarily reductionist in that it reduces the phenomenon under investigation in terms dictated by research questions or *problématiques*, as this is the only way to grasp or understand the complexity of things (see Bourdieu, Chamboredon, and Passeron, 1991). The point is, then, to reduce something in an appropriately scientific manner, rather than to reduce it simply for the sake of it in a manner not dictated by scientific reasons. The latter becomes the case when decisions are made prior to research, as in scholars' decisions to not investigate certain areas of congregational life on the basis of a theologically-informed perspective about what is central in congregations and what is not.

Understanding Diverse Congregations

Let me return to the ethnographic example with which I began this chapter. Joseph's behaviour in church worship, where he often took a leading role and presented himself as an active, jovial member of the congregation, was not especially revealing of his position and sense of belonging in the congregation. He held very critical views about the direction the British Methodist Church was taking and yet found himself little able to translate these into influence within the congregation. I have found this to be common amongst immigrants in London churches – even those who have worshipped in a congregation for most of their adult lives, having perhaps arrived from the Caribbean in the 1940s or 1950s. They tend to feel excluded from decision-making, despite holding important positions on committees.

It is by no means clear that worship is the most central activity in a congregation. In contrast to Korie Edwards, quoted earlier, I argue worship is not necessarily helpful in telling us "who belongs and who does not." A much greater sociologically understanding of the issue may be gained by looking at what happens in committees and other back regions of a congregation. In fact, doing so helps us see things during times of worship that we might otherwise miss, such as why certain ways of worshipping are absent or why certain people enact some roles but not others.

These issues are particularly salient in congregations with a diversity of ethnicities or nationalities, as there may be significant differences in views about church leadership, organisation, and worship. In such congregations, the back region behaviour of committee work involves complex contestations and negotiations which we should not assume lead to consensus or equality. Such committee work takes place behind closed doors and is largely unacknowledged by the wider congregation, which, nevertheless, is greatly affected by the decisions made in committees. This includes the sort of identities that can be constructed and expressed in the congregation. The parameters of religious, ethnic, and racial identities are strongly informed by decisions about what sort of worship is to be enacted (including its music and liturgy), who is selected in leadership roles, and which small groups may be formed and the regulations by which they must abide.[3] These are precisely the sorts of issues explored in studies of congregations by the previous generation of sociologists of religion, including Penny Edgell Becker (1999) on the conflicts that surround identities in congregations. In some London Methodist congregations, for example, the most heated debates arise over whether to allow the formation of national fellowships (such as for the members born in particular West African countries) and whether to favour the selection of a black minister. The outcome of these decisions, made in a variety of committees, has a substantial impact on the sort of belonging members feel in the church and the sort of identity they can articulate.

Conclusion: What do Congregational Studies Tell us about the Sociology of Religion Today?

What do congregational studies tell us about the sociology of religion today? In general, they are symptomatic of weaknesses that prevail in this field of study. Phenomena are increasingly presented as socially decontextualised: they are lifted out of the social contexts necessary to make sense of them but which researchers dismiss because they involve issues of social power or decision-making. Linked to this social decontextualisation is the way phenomena are presented – in a manner that strips them of their practical and interactional dimensions. There is frequently little interest in what people are doing and with whom, even though most congregational studies make use of participant observational research. Instead, analysis is based on people's views collected during interviews. By and large, these problems mirror those found in

---

3 Editor's note: the significance of ethnicity for the understanding of religion is underlined in some of Wood's previously published works (2006, 2010a; Wood and Eade, 2014).

sociological studies of "spirituality" or the "New Age," as I have discussed in a number of publications.[4]

One consequence is that sociological analysis increasingly appears as an insider's discourse. Studies of congregations often read like handbooks on how to run a successful congregation – indeed, Ammerman and her colleagues in the US have published a "handbook" on studying congregations that is "most directly addressed" to those "who work with and care about congregations" (Ammerman et al., 1998: 9), while Guest and his colleagues have edited a book about congregational studies in the UK that appears in a series on "Explorations in Practical, Pastoral and Empirical Theology," with several chapters by religious professionals (Guest, Tusting, and Woodhead, 2004). These developments require us to ask to what use sociology is being put, for it seems the discipline is being drawn upon to grant scientific prestige to theological concerns. In such cases, a sociological analysis is not pursued for its own sake, but is used in an uncritical and non-rigorous manner for other purposes. This explains why certain central sociological issues, particularly those relating to power, are ignored or downplayed. By drawing attention to the usefulness of Goffman's distinction between front and back region behaviours, we may attain a better sociological understanding of worship in congregations and, indeed, of congregational life as a whole.

References

Ammerman, Nancy. 1997. *Congregation and community*. New Brunswick; New Jersey: Rutgers University Press.

Ammerman, Nancy. 1987. *Bible believers*. New Brunswick: Rutgers University Press.

Ammerman, Nancy, Jackson Carroll, Carl S. Dudley, and William McKinney, eds. 1998. *Studying congregations: a new handbook*. Nashville: Abingdon Press.

Becker, Penny Edgell. 1999. *Congregations in conflict*. Cambridge: Cambridge University Press.

Bourdieu, Pierre, Jean-Claude Chamboredon, and Jean-Claude Passeron. 1991. *The craft of sociology: epistemological preliminaries*. Berlin; New York: Walter de Gruyter.

Edwards, Korie. 2008. *The elusive dream: the power of race in interracial churches*, New York: Oxford University Press.

Goffman, Erving. (1959) 1990. *The presentation of self in everyday life*. London: Penguin.

Guest, Mathew. 2007. *Evangelical identity and contemporary culture: a congregational study in innovation*. Milton Keynes: Paternoster.

---

4   Editor's note: see Wood (2007, 2009, 2010b).

Guest, Mathew, Karin Tusting, and Linda Woodhead, eds. 2004. *Congregational studies in the UK: Christianity in a post-Christian context*. Aldershot: Ashgate.

Harris, Hermione. 2006. *Yoruba in diaspora*. New York; Basingstoke: Palgrave Macmillan.

Knott, Kim. 1986. *Hinduism in Leeds*. Leeds: Community Religions Project, University of Leeds.

Marti, Gerardo. 2005. *A mosaic of believers: diversity and innovation in a multiethnic church*. Bloomington: Indiana University Press.

Stringer, Martin. 1999. *On the perception of worship: the ethnography of worship in four Christian congregations in Manchester*. Birmingham: University of Birmingham Press.

Toulis, Nicole. 1997. Believing identity: Pentecostalism and the mediation of Jamaican ethnicity and gender in England. Oxford; New York: Berg.

Warner, Stephen. 1988. *New wine in old wineskins: evangelicals and liberals in a small-town church*. Berkeley: University of California Press.

Warner, Stephen, and Judith Wittner. 1998. *Gatherings in diaspora*. Philadelphia: Temple University Press.

Wood, Matthew. 2015. "Shadows in caves? A re-assessment of public religion and secularization in England today," *European Journal of Sociology* 56: 241–270.

Wood, Matthew. 2010a. "Carrying religion into a secularising Europe: Montserratian migrants' experiences of global processes in British Methodism," *Anthropological Journal of European Cultures* 19(1): 9–23.

Wood, Matthew. 2010b. "The sociology of spirituality: reflections on a problematic endeavour." In *The new Blackwell companion to the sociology of religion*, edited by Bryan S. Turner, 267–285. Oxford: Blackwell.

Wood, Matthew. 2009. "The nonformative elements of religious life: questioning the 'sociology of spirituality' paradigm," *Social Compass* 56(2): 237–248.

Wood, Matthew. 2007. *Power and the new age: ambiguities of authority in neoliberal societies*. Aldershot: Ashgate.

Wood, Matthew. 2006. "Breaching bleaching: integrating studies of 'race' and ethnicity with the sociology of religion." In *Theorising religion: classical and contemporary debates*, edited by James A. Beckford and John Walliss, 237–250. Aldershot; Hants; Burlington: Ashgate.

Wood, Matthew, and John Eade. 2014. "La construction des religions publiques: ethnicité, Etat-nation et Méthodisme britannique." In *Le Protestantisme évangélique à l'épreuve des cultures* edited by Yannick Fer and Gwendoline Malogne-Fer, 67–85, edited by Yannick Fer and Gwendoline Malogne-Fer, 67–85. Paris: L'Harmattan.

CHAPTER 5

Unmasking the Relations of Power within the Religious Field

Christophe Monnot

Introduction

Last year, I was walking the corridors of my University with a colleague when we came across a new staff member. My colleague introduced me as a sociologist of religion. The question of my specialisation arose. My expertise lies in the institutionalisation of religion and the sociology of religious organisations; the colleague mentioned that I had recently worked on both Protestantism and Islam. The new staffer raised his eyebrows, turned to me and responded: "It is necessary to stay focused. Do not become too scattered!" In doing so, he gave voice to a common assumption amongst many scholars: in the field of the sociology of religion, specialisation generally refers to the tradition or the faith being studied, not to the methods or theories used during analysis. This anecdote illustrates the main point that I discuss in this chapter. As the study of religions is highly segmented into different religious specialities like the "sociology of Catholicism" or the "sociology of Islam," we may miss the fact that Catholicism in many countries in Europe occupies a privileged position or that Muslim groups encounter discrimination or suspicion all over Europe (see Hjelm, 2014: 863–865). My question is the following: By segmenting the study of churches, faith groups and minority communities into homologous disciplinary specialities, do we contribute to a masking of the dynamics of power at work in the religious field?

The purpose of the chapter is to show that the use of Bourdieu's perspective is helpful to connect the study of religious culture with the study of culture. In his attempt to elaborate a critical sociology, Bourdieu tried to reveal the social construction of first-hand experience and belief that leads us to accept the world as it is. In light of Bourdieu's statement that each field has its own *doxa* (Bourdieu, 1990), the chapter aims to further scholarly reflexivity[1] on the methods, theories and assumptions deployed in the analysis of religious fields.

---

1 A complete discussion of reflexivity and Bourdieu is available in Wood and Altglas (2010).

Surely a religious field, like other fields, contains relations of power, hierarchy, or cultural positioning that favour some groups over others. Questions about locating congregations in a specific cultural field are also important for a sociologist's understanding of his/her relationship to the field. I approach this problematic through a consideration of worship, one of the central productions of Christian congregations, by asking two questions. First, can we observe differences that distinguish specific agents? Second, does a routine religious service position a congregation in a particular cultural field?

Providing an overview of the relations of power and/or the cultural positioning of religious congregations may inspire sociologists of religion to bring a new reflexivity into their analyses. An important set of issues arises from taking reflexivity seriously. When the sociologist produces an analysis of relations of power and domination in a religious field without identifying the contours of that field and how agents are situated within it, he/she participates in the constitutive discourses of that field. In other words, the sociology of religion should carefully clarify the relations of power structuring the field to avoid the risk of reproducing them. In this chapter, I argue that the work of sociologists should not neglect the social positioning of congregations and denominations in the relations of power between them. Some have accumulated important cultural capital and recognition; others have not and find themselves dominated. The sociologist should continually work to recognise agents occupy positions in which they relate to others. For Bourdieu and Wacquant, recognising these relations prevents us from "rest[ing] on a relations of immediate belief in the facility of the world that makes us take it for granted" (1992: 73).

Historical congregations have obtained a privileged position in Europe that helps them share values close to those of society, unlike the minority groups who try to distinguish themselves from the mainstream values of society. The study of religious agents, groups, or denominations refers to relations of immediate belief. The salient issue for the sociologist in his or her analysis is to identify the social positions held by the studied cases in order to shed light on the relations of power in the field. This social identification helps the sociologist avoid isolating communities, taking them out of the social context in which they are positioned, thus contributing to the objectification of cultural distance and supporting groups trying to "impose" their views through relations of power.

To address these questions, the chapter approaches the social positioning of the various Christian congregations active in Switzerland through one limited, but crucial, activity: the cultural production of worship. Despite the abundance of cultural activities within the religious field, it is meaningful to study the routine production of worship as a marker of the cultural distinction of congregations. The chapter begins with a sociological account of worship as a cultural repertoire that structures congregational routines. Building on this account and using new data on Swiss churches, it then plots a social space of worship production. The data is from the National Congregations Study (NCS) conducted in Switzerland from 2007 to 2010. The study provides social and cultural indicators for each participating local congregation.[2] Working with this data allows a new understanding of the cultural position of congregations as determined by their denominational structures.

Cultural Dis-position and Religious Congregations

In the sociology of Bourdieu, the elements of worship provided by Christian congregations constitute a part of their cultural capital. As Bourdieu points out, cultural capital provides a position and distinction in a social space. In the context of cultural production, "denominations and, more generally, religious traditions provide an institutional source of structure in worship" (Chaves, 2004: 143), and "denominations are most similar, more distinctive, in their worship practices than in their demographic composition" (ibid: 164). It is important, therefore, to underline that I am interested in the routine cultural production of the usual worship by congregations. Obviously, I might choose to focus on the positions of particular agents within a church or a denomination. Or I could push the work to observe internal hierarchies, as do Bourdieu and de Saint Martin (1982) in "The Holy Family," a study shedding light on the relations of power within the French Catholic Magister. The cultural production discussed in this chapter does not take place in the shadows, however, but in the open, or on the "front stage" as Goffman (1959) would say. Certainly, there are other positions and relations of power on the "back stage" within denominations or churches, as Bourdieu and de Saint Martin argue or as Matthew Wood shows in his case study on Methodism in the preceding chapter of this volume. Nevertheless, even if we stay "front stage" by studying practices of worship, we can still perceive cultural positioning that distinguishes religious groups.

---

2 My definitions follow Chaves: "By congregations, I mean the relatively smallscale, local collectivities and organizations through which people routinely engage in religious activity: churches, synagogues, mosques, temples. Religionproducing organizations that are not congregations mainly include denominational organizations that serve, are supported by, or have authority over local congregations" (Chaves, 2002: 1523). See also Monnot and Stolz (Forthcoming) for the operationalisation of the definition.

In *Distinction,* Bourdieu (1984) argues cultural tastes are related to agents' social positioning. Accordingly, for Bourdieu, social agents with similar social or close positioning are subjected to similar social constraints and will display similarities in their cultural tastes:

> Social space is so constructed that agents who occupy similar or neigh-bouring positions are placed in similar conditions and subjected to similar conditioning, and therefore have every chance of having similar dispositions and interests, and thus of producing practices that are them-selves similar.
>
> BOURDIEU, 1989: 17

This is a significant point to make, because churches and religious groups can be seen as social agents who participate in cultural production. The number of artists who exert their musical skills within churches is very important as well. Consider Vivaldi, Bach, or more recently, Mahalia Jackson and Aretha Franklin, to name a few.

Just as like attracts like, so too Bourdieu shows agents distinguish them-selves by displaying a distance from others with different cultural capital. But distinction is simply a "relational mode of thinking" (Bourdieu, 1987: 4) under-stood in a specific social space. Bourdieu notes:

> The social world can be represented in the form of a (multi-dimensional) space constructed on the basis of principles of differentiation or distri-bution constituted by the set of properties active in the social universe under consideration, that is, able to confer force or power on their pos-sessor in that universe. Agents and groups of agents are thus defined by their relative positions in space.
>
> BOURDIEU, 1992: 226

The distinction between agents is manifested in this social space by the social distance between them. Each agent occupies a relative position in this social space; through relations of proximity, agents see they are culturally close with-out being oblivious to Bourdieu's important idea. They share stakes in power with the culturally proximal, more so than with those who are further away. These other agents consequently have a different positioning, a more powerful or a weaker one depending on the capital they have acquired. For Bourdieu, positions in a specific social field correspond to the distribution of power in the field; this, in turn, depends on agents' economic capital or cultural and social capital, as well as their symbolic capital. Thus, the space will offer more prestigious positions to agents with strong legitimacy than those without.

I focus on one social space, Sunday worship, and on the production of culture in that space. Specific forms of cultural production characterise local parishes and religious communities. The cultural production of worship is not only regular in time, but also distinguishes itself by a combination of speech, music, and prayer, with readings, gestures, and recitations. The selection of these elements affects the embodied style of the worship services produced by congregations and positions them culturally. In Bourdieu's terms, these elements constitute cultural capital. The musical style, the kind of speech used, and the type of member participation create a culture shared by the local congregation. The performance matches the cultural capital accumulated by the congregation. It provides a dis-position for the religious communities in a social space.

Communities are groups of agents in a particular social space. This social space characterises their cultural capital and distinguishes them from other agents, i.e., other religious groups offering a similar or different style of worship service. In other words, congregations select from a range of cultural elements to produce worship. Although the available cultural repertoire is "a collection of stuff that is heterogeneous in content and function" (DiMaggio, 1997: 267), a congregation's selection shapes its religious expression and leads to an identifiable style. Moreover, as Chaves says of American congregations, a common "social homogeneity forges links between worship elements" (Chaves, 2004: 139). Ultimately, a selection of cultural elements is combined in forms of praise, becoming an institutionalised cultural production that defines a congregation's position in a specific social field of worship: "The form assumed, at each moment ... defines the state of the relations of power, institutionalized in durable social statuses that are socially recognized or legally guaranteed, between agents who are objectively defined by their position within these relations" (Bourdieu, 1992: 226). Congregations provide a culture of worship, or following de Certeau, a frame, "an element whose experience receives its form and expression" (de Certeau, 2003: 47). According to Friedland and Alford, the form of worship is not random but part of an "institutional logic" (Friedland and Alford, 1991: 248). This logic determines the selection of elements from an assorted "set of material practices and symbolic constructions, liturgical elements, which constitutes its organizing principles and which is available to organizations and individuals to elaborate" (ibid: 248). The selection of cultural elements affects the cultural style of worship service produced by congregations and positions them socially. Songs, instruments, types of liturgy, prayers, and recitations composing worship are elements that characterise the positioning of local communities in a field of specific cultural production.

The institutionalisation of the range of choices by denominations themselves reduces the possibility of choices of local communities. For instance, in the Catholic Church, Vatican II decided to stop masses in Latin. All Catholic congregations began to worship in vernacular languages. Protestant congregations make similar decisions, such as the choice of a particular hymnbook, the ministers' wearing of a robe, or the recognition of particular religious training.

Data: National Congregations Study in Switzerland

To illustrate cultural positioning, I have selected several cultural elements from the Swiss National Congregations Study (NCS) dataset (Monnot, 2013; Stolz et al., 2011). The Swiss NCS (Stolz et al. 2011) follows the design of the original NCS, conducted by Chaves and colleagues (Chaves, 2004; Chaves and Anderson, 2008) in the United States in 1997–1998, with a second wave in 2006–2007. Two different ways of proceeding can generate a random and representative sampling. One is the classic census format: counting the units to obtain a comprehensive list of these units – here, the active congregations – in a defined territory. The Swiss NCS follows this procedure and maps all active congregations in the country. The other is hyper-network sampling, the method used by the NCS survey in the US. In the absence of a comprehensive list of all units, one simply starts with a random sample of individuals and asks them to name the organisation(s) to which they are attached (Chaves et al., 1999: 460). In Switzerland, the census was conducted from September 2008 to September 2009. The Swiss research team used all available lists, directories or databases. This was supplemented with data collected through fieldwork, using snowball sampling to identify previous undocumented congregations. Each congregation entered into the final database was verified by two independent sources of information. By combining these two data collection methodologies, the NCS achieved the most systematic documentation of Swiss congregations to date.

The census counted 5,734 congregations across all regions of Switzerland. In the second phase of the study, researchers took a random sample of 1,040 of these congregations. It was stratified by religious belonging to over-represent religious minorities. For each of the 1,040 congregations, they interviewed one key informant – in most cases the spiritual leader – by telephone in one of the three national languages. A close-ended survey was administered with 250 questions on concrete, routine practices (such as instruments played during worship), as well as the tangible characteristics of the organisation (such as number of congregants). This questionnaire was adapted from the American NCS (Chaves et al., 1999). Special care was taken to adapt the questionnaire to the range of religious traditions found in Switzerland (Forsyth et al., 2007; Behling and Law, 2000). The various religious federations supported the project by encouraging local leaders to take part, thereby producing a high response rate of 71.8 percent (Monnot, 2013: 244–255). The survey data, the questionnaire, and the variable coding are all available on the FORS database (https://forsbase.unil.ch/datasets/dataset-public-detail/12643/828).

The census allows us to observe a large majority of Christian congregations: more than eight congregations out of ten. Non-Christians represent 17 percent of the congregations (i.e., the local parishes). These are very diverse, including numerous religions of the world (like Islam, Buddhism, or Hinduism), many minority groups (such as Ahmadyyia and Bahaï) and new religious movements (such as UFO religions, neoshamanism, or scientology); however, fewer than 10 percent of all congregants in Switzerland converge into one of these minority groups (Monnot and Stolz, 2014). Given the lack of space and because congregations are mainly Christian in Switzerland, I hence focus on Christian worship. For a wider and more general comparison, the reader is referred to Monnot and Stolz (2014) or to Monnot's comparison of congregations, including elements of worship (2013: 148–166).

The diverse Christian faiths are categorised into groups, such as Catholic, Reformed, Evangelical, Pentecostal, Conservative Evangelical, Messianic, and "other" Christian congregations. For the Catholic faith, the survey identifies 1750 local congregations and linguistic "missions." Monasteries and religious communities are not included, as these are not considered usual congregations. The Reformed faith includes 1094 active congregations in the different Swiss Cantons. Following the work of Stolz and Favre (2005), the Evangelical faith includes 544 congregations derived from Anabaptism and Pietism. These Evangelical congregations are Methodists, Salvation Army (both born during the revivals of the 18th century), "Free" churches (born in 19th-century revivals), and Mennonites. The Pentecostal faith emerged in the 20th-century Holiness movement (Apostolic Church, Elim Church) and the Pentecostal awakenings (Assembly of God) and comprises 685 congregations.[3] The Conservative faith includes 194 congregations, such as the Bretheren and the Darbyst; these do not cultivate strong links with churches outside their denominations. The Messianic faith includes Jehovah's Witness, Mormon, and Adventist communities. In this chapter, I exclude the category "other" Christians; it would not be analytically meaningful to group small numbers of congregations in a single category, as their origins, language, and traditions are very different. To be more specific, the census identifies 58 Orthodox congregations (including Coptic,

---

3   The main Pentecostal group in Switzerland, *Pfingstmission*, is internationaly affiliated with the AOG.

Apostolic Armenian, Syriac, Greek, Russian, Serbian, and Romanian Orthodox faiths), 50 Lutheran congregations (originating from a range of countries such as Germany, Denmark, Sweden, Norway, and the United States), 35 congregations of the Christian Catholic of Switzerland (Union of Utrecht of the Old Catholic Church), and 12 Anglican congregations. Clearly, the sample size is too small for specific analyses.

Following a suggestion from Chaves in his analyses of American congregations (2004), here, I focus on elements of worship. Among other elements (like the architecture of the building, the paintings, the stained-glass windows, etc.), these both build and display cultural capital. On a cultural level, worship is a production that characterises both local parishes and larger religious denominations. The cultural production of worship is not only regular in time but is distinguished from other cultural productions by its unique combination of speech, music, and prayer. For instance, a graduation ceremony may include speech and some music, but not in a combination like a church liturgy, and certainly without the use of ritual gestures or spontaneous prayer. A worship service is a cultural production that characterises a religious community – on the broader stage or locally – and positions it in a specific social and cultural field.

A worship service, according to the NCS survey, lasts an hour, on average. It is composed of one-third singing and music, one-third speeches and readings, and one-third prayer, meditation, recitations, and liturgical gestures. For the purposes of this chapter, I have selected 18 elements to characterise the culture production of worship on three levels: the musical level, the ritual level, and the participation level. On the musical level, these elements are the worship's instrumentation and singing. On the ritual level, they refer to liturgical gestures, the distinctive robe of the minister, and the presence of a formal written program. On the participation level, the elements include spontaneous or individual gestures, applause, or spontaneous prayers by participants. Some elements, like a preaching a sermon, are not considered; every Christian service includes this kind of thing. One difference in Switzerland is the length of the preaching, running from nine minutes on average in a Catholic worship service to 48 minutes in an Evangelical Conservative worship service.

Table 5.1 offers an overview of the frequency of these 18 cultural elements in the individual congregations categorised by the faith to which they belong.[4]

Table 5.1 shows a range of cultural options to celebrate worship. On the music level, the Catholic and Reformed congregations are much more likely to celebrate with an organ than others. At the opposite end of the spectrum, the Pentecostal and some Evangelical groups play drums, rarely the case in other services.

---

4   For an overview of all worship elements, see Monnot (2013: 152).

TABLE 5.1   *Frequency of a selection of 18 cultural elements used during usual worship in six Christian faith categories.*

Elements	Catholic	Reformed	Evangelical	Pentecostal	Conservative	Messianic
N (sample size)	317	198	99	124	35	21
Organ	78%	85%	11%	3%	6%	32%
Drums	2%	5%	38%	57%	9%	5%
Choir	36%	24%	18%	35%	46%	5%
Hymnbook	90%	95%	30%	20%	91%	91%
Projection	9%	17%	83%	83%	31%	43%
Ritual gestures	95%	38%	21%	47%	9%	48%
Meditation	97%	75%	85%	71%	46%	52%
Written program	32%	27%	22%	22%	14%	52%
Special garments	99%	72%	11%	3%	0%	0%
Recitation	94%	86%	31%	32%	33%	27%
Reading	95%	63%	67%	65%	83%	73%
Speaking in tongues	1%	1%	9%	68%	0%	0%
Testimony	55%	62%	96%	95%	100%	100%
Spontaneous gestures	26%	19%	67%	89%	7%	10%
Spontaneous prayer	4%	6%	55%	61%	83%	27%
Jump or dance	2%	1%	6%	37%	0%	0%
Applause	24%	29%	37%	63%	6%	27%
Laughter	30%	53%	73%	72%	58%	52%

National Congregations Study in Switzerland, University of Lausanne, 2010. Bold numbers are those showing a significant difference (p<.001).

On the ritual level, we see the Catholic services have many more ritual gestures. Catholic priests and Reformed pastors wear robes or special garments, and their congregations read or recite a prayer, a creed, or a scripture together. In the Reformed, Evangelical, and Pentecostal services, participants read scripture or a prayer to the rest of the congregation. The Conservative and Messianic services devote much less time to silent prayer or meditation than any of the others. The Messianic services usually follow a program, whilst Pentecostal services distinguish themselves by having people speak in tongues.

On the participation level, the Reformed and Catholic services less frequently offer a time for participants to testify or speak about their own religious experience. In the Evangelical and the Pentecostal services, however, attendees make individual and spontaneous gestures, such as standing up, clapping hands, moving, and spontaneously expressing themselves aloud. These participants also offer up spontaneous prayers, but such involvement occurs most frequently in Conservative services. The Pentecostal services even feature adults jumping, shouting, or dancing spontaneously during the service, and applause can break out at any time. In contrast, participants rarely even laugh aloud at any point in the Catholic service.

Looking over the elements in Table 5.1, it is clear the actual worship services are not random subsets of these 18 elements; that is, "some of these elements are more likely than others to occur together" (Chaves, 1999: 13). A service with a minister wearing special garments, for instance, is more common when organs are a featured part of the service and less common when participants are likely to express a prayer spontaneously. The use of drums is linked with the non-use of hymnbooks, whilst the organ is linked with the non-use of any visual projection equipment during the service.

A Cultural Space in Two Dimensions

The combination of speech, musical style, type of prayer, and other ritual elements constitutes a worship service. As observed above, the worship service is a production that characterises religious communities. More precisely, it is a specific production that offers a specific position to a congregation in a particular social space. When worship elements are included in a factor analysis to identify those occurring together, two dimensions emerge. One corresponds to the formal expression of the liturgy. The other relates to the individual expression of the faithful. Table 5.2 gives an overview of the two dimensions.

In order to measure the first dimension, the formal expression of faith, a scale[5] can be built using such elements as ritual gestures, meditation time, the musical part of the worship (i.e., use of an organ, a choir, music in a hymnbook), readings by members in front of the church, and group recitation by the assembly. A second scale can be built with other elements to indicate the individualistic and spontaneous involvement of attendees; such elements include spontaneous gestures, dancing and jumping, applause, laughter, speaking in tongues, personal prayers, testimonies given by members of the congregations, and music played using drums with lyrics projected on a screen.

---

5   For each item: Yes = 1, No = 0.

TABLE 5.2   *Elements composing two cultural dimensions of worship.*

Formal dimension		Individual dimension	
Elements	%	Elements	%
Ritual Gestures	57%	Spontaneous gestures	36%
Hymnbook	74%	Projection	32%
Choir	33%	Jump or dance	6%
Organ	57%	Drums	15%
Meditation	83%	Spontaneous prayers	22%
Recitation	71%	Applause	29%
Reading	76%	Laughter	48%
Written program	27%	Testimony	69%
Special garments	61%	Speaking in tongues	12%
Scale mean (SD)	5.4 (2.1)	Scale mean (SD)	2.4 (1.9)
N of items	9	N of items	9
Cronbach's Alpha	.674	Cronbach's Alpha	.732

National Congregations Study in Switzerland, University of Lausanne, 2010.

As suggested by Chaves in his analyses of worship in American congregations (2004: 127–165), these two dimensions compose a cultural space in which religious congregations construct their worship services.[6] When all Christian congregations from the representative sample are combined and placed along these two dimensions by faith, their cultural position emerges, as shown in Figure 5.1.

To reiterate, Figure 5.1 diagrammatically represents where the expressions of the main faiths are situated in social space along two dimensions – individual and formal. The higher numbers on either axis refer to greater evidence of those elements listed in Table 5.2 for that dimension. The choice to represent the two dimensions on a schematic space follows Bourdieu:

> We can compare social space to a geographic space within which regions are divided up. But this space is constructed in such a way that the closer the agents, groups or institutions which are situated within this space, the more common properties they have; and the more distant, the fewer. Spatial distances – on paper – coincide with social distances.
> BOURDIEU, 1989: 16

6   Note that these two dimensions are weakly correlated: $r(1040)=-.370$; $p<.01$.

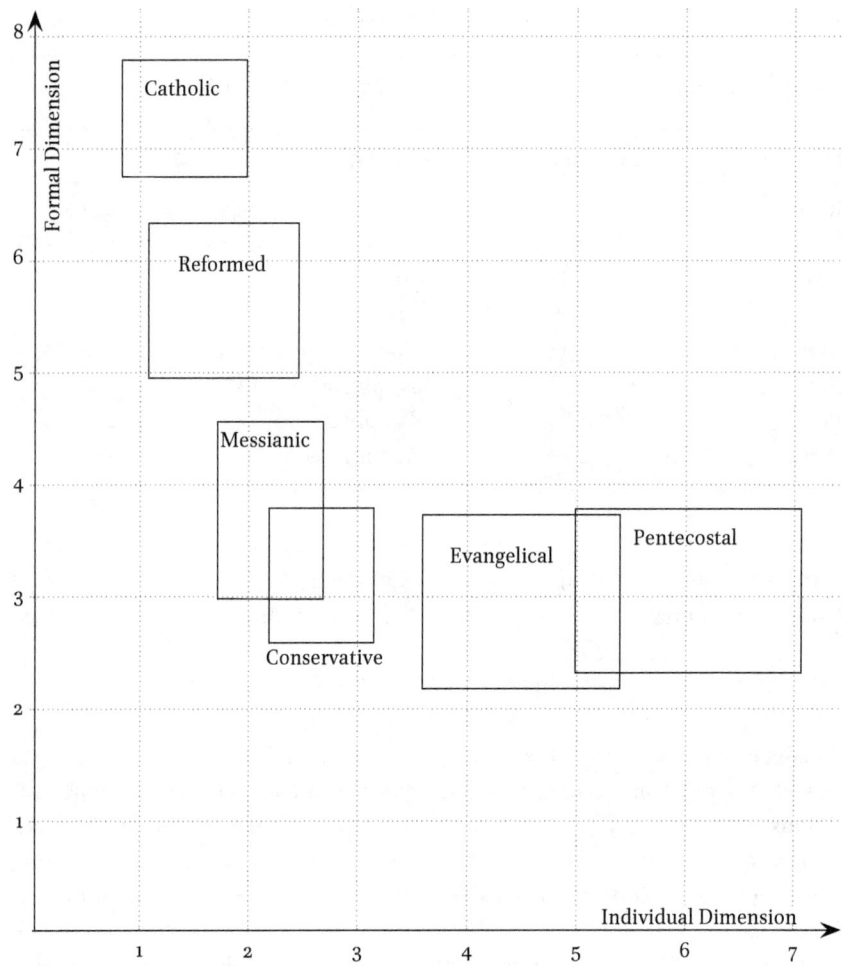

FIGURE 5.1   *Worship space of the main Christian faiths in Switzerland.*

Again following Bourdieu, the figure shows the social distance between Christian faiths in Switzerland. At the same time, it shows a degree of overlap on the cultural level of worship production for many, but not all faiths.

The congregations belonging to Catholic and Reformed churches are positioned at the top of the formal dimension and at the bottom of the individual or spontaneous dimension of forms of worship. The strong formality in both is perhaps a cultural consequence of their legal standing, whereby they are legally recognised by the state as institutions. Like other cultural productions supported by the state (e.g., opening of Parliament), their worship services are both ceremonial and official, following specified and institutionalised rules. In contrast, in the lower right of the figure, the services of Pentecostal and Evangelical congregations distinguish themselves with their low level of formality and high level of individual participation, as evidenced by the strong involvement of assembly members, including participation with the body, individual spontaneity, and a musical style rooted in pop culture. The Messianic community is the most formal of the non-recognised denominations, with less individual and spontaneous involvement than the other evangelical groups. Interestingly, it overlaps with the Conservative community. In the latter case, the involvement of the members can be summarised as the participation of individuals and spontaneous prayer spoken aloud. Citing Bourdieu, Chaves says such overlapping positions clearly express a "variation between 'popular' and 'bourgeois' entertainment style" (Chaves, 2004: 141; see Bourdieu, 1984: 487–488), reminding us that the selection of certain elements by a faith or an individual congregation reflects both how it sees itself and how others see it.[7]

A point to note in Figure 5.1 is the shape and size of the various denominations. The rectangles are neither uniform nor arbitrary. In fact, they have statistical significance, as they describe the dispersion around the mean (standard deviation). A long side (vertical or horizontal) indicates the cultural productions of the various congregations in that particular religious faith are more diverse and, therefore, can spread further from the mean; a shorter side indicates all congregations in that faith are more alike and, thus, are clustered closely around the mean. Generally, the deviation is little more than one point on the scale. The only exceptions are the Evangelicals and Pentecostals, but as noted above, these faiths cover several different denominations. Thus, they demonstrate a wider cultural range than the others in both dimensions. Whilst greater than that of other groups, however, the range is not that significant overall: less than two points on the formal dimension and slightly more than two points on the individual dimension. This suggests the well-defined cultural

---

7   Unfortunately, the connection between this cultural space and the social characteristics of attendees is missing. There are social or educational differences between people attending worship from these congregations but as Stolz, Könemann et al. (2016) underline, the link to the congregation is different, ranging from those who are really regular to those who are very distant from the local congregation. However, those who attend irregularly also have a social impact on the position of a group.

understanding of the individual congregations; a sense of cultural investment and social positioning is shared by the denominational/faith structure at the local level.

The overlapping of certain faiths suggests the cultural settings within them. For example, Adventists, cited as part of the Messianic faith group above, are actually positioned between the Messianic and Evangelical faiths, possibly explaining the overlapping of the Messianic and Conservative faiths. Meanwhile, the Charismatic renewal movements in some classical Evangelical congregations can explain the overlap of Evangelicals and Pentecostals, pointing to what Stolz et al. (2013) call the "competitive milieu" of Evangelicals.

Beside these confined overlapping spaces, some groups have more social homogeneity and others more heterogeneity. A Catholic congregation, for instance, will always be identifiable by the cultural elements it mobilises. To continue with the example, the elements of a Reformed congregation will be culturally close to those of a Catholic one, but distinguishing between the two is not difficult. The range of elements in a Reformed congregation will also distinguish it from an Evangelical one. A Pentecostal congregation will show an even greater cultural distance from an Evangelical congregation; only some Charismatic Evangelical services look like Pentecostal ones. For example, playing drums is a distinctive feature of Pentecostal services. Interestingly, this echoes the sense of belonging reflected in the use of the organ in Catholic or Protestant worship services.

Bourdieu observes: "In effect [these dispositions mark culturally] social distances [that] are inscribed in bodies or, more precisely, into the relation to the body, to language and to time – so many structural aspects of practice ignored by the subjectivist vision" (Bourdieu, 1989: 17). In the set of positions occupied by the various faiths and the congregations comprising them, then, we can read a distribution of cultural capital and its related powers. Bourdieu also alerts us to the thinking behind the distribution:

> The social space cannot be reduced to a simple "awareness context" in the interactionist sense, a universe of points of view reflecting each other *ad infinitum.* It is the relatively stable site of the coexistence of points of view, in the dual sense of positions in the distribution of capital (economic, informational, social, etc.) and of the corresponding powers, but also of *practical reactions* to or representations of that space, produced from these points through habitus that are structured, and doubly informed, by the structure of the space and by the structure of the schemes of perception that applied to it.
>
> BOURDIEU, 2000: 183; emphasis in original

In what Bourdieu calls a "practical reaction," congregations opt for the closest cultural tools, distinguishing themselves from others according to which elements they choose to draw from the available repertoire. Pentecostal congregations can justify the use of rock music in their worship services as a tool marking their distance from the "religious" and "boring" traditional worship services of other congregations belonging to other faiths. By using these items, they express their distance from a formal culture they see as spiritually negative. Culturally, Pentecostals seem closer to Johnny Cash than Jean-Sebastien Bach (the latter is closer to the culture of worship in Reformed churches). As Bourdieu observes, "The dispositions acquired in the position occupied imply an adjustment to this position, what Goffman calls the 'sense of one's place'" (Bourdieu, 1989: 17). For him, this "sense of one's place" leads some agents to maintain a certain style of worship, whilst others assert their distance by producing another one, whether consciously or unconsciously.

Dis-position of the Sociologist

Figure 5.1 shows the positioning of congregations sorted by the manifestations or productions of their faith. Briefly stated, each congregation has a position in a specific field represented by the rectangle, but as Bourdieu cautions: "The social field can be described as a multi-dimensional space of positions such that each actual position can be defined in terms of a multi-dimensional system of co-ordinates whose values correspond to the values of the different pertinent variables" (1992: 226). In other words, an agent (a specific congregation) or a group of agents (a faith) is involved in a number of different fields. For example, although I have been discussing worship space as revelatory of cultural or symbolic capital, the accumulation of economic capital is another possible field of enquiry. If we were to consider this capital, we would find a clear distance between the Catholic and Reformed churches and the rest, because the former two can charge taxes in Switzerland. Such privileges accrue from their special legal status, bringing us back full circle to a reminder of the symbolic capital they have amassed over time.

Once we consider their positioning in a wider social space, we find each congregation occupies a worship space very similar to another congregation of the same denomination or faith. The slight variations within faiths indicate the overall positions of the congregations and their distance from other congregations.

Yet we need to go beyond the social position of the religious group investigated to ask about the social position of the sociologist investigating it.

If positioning in a worship space shows distances, the sociological analysis has to take it into account. This is not always obvious when the study is focused on a single faith, denomination, or congregation. Some congregations/faiths have social privileges when others do not; some have distinctive positions on the formal dimension and others on the individual dimension. All of this suggests different cultural positions. In the study of majority faiths, it is also useful to shed light on the (religious) strategies that help the local congregations maintain their privileged position.

For the Swiss case, as discussed elsewhere (Stolz and Monnot, 2017) and underlined here through the Christian worship space, the majority groups provide a worship culture which is similar to the culture of ceremonies provided by the State's administration. The sociologist will necessarily be in homology or in heterology with the culture provided by the specific case he or she is investigating, but the analysis has to avoid describing the ceremony as the unique consequence of a specific theology or behaviour by the priest or by the members; rather, it must show that the ceremony is a historical construction, the fruit of the struggles of power to keep a privileged position.

When addressing minority groups, the analysis has to avoid the traps of social prejudices to show that the groups try to position themselves as cultural or religious alternatives to others in order to carve out a niche within which to survive, where members can participate in a kind of religious counterculture. In Switzerland, for instance, the struggle for power between the State-supported Reformed groups, along with the discriminatory treatment of the Anabaptist groups, historically led the Evangelical groups to withdraw from community affairs, wherein the individual connection of each member is essential. In this case, the participative ceremonial culture is both a theological predisposition and a fruit of the struggles to keep members and maintain legitimacy.

My main point is that religious groups are always in a social space in which they relate to each other; we cannot pretend that all these groups have the same position in society. It is a risk if we do not identify the contours of the religious field or a specific space by segmenting, for instance, the study of religion into specific faith without considering their social positioning.

A more pressing issue is articulated by Bourdieu. Speaking to sociologists of religion, he says:

> The question is not to know, as we often pretend, whether those who practise sociology of religion have faith or not, nor even whether they belong to the Church or not.... It is for each sociologist of religion to ask, in the interest of their own research, when he speaks about religion,

whether he wants to understand the struggles in which religious things are at stake, or to take part in these struggles.

BOURDIEU 2010:2

Following Bourdieu's logic and reading Figure 5.1, then, the question raised earlier about the segmentation of sociology into different denominational specialities seems a good one.

The sociologist has to identify how groups are situated within a social field and to understand if his/her social position is culturally close to or distant from the culture of the case under study. Like the larger denominations and the local congregations, the sociologist is positioned in a social field. As noted by Bourdieu:

> Thus the representations of agents vary with their position (and with the interest associated with it) and with their habitus, as a system of schemes of perception and appreciation of practices, cognitive and evaluative structures, which are acquired through the lasting experience of a social position.
>
> BOURDIEU, 1989:19

More specifically, this means sociologists will categorise the object of study in different ways, depending on their perception of distance. For instance, the sociologist of religion may, in some cases, find a particular liturgy style aristocratic or "petit bourgeois" (Chaves 2004: 141). To follow Bourdieu, "This makes for the fact that nothing classifies somebody more than the way he or she classifies" (1989:19). In this perspective, a particularly provocative example comes from the church-sect typology of Max Weber (1973). Some may categorise the churches of the aristocracy and high bourgeoisie to which they are close as part of a "church type," contrasting them with the communities of "others." This example suggests it is certainly a risk for the sociologist's consideration to reflect his/her position when he/she studies individual groups without recognising that groups commonly have a position in a social or cultural field in which they relate to others.

This is fundamental for Bourdieu in his attempt to elaborate a critical sociology. Critical of what? Simply stated, critical of the social construction of first-hand experience and belief that leads us to accept the world as it is. To be scientific, sociology needs to address the religious field's *doxa*. Only by revealing the *doxa*, by shedding light on the ways social actors "naturally" take the world for granted, can sociology go forward. According to Bourdieu, if sociological analyses do not shed light on this *doxa*, they will simply supplement it. The sociologist will be culturally prone to have a "natural" penchant for one religious group rather than another. Depending on the group he/she studies, he/she will have a close or distant positioning with respect to his/her object of study.

This applies to groups being compared using a macro perspective. The cultural distance involves a distinction, from which "one can immediately understand that practices or goods associated with the different classes in the different areas of practice are organized in accordance with structures of opposition which are homologous to the structure of objective oppositions between class conditions" (Bourdieu, 1984: 171). The stakes of power have to be analysed in relation to groups with social legitimacy and others seeking this legitimacy, but who differentiate themselves by selecting different strategies which, in turn, will position them differently in the social space. To give an example from Figure 5.1's social space, we see Pentecostal community groups value individual expression; accordingly, they will find legitimacy among those who perceive them as a community that takes care of its members as individuals.

But in social space, the strategy conforming to a much more formal liturgy gains legitimacy, so when sociologists examine this type of group, they need to consider power dynamics to free themselves from various *doxa* (such as the one taking for granted that a more formal liturgy has more legitimacy) to avoid being at the beck and call of the dominant (ruling) class. If they do not, they may contribute to the *illusio*, the immediate adhesion to the beliefs of a field, giving it scientific support.

Although I emphasise the cultural positioning of the individual congregations and their overarching faiths observable here, if we are considering the cultural production during worship, segmenting the sociology of religion into different specialities, such as Catholicism, Methodism, or Lutheranism, can fracture the larger field into numerous homogenous cultural fields and obscure the contours of a broader space in which they have a position. It obscures the relations with power, as well as the positioning of a particular faith in the larger religious field, not to mention the positioning of a particular community within the larger religious faith. Because there is no knowledge of the positions of religious groups, the actual position of any given group may be interpreted as a specificity of that religious group, not indicative of the position it occupies in the religious field. For instance, when sociologists speak about Catholicism without recognising its embeddedness in a cultural space in which it relates to other groups and do not discuss it in the light of the social position and legitimacy it has gained during its history, they run the risk of considering Catholicism outside the relations of power it has with other religious groups.

Moreover, the segmentation of the field into faiths affects the social representation of these faiths, including in social research. Accordingly, the work of sociologists may contribute to positive or negative portrayals of religious agents, rather than objective analyses. As Bourdieu argues, "The representations of agents vary with their position ... and with their habitus" (1989:19). For Bourdieu, the habitus may be a system of schemes of practices, but it is also a system of perception and appreciation – in other words, the gaze of the analyst, whose appreciation of certain practices expresses a social position. More important for the present discussion, however, "habitus produces practices and representations which are available for classification" (Bourdieu, 1989:19). Some practices are close to the habitus of the sociologist and influence his/her categorisation. Such practices will be discussed differently from those showing a cultural distance. This is important, as the work of the scientist is to observe those distances between agents or religious groups that show the relation of power between these agents.

Consequently, the description of a religious faith or an individual congregation by the sociologist may not be indicative of its social position or its position within the larger religious field. If these relationships are obscured, especially by segmenting the field of religion into different denominational disciplines, the work of the sociologist may simply reproduce the structures in sociological words. The work of sociologists should not neglect the social positioning of congregations and denominations in the relations of power between them. Some have accumulated important cultural capital and recognition; others have not and find themselves dominated. In this situation, some groups present a cultural homology with the academic field and others look bizarre or singular. For example, the use of an organ is rarely a topic in the social science literature, but the use of pop-rock bands in churches is a subject for research (see Wagner, 2014a, 2014b).

In this situation, it is helpful to remember once more that the denominations and religious groups are historically and socially in different positions. The scholar is also in a social position, either near or far from the studied case. The cultural production and/or practices of a congregation will be described as self-evident, with some considered "interesting" because they are "different." This fact must be addressed in religious studies, which, as I underlined in the opening of this chapter, is highly segmented into specialities covering a specific faith or denomination.

Admittedly, by specialising in specific denominations, the sociology of religion runs the risk of removing the object of analysis from its social context, with the possibility of missing out on good information, including the logic of actors. Sometimes, this specialisation allows the highlighting of issues of power within a faith (Bourdieu and de Saint Martin, 1982). Yet it may fall into

another trap – simply reproducing in academic discourse the cultural positions occupied by religious groups.

My purpose here has been to show that the use of Bourdieu's perspective
is appropriate and helpful to connect the study of religious culture with the
study of culture. We definitely miss something when we study individual
groups without acknowledging the cultural or social positions they occupy in
which they have relations to others. For sociologists, the work is also to identify
the contours of a cultural space and to show how groups are situated within
it. With the representative data of the NCS in Switzerland, I have shown there
are clear social positions within and across denominations. The work of the
sociologist is to emphasise these distances to underline the strategies of the
agents involved. But the possible homology between sociologists and the cultural capital of some collective religious entities force the good sociologist to
identify the relations of power between different positions within the religious
field to avoid participating in the *doxa* of the field. In this case, the sociologist
will bring legitimacy to some practices and question others simply because of
the distance between the social position of the academic field and the position
of the studied group.

The work obviously deserves to be widened to include non-Christian communities, but the data is too limited to supply a significant profile of other
traditions. First, minorities can be diverse; Switzerland has 33 Jewish communities, with some Reform, others Conservative, or Reconstruction, and
still others belonging to the Hassidism tradition with the "Chabad-Lubavitch"
movement. The situation is even more complex with Islam. Even if the large
majority has origins in the Balkans or Turkey (Sunni Hanafi school), the inner
diversity of Islam is important. As well as Sunni, the country also has Alevi,
Shia (Ismaili, Shia loyal or dissident to Iran), Wahhabi, and groups of Swiss
converts. We would have to find cultural indicators of worship relevant for this
wide range of traditions. The next wave of NCS will focus on these minorities
to ensure a better understanding of the cultural productions of the plethora of
diverse traditions. At that point, we will be able to define their worship space
and determine their actual positioning.[8]

Conclusion

The most crucial cultural production of a congregation is its worship service.
As the Swiss NCS data indicates, congregations select certain cultural elements

---

8   An attempt to paint a general picture is available in Monnot (2013: 148–166). See also the wor-
    ship space proposed by Chaves for American congregations (Chaves, 2004: 147).

from a larger repertoire to compose a service. The selection of elements defines the worship and is not random. Some cultural elements are more likely than others to occur together. A service has two dimensions: formal liturgy vs. individual and spontaneous involvement. It may be better to think in terms of a spectrum, with those dimensions at opposite ends. In their selection of options, religious congregations position culturally their worship service somewhere on the spectrum.

The space distribution of the congregations is consistent, however, indicating worship services occupy, by denomination, a distinctive niche in a cultural field. In other words, congregations demonstrate a "sense of place" (Goffman cited by Bourdieu, 1989: 17) guided by the cultural capital they have accumulated and by the larger faith structure to which they belong. Recall Figure 5.1. In this schematic representation, certain bodies clearly position themselves at the top of the formal dimension of worship based on their selection of which items to use during their production of worship; others just as clearly position themselves at the extreme end of the individual dimension, based on the much more participatory and individual elements they prefer. From a sociological perspective, the cultural positioning is not surprising; more surprising is the lack of literature on this specific topic. Fortunately, data are now available, and more studies should appear in the near future.

The cultural positioning of congregations affects the type of practices they select; it also affects how they are represented. The particular musical and liturgical selections comprising a religious ceremony are often ranked on a spectrum of legitimate practices. The sociologist, because of his/her social position, is culturally in homology with or at a variable distance from the culture of the case he/she is studying. The cultural distance involves a distinction; the sociologist must consider this to escape the ruling interests of the dominant religious and/or sociological field. For example, the cultural positioning of confessions appears in the discourse of sociologists as natural or is taken for granted.

To paraphrase Bourdieu, the work of sociologists often participates in positive or negative portrayals of religious agents. In such instances, it will exceed the *doxa,* which describes social space as something other than that which is taken for granted in the relations of power between groups. It is important to show the cultural hierarchy among the denominations that may be hidden by the segmentation of the discipline into faith specialisations or that are reinterpreted uniquely as specific religious attributes. The critical sociology proposed by Bourdieu is important for a better understanding of the religious field because it always reminds the sociologist to consider the struggles of power within a specific field and also the position of the sociologist in relation to that specific field.

References

Behling, Orlando, and Kenneth S. Law. 2000. *Translating questionnaires and other research instruments: problems and solutions*. London: Sage Publications.

Bourdieu, Pierre. 2000. *Pascalian meditations*. Stanford: Stanford University Press.

Bourdieu, Pierre. 1992. *Language and symbolic power*. Cambridge: Polity Press.

Bourdieu, Pierre. 1990. *The logic of practice*. Cambridge: Politis.

Bourdieu, Pierre. 1989. "Social space and symbolic power," *Sociological Theory* 7(1): 14–25.

Bourdieu, Pierre. 1984. *Distinction: a social critique of the judgement of taste*. Cambridge: Harvard University Press.

Bourdieu, Pierre. 1987. What Makes a Social Class? On the Theoretical and Practical Existence of Groups. *Berkeley Journal of Sociology* 32: 1–17.

Bourdieu, Pierre. 2010. Sociologists of Belief and Beliefs of Sociologists *Nordic Journal of Religion and Society* 23: 1–7.

Bourdieu, Pierre, and Monique de Saint Martin. 1982. "La sainte famille," *Actes de la recherche en sciences sociales* 44(1): 2–53.

Bourdieu, Pierre, and Loïc J.D. Wacquant. 1992. *An invitation to reflexive sociology*. Chicago: University of Chicago Press.

Chaves, Mark. 2004. *Congregations in America*. Cambridge: Harvard University Press

Chaves, Mark. 2002. "Religious organizations: data resources and research opportunities," *The American Behavioral Scientist* 45(10): 1523–1549.

Chaves, Mark. 1999. *How do we worship?* Bethesda: Alban Institute.

Chaves, Mark, and Shawna L. Anderson. 2008. "Continuity and change in American congregations: introducing the second wave of the National Congregations study," *Sociology of Religion* 69(4): 415–440.

Chaves, Mark, Mary Ellen Konieczny, Beyerlien Kraig, and Emily Barman. 1999. "The national congregations study: background, methods and selected results," *Journal for the Scientific Study of Religion* 38(4): 458–477.

de Certeau, Michel. 2003. *La faiblesse de croire*. Paris: Seuil.

DiMaggio, Paul J. 1997. "Culture and Congnition," *Annual Review of Sociology* 23(1): 263–288.

Forsyth, Barbara H., Martha Stapleton Kudela, Kerry Levin, Deirdre Lawrence, and Gordon B. Willis. 2007. "Methods for translating an English-language survey questionnaire on tobacco use into Mandarin, Cantonese, Korean, and Vietnamese," *Field Methods* 19(3): 264–283.

Friedland, Roger, and Robert R. Alford. 1991. "Bringing society back in: symbols, practices, and institutional contradictions." In *The new institutionalism in organizational analysis*, edited by Walter W. Powell and Paul J. DiMaggio, 232–263. Chicago: University of Chicago Press.

Goffman, Irving. (1956) 1959. *The presentation of self in everyday life*. New York: Anchor Books.

Hjelm, Titus. 2014. "Religion, discourse and power: a contribution towards a critical sociology of religion," *Critical Sociology* 40(6):855–872.

Monnot, Christophe. 2013. *Croire ensemble : analyse institutionnelle du paysage religieux en Suisse*. Zurich: Seismo.

Monnot, Christophe, and Jörg Stolz. Forthcoming. "How do you recognize a 'congregation'? Definition and operationalization strategies of the Swiss congregation census." In *Congregations in Europe,* edited by Christophe Monnot and Jörg Stolz. Heidelberg: Springer International Publishing.

Monnot, Christophe, and Jörg Stolz. 2014. "The diversity of religious diversity: using census and NCS methodology in order to map and assess the religious diversity of a whole country." In *Religious pluralism,* edited by Giuseppe Giordan and Enzo Pace, 73–92. Heidelberg: Springer International Publishing.

Stolz, Jörg, and Olivier Favre. 2005. "The evangelical milieu: defining criteria and reproduction across the generations," *Social Compass* 52(2): 169–183.

Stolz, Jörg, and Christophe Monnot. 2017. "The established and the newcomers. A Weberian-Bourdieusian view of congregations in the Swiss religious field." *Revue d'Histoire et de Philosophie Religieuse* 97(1): 69–90.

Stolz, Jörg, Mark Chaves, Christophe Monnot, and Laurent Amiotte-Suchet. 2011. *Die religiösen Gemeinschaften in der Schweiz: eigenschaften, aktivitäten, entwicklung,* Religions, the States, and Society Series, National Research Program 58. Berne: Swiss National Science Foundation, accessed 24 December 2017, from http://www.nfp58 .ch/files/news/126_Schlussbericht_Stolz_Chaves.pdf.

Stolz, Jörg, Olivier Favre, Caroline Gachet, and Emmanuelle Buchard, eds. 2013. *Le phénomène évangélique: analyses d'un milieu compétitif.* Genève: Labor et Fides.

Stolz, Jörg, Judith Könemann, Mallory Schneuwly Purdie, Thomas Englberger, and Michael Krüggeler. 2016. *(Un)believing in modern society : religion, spirituality, and religious-secular competition*. London: Routledge.

Wagner, Thomas. 2014a. "Branding, music, and religion: standardization and adaptation in the experience of the 'hillsong sound.'" In *Religions as brands: new perspectives on the marketization of religion and spirituality,* edited by C. Usunier and Jörg Stolz, 59–74. London: Ashgate.

Wagner, Thomas. 2014b. "Music, branding, and the hegemonic presumption of values of an evangelical growth church." In *Religion in times of crisis, critiques and change,* edited by Gladys Ganiel, Heidemarie Winkel, and Christophe Monnot, 11–32. Leiden: Brill.

Weber, Max. 1973. "On church, sect, and mysticism," *Sociological Analysis* 34:140–141.

Wood, Matthew, and Véronique Altglas. 2010. "Reflexivity, scientificity and the sociology of religion: Pierre Bourdieu in debate," *Nordic Journal of Religion and Society* 23(1): 9–26.

CHAPTER 6

An Affective (U-)Turn in the Sociology of Religion? Religious Emotions and Native Narratives

Yannick Fer

Introduction

In short, what individuals and groups invest in the particular meaning they give to common classificatory systems by the use they make of them is infinitely more than their "interest" in the usual sense of the term; it is their whole social being, everything which defines their own idea of themselves, the primordial, tacit contract whereby they define "us" as opposed to "them."[1]

BOURDIEU, 1984: 478

The concept of emotion appears to work in the sociology of religion as a pre-notion linked with processes of (dis)qualification and distinction. These processes determine the scientific (and social) classification of "emotional" religious actors. They also shed light on the role that sociologists themselves play as "ranking agents ranked by their own ranking" (Bourdieu, 1979: back cover). Through the distinctions they make, they reveal the position they occupy within the scientific field and the relations they have with the religious field.

During the 1990s, the emergence of a new affective economy in western societies – and the rehabilitation of emotion as an authentic expression of self – fostered an "affective turn" (Clough, 2007) marked by an "explosion of academic fascination with the emotions" (Woodward, 1996: 759). This renewed interest in the study of emotion has crossed all disciplines in social and human sciences. It draws on a set of theoretical and epistemological trends, such as poststructuralist feminist theory, linguistics (Lutz and Abu-Lughod, 1990), psychological anthropology (Schweder and LeVine, 1984), and cognitive science (Damasio, 1994). By "challenging the conventional oppositions between emotion and reason, and discourse and affect" (Athanasiou et al., 2008: 5), this reflection questions the complex relationships between emotion, subjectivity, embodiment, and social domination.

---

1 Unless otherwise indicated in the reference list, the translations are my own.

This affective turn is scarcely noticeable in the sociology of religion. Of course, emotions are mentioned in numerous empirical works, especially those examining religions in connection with gender relationships or the body. But despite a few recent publications focusing on religion and emotion (Riis and Woodhead, 2012; Davis and Warne, 2013) and an older volume, *De l'émotion en religion: renouveaux et traditions* (Champion and Hervieu-Léger, 1990) – which was, in a sense, a pioneering one – published in French in 1990, the sociological understanding of religious emotions largely stays away from the general evolution of social theory on these issues. And as historian John Corrigan notes, even if "feeling" of one sort or another was integral to religion in the work of American sociologists of religion like Robert Bellah or Rodney Stark, "in these theories, and others of the time, emotion itself remained largely undefined" (Corrigan, 2007: 7).

Emotion is caught in the middle of classification struggles and field effects associated with sociologists' specific interests and a *doxa* shared by sociologists so fully invested in the field of social sciences of religion that they have developed a common *illusio* – a disposition "to play the game" which points out "the relationship of ontological complicity" between the habitus and the field (Bourdieu 1994: 154). The influence of this *doxa* is particularly evident at the national scale, and, in this chapter, I pay special attention to the French case, through an analysis of the book mentioned above, edited by Champion and Hervieu-Léger.

I open the chapter by asking why the French sociology of religion has mostly ignored the affective turn and the theoretical challenges it raises, seeming to prefer the established – we could say canonical – interpretations of classical authors over empirical research. These canonical interpretations closely link the issue of religious emotions with a set of pivotal concepts of the disciplinary *doxa*, such as legitimacy, institution, charisma, or modernity. The dominant understanding of religious emotions is not simply a blind spot in sociological analysis; rather, it constitutes the cornerstone of an intellectual construction which, in the eyes of many sociologists in this field, "engage everything which defines their own idea of themselves," to quote the epigraph of this chapter.

Then referring to the specific case of Pentecostalism – usually described as an "emotional religion" – I go on to consider how these canonical interpretations go hand-in-hand with strategies of categorisation and (dis)qualification. As I show, these strategies are intertwined with interests in the academic or religious field and with social relationships of domination. They highlight the social distance between the academic position (and the intellectual figure, classically associated with reason) and the religious "emotional" field. They also point to classification struggles between religious actors themselves.

Finally, I suggest how to disentangle the sociology of religious emotions from the influence of beliefs, distinction effects, and academic *doxa* and connect this field of research to wider social dynamics, such as the evolution of the relationships between individual and institution, the contemporary ideology of the "society of communication" (Neveu, 2001), and the norms of self-control in relation to the body.

Religious Modernity and the "Return" of Emotion

De l'émotion en religion: renouveaux et traditions[2] was published in 1990 by two French sociologists, Champion and Hervieu-Léger, respectively specialists in new religious movements and French Catholicism. It was the outcome of a network "initiated by Danièle Hervieu-Léger and led by Françoise Champion" that aimed to study "the emotional dimension of new religious movements," in the frame of the research group "Religion and Modernity" formed in 1985 by the CNRS to "explore a set of contemporary religious phenomena" (Champion and Hervieu-Léger, 1990: 8). The origin of this collective reflection was a "religious resurgence in the 1970s" questioning sociologists who thought of the religion of "modernity" in terms of rationalisation and secularisation. In contrast, the contributors to this volume tend to interpret "emotional resurgences" as symptoms of a double process: first, the decline of institutional systems, which generates a dispersion and a "privatisation of beliefs" ("the primacy of face-to-face relations"); second, a rejection of modern rationality expressed through the "return" of "emotional effervescence" ("the primacy of feeling over reason") (Champion and Hervieu-Léger, 1990: 8).

The chapters of this volume examine various emotional contemporary manifestations within Catholicism, Judaism, Sufi Islam, and the "mystical-esoteric nebula." The case studies show how emotional experiences contribute to religious re-commitment by fostering believers' voluntary reappropriation of religious tradition, rituals, and doctrines. The range of emotional styles offered by the mystical-esoteric movements analysed by Champion underlines the malleability of emotion in religious elaborations. Mystical-esoteric believers can, for example, "choose between disciplines of emotional control and groups ... where it is understood that spiritual development cannot do without a *catharsis*-expression of all emotions: love, joy, hate, anger, jealousy, etc." (Champion: 1990: 63–64).

---

2   Translated as "Emotion in religion: resurgences and traditions."

Yet despite this diversity of religious emotions, the conclusion of the volume – written by Hervieu-Léger – confines the understanding of religious emotion to the sole paradigm of regression and (de)secularisation, interpreting the "return" of emotion as an univocal symptom of "de-modernisation." This fall-back position (the opposite of the academic fascination with the emotions that prevailed at the same time in Anglophone social sciences) can be seen as a refusal to consider religious emotion as a true scientific object. While one can note (and deplore) the resurgence of *emotion* – understood as a rough and universal material – in contemporary religious practices, that alone is not enough to establish religious *emotions* (and their various contents) as an object for sociological analysis.

The definition of emotion, in the western intellectual tradition, is embedded in a cultural background deeply influenced by the Christian opposition between soul and body, mind and heart, reason and passion. It also frequently implies a concept of the person which locates emotions in an inner self that resists any scientific objectivisation ("no one can know"). Religious emotion is associated with a series of prenotions: beliefs or, more generally, an intellectual and religious culture, which remains unquestioned and shapes the sociological understanding of emotions. In her ethnography of everyday sentiments on the Micronesian atoll of Ifaluk, anthropologist Catherine Lutz, who has conducted extensive research on emotions, both empirically and theoretically (see, for example, Lutz and White, 1986), considered a radical decentring from the "Euramerican construction of emotion" was a necessary first step to break with the idea of emotion as essence and capture the cultural and social dimension of emotions (Lutz, 1988: 53–55).

Although anthropology is a major resource for this reflexive work, several academic productions prove it can also be done through a methodical exploration of western thought and history. Medievalist historians, for example (following the seminal work of Lucien Febvre and the Annales School), have elaborated a history of a "sensible Middle Age" which, by associating religious emotions with "other cognitive processes (imagination, memory, reasoning, etc.), finds its place within a history of experience, this total psychological fact, and is articulated with social history" (Boquet and Nagy, 2015: 17). This historical detour helps to measure the complexity of the transformations undergone by Christian emotions in tandem with the evolution of the patterns of political and religious power or the western history of consciousness (Selzner, 2010).[3]

---

3 As Selzner points out, Luther located consciousness "at the centre of man and soul, less as a moral faculty intimately linked with reason and cognition (like Thomas d'Aquin did), but

But part of the difficulty encountered in the social sciences of religion is not rooted in the long history of western thought; rather, it stems from what Nussbaum describes as "a kind of professional routine that contributes to dismiss the emotions without having the [western intellectual] tradition's deep, and controversial, reasons for doing so" (Nussbaum, 1992: 210). Indeed, the idea that

> emotions are irrational in the normative sense because they have nothing to do with judgment and cognition at all ... has never been strongly supported by major western philosophers who have done a good deal of their most serious work on the emotions: they have notably underlined the role played by emotions in the formation of a judgement that is not "blind." *And by now, contrary to what may be inferred from many sociologists of religion's writings, this interpretation of emotions* has been widely discredited even where it once was popular – in cognitive psychology, for example, and in anthropology.
>
> NUSSBAUM, 1992: 205–206

The main objection is, in fact, formulated by philosophers who think that emotions are not innate, but socially learnt, not blind impulses, but complex cognitive operations. Nussbaum says:

> These philosophers hold, however, that the judgments with which emotions are connected are *false*. They are false because they ascribe a very high value to external persons and events that are not fully controlled by the person's virtue or rational will.
>
> NUSSBAUM, 1992: 206; emphasis in original

Canonical Texts and Established Interpretations: Religious Emotions Trapped in a Disciplinary Field

How, then, can we understand the lasting influence of the irrationality-regression paradigm in most of the sociological literature on religious emotions? Part of the explanation for this inertia may lie in the functioning of the sociology of religion as a disciplinary field. For one thing, the distinctive positions of sociologists and their objects of study obviously influence the understanding

---

rather as a sensible and affective faculty that determines the fundamental emotional context of the whole soul" (2010: 189).

of emotion. From this perspective, the sociology of new religious movements – one of the most fertile grounds for the study of the emotional "resurgence" – differs significantly from the sociology of Catholicism: while the first is a relatively new field of research, marked by the influence of British and American sociology of "religious innovations" (Altglas, 2005: 165), the second is much older and dominated by the theoretical horizon of a "decreasing (western) religious field" under the effects of modernity (165). In the first case, the "return" of emotions is potentially one of the features defining an emerging domain of investigation, while in the second, the rise of "emotional movements" tends to contradict the hitherto dominant analytical framework. Thus, instead of questioning the limits of this framework (and its affinities with her own position, as an intellectual critical of the Catholic institution), Hervieu-Léger spontaneously sees this kind of movement as an ultimate consequence of the secularisation process – a sort of "end of religion," as religious doctrines lose their social relevance and give way to "inarticulate" and emotional religious forms. The charismatic renewal and the new catholic communities it has inspired are, therefore, mostly absent from her subsequent work.

Beyond these individual positions, the lack of interest amongst sociologists of religion in the analysis of emotions underlines a disciplinary closure separating the sociology of religion from general social theory. The historical shaping of the sub-disciplines dedicated to the study of religion partly explains this closure, as it has often reproduced the common sacred/profane distinction within the academic field, or has even explicitly proceeded from the assumption that religious facts should not be regarded as "ordinary" social facts. The collective interest of sociologists of religion in maintaining this disciplinary boundary manifests itself in at least two different ways: the recurring temptation to elaborate specific analytical tools rather than submitting religious facts to the general theoretical frameworks of sociology and the use of a restricted corpus of common bibliographical references and interpretations that constitutes the *doxa* of the disciplinary field and therefore functions as a sign of belonging.

A volume edited by Davies and Warne (2013) exemplifies the first of these trends. Trained in anthropology and theology, Davies has been teaching Religious Studies at Nottingham University and Study of Religion at Durham University's Department of Theology. The volume, which results from a research program funded by the UK's Arts and Humanities Research Council, presents 11 case studies on the emotional dimension of religious experience, mainly written by teachers in theology or religious studies (an indication of the ambiguous position of the social sciences of religion within the British academic field). Despite a brief chapter on William James' reflection on religion and emotion, the book doesn't offer a precise definition of religious emotions or any clear analytical framework, except Davies' introductory reflections on "the capacity of any religious group to prefer certain emotions and foster their affinity with particular doctrinal clusters of ideas" (Davies and Warne, 2013: 2). These reflections, by and large, deal with the relations between emotion and religious identities through the study of the theological, pastoral, and ethical attitudes developed by different religious communities.

In contrast, a book edited three years earlier by Ole Riis, a Danish sociologist, and Linda Woodhead, Professor of Sociology of Religion at Lancaster University (Riis and Woodhead, 2010), deploys a plethora of theoretical references, going well beyond the range of the social sciences of religions. However, it also reflects the embryonic stage of much research on religious emotions. Because of a lack of available ethnographic studies on the various emotional regimes elaborated in the religious field, the authors only develop a general analysis of religious "feelings." And the prominent place their analyses give to the mediating role of religious objects and rituals reinforces the closure of the religious field, instead of connecting it to the debates of social theory. Nevertheless, religious emotions are constructed here as a fully sociological object and analysed in terms of "emotional regimes" linking emotions with systems of relationships and significations, individual embodiment, and religious control of their expression.

Nothing similar has been produced in France in recent decades, and others did not follow up on the 1990 volume edited by Champion and Hervieu-Léger. In fact, the French sociology of religion remains relatively impervious to the debates of the Anglophone social sciences and even to the French ones. The dominant discourse on religious emotions is still shaped by an "intellectual routine" based on common interpretations of classical authors: Durkheim and, above all, Weber. Thus, sociologists of religion build their own "native" references, using a set of established texts and interpretations they regularly "rediscover" but never question.

Emile Durkheim, Religious Emotions and the "Unknown Thesis"

In 1990, on the occasion of the publication of a special issue of the *Archives de Sciences Sociales des Religions* on Durkheim, Isambert wrote:

> If there is a part of Durkheim's work that seems outdated, this is his theory of religion. Not that the general idea of the social character of religion has not progressed, and that a religious sociology has not experienced

important developments, but the idea of looking into their "elementary forms" to find the secret of religions, and of explaining religious feeling by the respect society inspires us seems now to appeal to a demonetised rhetoric.

ISAMBERT, 1992: 443

His quest for the "elementary forms of religion" led Durkheim to regard the emotional effervescence of specific community gatherings in aboriginal Australian societies as an archetype of religious feeling. For Durkheim, this feeling, in its original form, has no other content than "the feeling that the collectivity inspires in its members" (Durkheim, 1995: 230). These feelings, he says, are "projected outside the minds that experienced them, and objectified" (230), with society coming to nurture the belief in a transcendent power.

Beyond this outdated genealogical perspective which considers "primitive" peoples a field for the observation of social "elementary" forms, the sociological approach of Durkheim aims to understand religion as a social fact and to show how it is a foundational component of society – or, more specifically, the relationship between individual and society. His analysis, Mellor says, draws on a "conception of the dual nature of human beings ...: Durkheim suggests that 'man is double' in the sense that we are comprised of both 'an individual being that has its basis in the body' and 'a social being that represents within us the highest reality'" (Mellor, 2001: 170–171). And the notion of "collective soul" he develops in *The Rules of Sociological Method* helps to distinguish "beliefs, tendencies and practices of a group taken collectively" from the forms these collective states take when "refracted through individuals" (Durkheim, 1982: 54). So the attention Durkheim gives to the "non-rational dimensions of social life" (Mellor, 2001: 167) is part of a wider reflection on what "makes society." Religious life is, according to Durkheim, the "eminent form and, as it were, the epitome of collective life" (Durkheim, 1995: 421).

In the Australian context, the totemic figure materialises as the permanence of social life. The religious emotion associated with this figure doesn't create society; rather, it expresses society and makes it sensible to its members. Durkheim describes this experience as "elementary" because of the "unformed mind" of the "primitive." He says: "Since the emotional and passionate faculties of the primitive are not fully subordinated to his reason and will, he easily loses his self-control" (Durkheim, 1995: 217). Put otherwise, the primitive "feels that he is lifted above himself" but he is unable to clearly understand the social origin of all these extraordinary impressions (222).

We might expect sociologists of religion to leave this outdated representation of "primitives" aside and focus on the social dimension of religious emotions, especially the ability to shed light on the articulation of individual, body, and society. In fact, the dominant interpretation amongst French sociologists of religion links religious emotion, understood as "an extra-social or at least pre-social experience" (Hervieu-Léger, 1990: 221), to a cultural or psychological, elementary, and archaic state. Emotion frequently remains embedded in a set of schematic oppositions structured by an evolutionist scheme. If emotion was present at the origin and is still significant amongst the social or cultural categories supposedly closer to this "origin" (i.e., "traditional" societies and popular classes), its resurgence in the context of "advanced modernity" can only be explained as an anomaly caused by processes of regression, destabilisation, or disintegration of institutions, religion, social links, etc.

At the same time, this idea of an original emotion opens up the possibility of a religious reinterpretation of Durkheim, which reveals – as Lassave remarks – the reluctance of the French sociology of religion to sever all its affinitive ties with its object of study (Lassave, 2012: 5–6). Thus, in 1969, sociologist (and former Dominican) Henri Desroche, who initiated the group for the sociology of religion (founded in 1954) and its journal, the *Archives de sciences sociales des religions*, published a transcription of a 1914 conference entitled "Religious feeling at the present time" given by Durkheim at the Union of Free Thinkers and Free Believers. During this conference, Durkheim presented his theory of religion, also expressed in *The Elementary Forms of Religious Life* (1912). A rational explanation of religion, he said, should look for "a source of energy superior to what an individual can get by his own," and this source is to be found in collective life (Durkheim, 1969: 74). Rather than "imagining extra-human forces on which he could rely," man should, Durkheim concluded, "be convinced that humanity itself can provide him this support" (77).

However, the traditional interpretation established by Desroche and the *Archives* team – whose influence is still discernible three decades later, notably in a handbook coedited by Hervieu-Léger and Willaime (2001) – qualifies this eminently social understanding of religion to forge the "unknown thesis" of a more religious Durkheim, by reinterpreting a passage in the conference proceedings where Durkheim seems to present personal religious feeling as an epistemological prerequisite for a true comprehension of religion.[4] As Lassave points out:

---

4   "In short, I ask the free thinker to stand in front of religion in the state of mind of a believer. Only then can he hope to understand it. He needs to feel it as a believer feels it, because this is what religion is for the latter. So anyone who doesn't bring in the study of religion this kind of religious feeling cannot speak about religion! He would be like a blind man speaking about colours!" (Durkheim, 1969: 75).

> Desroche is not afraid to evoke ... the religious dimension of Durkheim-
> ian theory, "with the centrality it gives to the foundational moments of
> collective religious experience, its intertwining of the social phenom-
> enon and the religious phenomenon, its latent or explicit adventism ...
> through the analogy that it elaborates ... between religion, morality and
> science: three interlaced rings."
>
> LASSAVE, 2012: 11, citing Desroche, 1969

What Durkheim describes as the "dynamogenetic influence" of society, through religion, on human minds, can, then, be reformulated as an "emotion of the depths," a "primary layer, consisting in an emotional contact with the divine principle" (Hervieu-Léger, 2001: 177). Hervieu-Léger writes: "From the durkeim-ian perspective social life is nurtured, even remotely, by this religious source, a prodigious reservoir of energy resulting from the fusion of minds in the ex-perience of the sacred" (177). Whilst recalling that for Durkheim "the god that men adore and worship is in fact the society itself" (172), this interpretation nevertheless suggests a reasoning that subtly reverses the perspective. Above all, it is the religious feeling (now understood as the ineffable experience of the encounter with God) that finally appears as the foundation of the social link. And this emotion, closely associated with the original locus of religious truth, slips outside the social and, therefore, outside the scope of social sciences.

Max Weber: Emotions, Charisma and the Routinisation of Sociological Thought

This dominant interpretation of religious emotion in Durkheim's writing sheds light on a gesture of appropriation also observable, to a lesser extent, in Weber's writing – still the major reference in the French sociology of religion. This gesture, through which the sociology of religion shapes its "native" refer-ences, consists firstly in minimising the distance that separates the sociologist from the believer. This is easier to do with Weber than Durkheim (the latter was the son of a rabbi but also a rationalist and atheist).[5] Even though Weber declared himself a non-believer, his interest in religious issues originated in a personal interest, deeply rooted in an educational and familial context (on his

---

5 Nevertheless, Hervieu-Léger describes Durkheim as "probably attracted at one time by Catholicism" and notes that "numerous commentators have strived to find in the personal trajectory of Durkheim the religious bedrocks of his moral preoccupation as well as a pos-sible source of his interest in religion as a social fact" (Hervieu-Léger, 2001: 149–150).

mother's side), an interest openly recognised by Weber, as shown in a fascinating correspondence with Tönnies:

> Surely I am completely "insensitive to the music" of religion and I feel neither the need nor the ability to build in me religious psychic "constructions" of any sort; this doesn't work or I refuse to do so. But on further consideration, I am neither antireligious nor *unreligious*.
>
> GROSSEIN, 1996: 72; emphasis in original

Seizing on this quotation, Willaime interprets it as a "methodological agnosticism" associated with a "comprehensive sympathy with the religious phenomenon" – thus suggesting that no sociology of religion might be practicable without this "sympathy" (Willaime, 2001: 62).[6] But the "axiological neutrality" so often attributed to Weber doesn't exclude "taking sides" (Grossein, 1996: 71). And Weber's "sympathy" towards religion, far from being a general principle, is very selective and based on social and political considerations that sociologists of religion frequently ignore. The convictions of Weber on the political role of German Protestantism lead him to condemn Catholicism and Lutheranism, whilst praising Calvinism: "The fact that our nation has never gone through *any kind* of rigorous asceticism," he writes in the 1906 letter to Harmack, "is the cause of what I find hateful in her (as well as in me)" (Grossein, 1996: 73). And in the same letter, although he considers the time of "sects" is now out-of-date and the superiority of the church-institution needs to be recognised when "measured in terms of *non* ethical and *non* religious values," Weber maintains his preference for Protestant asceticism (Grossein, 1996: 73).

This specific position, articulated with the primordial interest of Weber in the analysis of the historical processes of rationalization, strongly influences his approach to religious emotions. He describes religious emotion as an intense and ephemeral phenomenon occurring before or against the historical process of institutionalisation and ethical rationalisation that leads to modernity. Religious emotion doesn't completely disappear but is progressively reshaped into more elaborate symbolic constructions as it takes place in everyday life and loses its initial intensity. From Weber's point of view, emotion has no real content and no lasting effect on individual lives. Therefore, religions seeking "the integration of one's pattern of life in subjective states and in an inner reliance upon god, rather than in the consciousness of one's continued ethical probation [must have] a completely anti-rational effect upon the

---

6 Reasoning similarly to Hervieu-Léger about the "religious bedrocks" as a necessary explanation of any sociological interest in religion, Willaime finally states that "as many liberal Protestants of his time, Weber can be regarded as a churchless Protestant" (2001: 62).

conduct of life" (Weber, 1978: 571). So religious emotion should be, above all, understood as a sign of regression or protest. Weber describes, for example, the Hindu traditions of *bhakti* as a popular protest against "the proud and noble intellectualistic religion of Buddhism from the fifth and sixth centuries" (Weber, 1993: 201). The "overflowing emotions" of the Protestant pietism of Moravian Brothers causes him visible difficulties (Radkau, 2011: 195), as does the "whining cadence of typical Lutheran sermons in Germany which has so often driven strong men out the church" (Weber, 1978: 571).

In fact, Weber is in line with the dominant mood of his time. During the second half of the 19th century (Weber was born in 1864 and died in 1920), "there was a slow transformation of sensibility into sentimentality" (Vincent-Buffault, 1986: 9). As a result, the expression of emotions and tears became confined to the intimate sphere, with a concomitant stigmatisation of the "excessive emotionality of women" (9). Weber's understanding of emotion is also influenced by a theory of action which considers thoughtless submission to tradition or affective effusion as two non-conscious behaviours. As Favret-Saada remarks, "Weber is a man of Enlightenment ...: above all, he is interested in conscious, voluntary, responsible activity" (1994: 102). In Weber's consideration, emotions are the symbolic feature of a religious experience mostly defined by default:

> In Weber's thought, the category of affect is a residual category, designed to accommodate everything that doesn't fit in the other categories. And sensibility is the faculty of soul in charge of everything that is beyond the control of reason or tradition.
>
> FAVRET-SAADA, 1994: 104

The Weberian analytical framework commonly used by French sociologists of religion in their descriptions of religious emotions doesn't simply rely on an uncritical and non-contextualised reading of Weber. The work of Weber is itself ambivalent and complex; its "multiple and continuously reconstructed reasoning" (Passeron, 1996: 7) allows various interpretations, not of religious emotion itself, but of its relations with the Weberian typology of legitimacy and notions such as institution or charisma. Among all these possibilities, sociologists of religion make a self-interested selection that emphasises the singularity of religious facts and confines emotions in an exclusive relationship with charisma. And yet,

> Weber has never delivered a systematic presentation of his theory of charisma, which could bring full coherence amongst the numerous passages that Weber has dedicated to this notion in his work. In fact, charisma is

approached from various perspectives that make it very difficult to understand precisely, as the definition of the concept varies.

LAIGNOUX, 2014: 14

The most frequently cited mention of charisma appears at the beginning of the section on "charismatic domination" in *Economy and Society*[7] and raises many questions: on the personal qualities of the "holder of charisma" (are they intrinsic or built through a discourse of legitimation and the recognition of disciples?); on the limited and extraordinary character of this charismatic domination; on the possibility of an institutionalisation of this charismatic domination; and on the association of charisma and "revolutionary" times (Laignoux, 2014: 16–20).

The "native" narrative on charisma is less ambivalent and focuses on a few texts dealing specifically with religious facts emphasising the extraordinary, "emotional" and personal character of charismatic legitimacy. This narrative keeps the sociology of religion at a distance from the interpretations and debates in other fields of sociology (and in political science). It pays little attention, for example, to the notion of "charisma of the office," or to the social and institutional conditions likely to produce asymmetric relations between the charismatic leader and his or her disciples (Laignoux, 2014: 18–19). This disciplinary narrative draws on Weberian ideal types to reinforce the ontological opposition between, on the one side, institution, reason, and modernity, and on the other, charisma, emotion, and archaism. According to Hervieu-Léger:

> Weber's conception of the religious trajectory of humanity's emotion is a step of an historical process leading from the "emotional density of the initial charismatic relation" to institutional and ethical religion through an ineluctable – or at least necessary – "routinisation" or this primitive emotion.

HERVIEU-LÉGER, 1990: 233–235

Put in other words:

> The poor, asocial and unsustainable affect needs to be domesticated through a process of institutionalisation whose task will be to enrich it,

---

7   "The term 'charisma' will be applied to a certain quality of an individual personality by virtue of which he is considered extraordinary and treated as endowed with supernatural, superhuman, or at least specifically exceptional powers or qualities. These are such as are not accessible to the ordinary person, but are regarded as of divine origin or as exemplary, and on the basis of them the individual concerned is treated as a 'leader'" (Weber, 1978: 241).

to make it socially viable, to root it in temporality and, by doing so, to introduce it into the scope of social sciences studies.

FAVRET-SAADA, 1992: 225

However, this idea of a necessary progression from the origin, the elementary and immediate experience (the emotion), to a complex and stable state of religion (the institution) is contradicted by a large part of contemporary religious evolutions – first of all, by the "return of emotions." The constant reference to the "routinisation of charisma," which supposedly leads to the decline of the original emotional "irrationality," becomes a call to a "normal" order of things that observation can hardly confirm. Similarly, the normative (or predictive) use of Weberian ideal types prevents sociologists from discerning in the religious field other kinds of relations between emotion and institution than this sole antinomy. This intellectual routine becomes particularly counterproductive when it turns to the study of so-called "charismatic" movements. In this case, the confusion between the Christian concept of charisma (as a gift of the Spirit) and its sociological use opens the way to all sorts of "default assumptions": as Bourdieu remarks, it is notably through the introduction of words borrowed from religious language that the "tacit presuppositions of the native relationship to the object" tend to slip into the sociology of religion. (Bourdieu, 2010: 6).

Pentecostalism as "Emotional Protestantism"

Weber's use of the concept of charisma was inspired by the work of German jurist and theologian Rudolf Sohm:

[Sohm] elaborated a theory of the essence of primitive Christianity which emphasises the spiritual dimension as opposed to any institutionalisation: the original Christian *ecclesia* would have relied on the personal charisma of some teachers, and the origin of this charisma is to be found in the divine grace that they received.

HEURTIN, 2014: 55

In an historical context marked by the official foundation in 1817 of the Evangelical German Church (an union of Reformed and Lutheran churches) and by strong tensions between Protestants and Catholics, Sohm's stance can be interpreted as an opposition to the institutionalisation of churches by the political authorities, and as a plea for a church "based on the individual believer" and "the spirit." Indeed, "according to Sohm, the spirit is what makes the church exist; a spirit manifested through gifts" (Heurtin, 2014: 57–59). Sohm questioned the legitimacy of a transformation of personal charisma (understood as a personal gift) into an institutional charisma independent from the personal qualities of the minister. Weber saw in this distinction a means to express the ontological tension between, on the one hand, a rationalised and institutionalised management of salvation goods, and on the other, an "authentically personal charisma, attached to the person as such, which fosters and teaches an autonomous path to God" (Heurtin, 2014: 66–67). Thus, both Sohm's definition of charisma and its outcome in Weber's sociology are embedded in a specific historical and theological debate on the relationships between religious authenticity, individual, and institution.

Pentecostalism emerged in the early 20th century as a "revival" within the context of North American Protestantism. It defines itself as a charismatic movement and claims the "gifts of the Holy Spirit" (*charisma*) mentioned in the Bible are available today, manifested as speaking in tongues, prophecies, miraculous healing, and the discernment of spirits. Its distinctive identity has been built on "baptism in the Holy Spirit," a reference to the day of Pentecost described in the New Testament (Acts 2), when the disciples of Jesus Christ were visited by "tongues of fire …[and] filled with the Holy Spirit [they] began to speak in other tongues as the Spirit enabled them." In the Pentecostal experience, this baptism becomes a highly emotional moment when the Holy Spirit visits the believer and, for the first time, "speaks in tongues," which is an incomprehensible and elementary language interpreted as a sign of God. Against the new ways of thinking accompanying urbanisation and the development of the railways at the end of the 19th century and against the theory of evolution, the historico-critical biblical exegesis, and the Social Gospel then in vogue among the urban churches of the Northeast (Ladous, 1995), Pentecostals proclaimed a return to the earliest times of Christianity, and a "religion of the heart," cleared of any institutional constraints. In some way, this Pentecostal credo is close to Sohm's position, in that "the spirit is what makes the church exist; a spirit manifested through gifts" (Heurtin, 2014: 57–59). In Pentecostalism, this implies a quest for emotion as an experimental proof of and means of communication with God, as the "action of the Holy Spirit" in individual bodies and amongst the community of believers is associated with highly emotional moments.

When it comes to the sociological analysis of a "charismatic" religious movement such as Pentecostalism, the entanglement of the theological understanding of charisma designed by Sohm with the Weberian descriptions of charismatic authority (especially those linking charisma and the prophetic figure) generates a knot of prenotions and confusions. This is made all the more difficult as academic and religious interests are intertwined, as are the relationships of domination classically associated with the perception of emotions by agents who occupy dominant social positions and are situated *ex officio* on "reason's side." When interpreted in a normative and predictive way, the Weberian ideal type of charismatic legitimacy leads to an inference of "charismatic" identity (in a biblical sense) as containing a set of immutable characteristics and ranking principles which confine the diversity of contemporary Pentecostal/charismatic movements within a narrow theoretical scheme elaborated by and for the sociology of religion's disciplinary field. According to this scheme, Pentecostalism is inextricably charismatic and emotional, based on the immediate (and unelaborated) experience of the "gifts of the Spirit," outside any stable institutional framework and under the leadership of prophet-ministers who draw their "personal" legitimacy from their ability to make God act here and now. This "charismatic" configuration combines, in a seemingly paradoxical fashion, the individual and the collective (in reference to Durkheim's "emotion of the depths"), a paradox that can only be resolved by postulating an implicit distinction between strong individuals (the holders of charisma) and weak individuals (believers who give up their personal freedom to take shelter in an "emotional community") – as if the boundary between the two categories could be so clear-cut. But despite evident inconsistencies, this paradoxical description of Pentecostalism at least helps to preserve the dominant native narrative, which opposes the archaic (or regressive) emotional community to rational individuals and modern institutions.

This opposition is not only chronological, but also diachronic, when the charismatic experience is associated with (popular) social categories or cultural categories ("traditional societies"). Pentecostalism first grew amongst the poorest social groups and in non-western societies. These circumstances fostered theoretical elaborations inspired by the ranking principles of social domination well described by Bourdieu: the opposition between the fighting strength the dominated attribute to themselves and the reduction of this strength by dominant classes to "brute strength, passion and instinct, a blind, unpredictable force of nature" and "the unreasoning violence of desire" (Bourdieu, 1984: 479). At the same time, these dominant classes attribute to themselves "a self-control that predisposes them to control others and allows them to conceive their relationship to the dominated – the 'masses,' women, the young – as that of the soul to the body, understanding to sensibility, culture to nature" (479).

The spread of Pentecostalism into the middle classes and the effects of upward social mobility that it produces in many contexts have not really modified these prenotions, based on canonical readings of Durkheim and Weber rather than on fieldwork observation.[8] Pentecostalism, as a religion of the poor, has thus been described as a poor and elementary religion, an "illiterate and effervescent religion of orality" (Bastian, 2001: 205), with speaking in tongues called a "fantastic revenge of 'illiterate' on literate persons" (Willaime, 1999: 116).

The stakes of (dis)qualification and ranking struggles implied by the sociological classification of Pentecostalism (and more generally of charismatic Protestantism) are never more clearly illustrated than in the progressive elaboration of ideal types designed by sociologists to separate the wheat from the chaff. In 1992 – and in more detail in 2005 – Willaime proposed a translation of the Weberian ideal types of legitimacy into the native language of the sociology of religion by combining theological and sociological criteria (Willaime, 1992: 22–25; 2005: 32–44). In this typology, Lutheran-reformed Protestantism is defined as an institutional ideological model. This socially dominant Protestantism, to which Willaime is personally close,[9] enjoys symbolic benefits deriving from its institutional label (a "desacralised and functional" institution) and rationality. Its adherents submit to the authority of the Bible and to the intellectual leadership of the theologians. Catholicism, also categorised as "institutional," is described as based on ritual and traditional legitimacy (ritual institutional model). Adopting Weber's analysis, Willaime associates the Catholic Church with "charisma of the office" and "institutional grace [which] by nature tends to regard obedience and submission to the authority as a cardinal virtue and a condition for salvation" (Willaime, 2005: 36).

In the original version of this typology (in 1992), a third category, the associative charismatic model, is used by default to define everything not falling into the categories of institution, tradition, or reason – what everyday language more simply calls a "sect." Here, the power is "personal;" the adepts are in "absolute dependence to the leader," with "close supervision" of their relations with the outside world and their individual behaviours (Willaime, 2001: 24). Following the established interpretation of Weber, these "charismatic" groups

---

8 However, the sociological profile of the members of French Catholic charismatic renewal, which hardly fits into this normative description of emotional Christianity, leads Hervieu-Léger to imagine the "return of emotion" as an ultimate outcome of the individualisation and secularisation processes. Thus, when charismatic emotion can't be described as a religious expression of social poverty, it is still a symptom of an impoverishment of the religious culture itself: amongst believers well integrated into modern society, speaking in tongues expresses an inability to "appropriate by the language the symbols of a religious tradition" (Hervieu-Léger, 1990: 246).

9 Doctor in religious sciences from the Strasbourg Protestant Faculty of Theology, Willaime is also President of the supervisory board of the weekly journal *Réforme*.

are, nevertheless, "instable" by nature and can only last if they profoundly change (24).

In 2001, Fath suggested a modification of these ideal types, drawing on his PhD thesis on the history of French baptism (with which he has close personal links). His suggestion refines the categorisation of Protestant expressions by proffering a fourth model, the "associative ideological." It also helps to symbolically redeem non-charismatic Evangelism by crediting it with a rational dimension. From the institutional ideological model, this complementary model borrows an

> emphasis on ideology, a particular, perennial theological orientation, based on the exegesis of the Bible, which represents for all Protestants the main source of legitimacy. But this model opposes to institutional structures the primacy of the local association, the congregation of believers.
>
> FATH, 2001: 381

Pentecostalism, as it belongs to the charismatic side of Evangelism, is therefore described as "oscillating between the two models: the 'associative ideological' and the 'associative charismatic'" (Fath, 2001: 382). But the two ends of this oscillation are not really equivalent. In fact, Pentecostalism, by nature, is subject to the risk of "drifting towards a personal power oppressing believers" and seems attracted to the associative charismatic model.[10]

The influence of personal interests and strategies of distinction in such constructions of ideal typical categories doesn't completely shatter their scientific relevance. But it illuminates the pitfalls of a too normative (or predictive) use of ideal types, notably the tendency to create "self-fulfilling prophecies" when one sees only what one is sure of finding. As Roa Bastos notes: "Eventually, charisma is only useful if it is regarded as a temporary concept, as part of these notions that Weber himself defined as 'simple ports of call (*Nothäfen*) on the wide sea of empirical facts'" (Rao Bastos, 2014: 232).

The systematic oppositions that an ideological interpretation of reality tends to build inevitably encounter contradictions difficult to overcome. Willaime notices a contradiction (in Weberian terms, a "tension") between, the "often instable emotion" of Pentecostal services and Pentecostalism's production of "a moralisation through individual responsibility," an "ethical qualification ... that fosters social advancement and public responsibilities" (Willaime,

---

10　In the same article, Fath says Pentecostalism might be moving "towards an institutional charismatic type, ... a quite unprecedented form of Christian socialisation" (Fath, 2001:387). However, he does not explore this heterodox hypothesis further.

1999: 23) – in other words, a rationalisation of personal lives. Such a contradiction is *de facto* irreducible without a critical examination of the use of Weberian ideal types by sociologists of religion and a reflexive approach to the distinction's stakes and field effects associated with the sociological (dis)qualification of "emotional" religious forms. Native interpretations of canonical texts, when confronted by empirical facts, persist in producing paradoxes instead of looking for coherence. Only by casting off this disciplinary *doxa* can we eventually reinsert the sociology of Pentecostal/charismatic movements into the wider framework of social theory.

Three Proposals for a Sociology of Pentecostal/Charismatic Emotions

According to Mellor, an analysis of the forms of charismatic religiosity suggests the need to rethink "the apparent theoretical gulf between James and Durkheim" (Mellor, 2007: 591) in their understanding of religious emotions – seen as an individual experience by the first and as a collective phenomenon by the second:

> It is generally acknowledged that this religiosity has a highly *personalist* character in the sense that it is focused on the transformation of individuals through powerful religious experiences [and] the foundation for this experiential focus is an intensely emotional encounter with Christ and the Holy Spirit.
>
> MELLOR, 2007: 591; emphasis in original

Referring to the work of Percy (1996), Mellor underlines that "the range of extreme physical and emotional symptoms individuals experience as they encounter the Holy Spirit are *collectively nurtured*," so personal experience should not be opposed to but articulated with the patterns of collective emotional stimulation to describe the genesis of charismatic emotions (Mellor, 2007: 591–592; emphasis in original).

My first proposal is to approach Pentecostal emotions as a modality of personal commitment located at the intersection of individual, community, and institution (Fer, 2010). This conception of emotion relies on Bourdieu's notion of habitus and includes in the analysis the role of the Pentecostal institution as an apparatus of socialisation inculcating specific embodied dispositions, which are "as much bodily as mentally constituted" (Rey, 2007: 128). It is also inspired by Rosaldo's definition of emotions as "hot thoughts":

What distinguishes thought and affect, differentiating a "cold" cognition from a "hot," is fundamentally a sense of the engagement of the actor's self. Emotions are thoughts somehow "felt" in flushes, pulses, "movements" of our livers, minds, hearts, stomachs, skin. They are *embodied* thoughts, thoughts seeped with the apprehension that "I am involved."

ROSALDO, 1984: 143; emphasis in original

Such a theoretical perspective allows an analysis of both the content of Pentecostal emotions and the modalities of their expression, by connecting them to the institutional work and community dynamics that produce the incorporation of a system of belief focused on the subjective experience of a "personal relationship with God." Far from being rough material or an elementary form of religious experience, individual emotions aroused by this "relation" – and by all the "evidences" of the Holy Spirit's action that believers learn to recognise – can be described in terms of an "intentionless invention of regulated improvisation" (Bourdieu 1992: 57). These emotions are spontaneous manifestations of a religious habitus in ritual behaviour, through the mediation of "incorporated images" (Csordas 2002:72). They are the expression of a set of embodied dispositions, mobilised by the individual to give shape to her personal commitment. When the collective enthusiasm of the community or the intensity of personal prayer seems to prove the tangible presence of God, the Pentecostal believer responds to this "evidence" religiously learnt by appropriate thoughts, behaviours, and emotions. She feels moved when "God speaks to her" and sometimes cries as she strives to express the recognition inspired by the sacrifice of Jesus Christ (who died for her "sins") or the "presence" of the Holy Spirit.

My second theoretical proposal is to consider Pentecostal emotions as a field of observation of the contemporary reshaping of institutional work, in connection with anthropological and sociological analyses of communication. The contemporary desinstitutionalisation of religion, or more accurately the "crisis of institutional regulation," produces, as Hervieu-Léger remarks, "a shift in the repository of the truth of belief from the institution to the believer" (Hervieu-Léger, 1993: 245). This process of subjective personalisation of religious experience doesn't systematically imply a decline of institution, however, but a reshaping of its modalities of intervention. So we need, as Wood notes about the sociology of New Age movements, to overcome "the theoretical presupposition that a distinction can be drawn between external authority and self-authority" (Wood, 2009: 240), to be able to re-examine Pentecostal emotions from the perspective of an institutional work producing a subjectivisation of religious experience (Fer, 2015a).

The major part of the Pentecostal/charismatic affective economy is organised around the belief in a communication with God which makes possible God's effective presence in the convert's personal life. To understand the supposedly paradoxical coexistence of emotional intensity and ethical rationalisation, these two dimensions of Pentecostalism have to be considered within what Boutter (drawing from Bateson's work) has defined as a "system of complementary interactions between the individual and God." Previously engaged in "symmetrical relations," the individual has had to cope with the limitations of his own will and the conflictive nature of ordinary social relations. As he becomes a Pentecostal, he strives to cast off this direct confrontation by establishing a triangular communication in which God intervenes as an omnipresent mediator (Boutter 1999: 251–254). Between the "new person" (the new identity gained through conversion) and the "old nature" (associated with the convert's former identity "in the world"), as well as between the convert and the society, God is an omnipresent mediator: God "talks" through a set of "invisible mediations" that enable the church, as a community and an institution, to intervene in the personal lives of its members. Messages "received from God" for a "sister in Christ" and, above all, the "voice of the Holy Spirit," function as the voice of the Pentecostal habitus linked with the Pentecostal ethos. "Is that thought from you, God, or does it come from the world?" "God, tell me how to react to this situation according to your will!" Ideally, this system of communication will contribute to a moderation of personal behaviours (more thoughtful and less reactive, less directly involved with "worldly" stakes), part of the ethical rationalisation of lives promised by the Pentecostal conversion. However, the intense emotions experienced during the church services express the conviction of being in a direct and immediate communication with God. This becomes the time to tell God everything, often overflowing the limits of ordinary language (through prayer in tongues), whilst also receiving messages from God (through the messages in tongues, followed by interpretations).

This system of communication can only produce concrete effects because Penecostal converts share a common belief in an ideal of transparency and the virtues of communication. This Pentecostal system of belief is attuned to the contemporary ideology of the "society of communication," defined by Neveu as "a process of reduction of the conflictive nature of social relations,... a social anomaly [which] requires therapists [to be] able to help the ill-adapted progress, and to improve communication flows that provide exchange and consensus" (Neveu, 2001: 81). As a Pentecostal discipleship training program explains, "An unresolved conflict becomes a problem. A problem can be defined as a broken relation" (Venditti and Venditti, 1996: 278). Communication is always the solution, and no conflict can withstand an open and transparent dialogue.

An individual needs to restore and improve her communication flow with God, to learn how to listen to God's voice, and to maintain with her "brothers and sisters in Christ" what the training program calls a "fourth level of communication." This "communication of emotions" enables "the word of God to have an impact and change lives" (Venditti and Venditti, 1996: 284).

Finally, the affective economies, or "emotional regimes" (Riis and Woodhead, 2010:10), observable in the religious field cannot be understood independently from the more general evolutions of the social norms of self-control. The notion of "informalisation of manners" elaborated by Wouters (2011: 152), continuing the sociohistorical analysis of Elias, provides a crucial theoretical tool for an understanding of religious emotions that is not confined to the sociology of religions. This notion describes a historical evolution of the social forms of self-control inspired by a quest for "naturalness" (Wouters, 2011: 152) that leads to the abandonment of formal systems of constraints which ensure the respect of rules of manners and the adoption of an individual self-regulation based on the incorporation of behavioural norms. According to Wouters, "the long-term trend of formalization reached its peak in the Victorian era, from the mid-nineteenth century to its last decade" (148).

This "second nature" regime strives to domesticate the spontaneous impulses of "human nature" and bases moral reputation on the personal ability to self-discipline. The dominant social norm (influential in western societies at least until the 1960s) is marked by "a fear of the slippery slope" (Wouters, 2011: 148) leading to immoral pleasure. This same fear leads classical Pentecostalism to closely control the manifestations of the Holy Spirit and the emotional effervescence associated with them. It aims to combine an openness to supernatural manifestations, which implies an ability to "let go" and be ready for emotional experiences, with a quest for social respectability based on the reformation of personal lives. So classical Pentecostalism can be located at the intersection of two inseparable constraints that define the "second nature" regime. As Wouters puts it, "the constraint towards becoming accustomed to self-constraint is at the same time a constraint to be unconstrained, to be confident and at ease" (Wouters, 2011: 151). "Feel free amongst us," Pentecostal ministers often tell those who attend a church service for the first time. This elaboration of a church where one can be free relies on a set of mechanisms through which classical Pentecostalism produces specific forms of self-constraint, or "invisible" constraints, likely to be subjectively experienced as individual liberation (Fer, 2005: 186).

In contrast, the charismatic movements (also called "neo-charismatic" or "independent charismatic") that have developed as an alternative to classical Pentecostalism minimise the role of institution in the elaboration of personal religious experience, whilst emphasising the freedom of self-expression. Less concerned about social respectability than individual virtuosity, they are attuned to what Wouters calls the "third nature" regime. This shift, which occurred between the 1950s and the 1980s, enables "people to admit to themselves and to others to having "dangerous" emotions, without provoking shame, particularly the shame-fear of losing control, and having to 'give in to' and act upon these feelings" (Wouters, 2011: 153). These experiences are felt by individuals who "can take the liberty" of allowing them because they own (and are seen as owning) an inalienable capacity of self-regulation, based on a set of embodied dispositions. The liberation of emotions that they seek expresses, in Wouters' terms, "an attempt at reaching back to 'first nature' without losing any of the control that was provided by 'second nature'" (Wouters, 2011: 153). This new orientation fosters a diversification and a radicalisation of emotional experiences, including "the evocation of bodily possession by powerful, externally derived and divine forces" (Coleman, 2000: 139) seen as a new means of intense communication with the Holy Spirit. At first glance, this global charismatic culture seems to deviate from mainstream western habitus, as its styles of faith and bodily deportment involve "the evocation of bodily possession by powerful, externally derived and divine forces" (Coleman, 2000, 139). This is (implicitly or explicitly) inspired by a desire to move closer to the forms of bodily experiences commonly associated with non-western spiritual realms, such as trance (Fer, 2015b: 234–235).

Without a reflexive re-examination of the prenotions implied by the native narrative of the sociology of religion on emotions, this charismatic desire to reach back to the "first nature" might be interpreted at face value as a regression towards the most "elementary" forms of religious experience, associated here with a primitive and exotic authenticity. It is clear that such a perspective would be both reductionist and lazy, contenting itself with the features of believers' discourses which most easily fit the established interpretations of a disciplinary *doxa*. Rather than a systematic use of ideological oppositions between tradition and modernity, body and mind, etc., the scientific understanding of these kinds of emotional phenomena requires a detailed sociological analysis of how religious emotions are built though the articulation of individual commitment, community socialisation, and institutional work.

References

Altglas, Véronique. 2005. "'Les mots brûlent': sociologie des nouveaux mouvements religieux et déontologie," *Archives de Sciences Sociales des Religions* 131–132: 165–188.

Athanasiou, Athena, Pothiti Hantzaroula, and Kostas Yannakopoulos. 2008. "Towards a new epistemology: the 'affective turn,'" *Historien* 8: 5–16.

Bastian, Jean-Pierre. 2001. "De l'autorité prophétique chez les dirigeants pentecôtistes," *Revue d'Histoire et de Philosophie Religieuse* 81(2): 189–202.

Boquet, Damien, and Nagy Piroska. 2015. *Sensible Moyen Âge. Une histoire des émotions dans l'Occident médiéval.* Paris: Seuil.

Bourdieu, Pierre. 2010. "Sociologists of belief and beliefs of sociologists," translated by Véronique Altglas and Matthew Wood, *Nordic Journal of Religion and Society* 23(1): 1–7.

Bourdieu, Pierre. 1994. *Raisons pratiques, sur la théorie de l'action.* Paris: Le Seuil.

Bourdieu, Pierre. 1992. *The logic of practice.* Stanford: Stanford University Press.

Bourdieu, Pierre. 1984. *Distinction: a social critique of the judgement of taste.* Boston: Harvard University Press.

Bourdieu, Pierre. 1979. *La distinction, critique sociale du jugement.* Paris: Editions de Minuit.

Boutter, Bernard. 1999. *La mission salut et guérison à l'île de la Réunion: dontribution à une anthropologie du pentecôtisme dans les sociétés en mutation.* Ph.D. dissertation in Ethnology, University Strasbourg II.

Champion, Françoise, and Danièle Hervieu-Léger, eds. 1990. *De l'émotion en religion: renouveaux et traditions.* Paris: Centurion.

Champion, Françoise. 1990. "La nébuleuse mystique-ésotérique: orientations psychore-ligieuses des courants mystiques et ésotériques contemporains." In *De l'émotion en religion: renouveaux et traditions,* edited by Françoise Champion and Danièle Hervieu-Léger, 17–69. Paris: Centurion.

Clough, Patricia. 2007. Introduction. In *The affective turn: theorizing the social,* edited by Patricia Clough and Jean Halley, 1–33. Durham: Duke University Press.

Coleman, Simon. 2000. *The globalization of charismatic Christianity: spreading the gospel of prosperity.* Cambridge: Cambridge University Press.

Corrigan, John. 2007. "Introduction: the study of religion and emotion." In *Oxford handbook on religion and emotion,* edited by John Corrigan, 3–12. Oxford: Oxford University Press.

Csordas, Thomas J. 2002. *Body/meaning/healing.* Houndmills: Palgrave Macmillan.

Damasio, Antonio R. 1994. *Descartes' error: emotion, reason, and the human brain.* New York: G.P. Putnam's Sons.

Davies, Douglas J., and Nathaniel A. Warne, eds. 2013. *Emotions and religious dynamics.* Farnham: Ashgate.

Durkheim, Émile. (1912) 1995. *The elementary forms of religious life.* New York: The Free Press.

Durkheim, Émile. (1937) 1982. *The rules of sociological method.* New York: Macmillan.

Durkheim, Émile. 1969. "Le sentiment religieux à l'heure actuelle," *Archives de sociologie des religions* 27: 73–78.

Fath, Sébastien. 2001. « L'autorité charismatique au ceur de l'Eglise : pentecôtisme et débat sectaire », *Etudes théologiques et religieuses* 2001/3: 371–390.

Favret-Saada, Jeanne. 1994. "Weber, les émotions et la religion," *Terrain* 22: 93–108.

Fer, Yannick. 2015a. "Pentecostal prayer as personal communication and invisible institutional work." In *A sociology of prayer*, edited by Linda Woodhead and Giuseppe Giordan, 49–65. Farnham: Ashgate.

Fer, Yannick. 2015b. "Charismatic globalization, morality and politics in Polynesian Protestantism." In *The anthropology of global Pentecostalism and evangelicalism*, edited by Simon Coleman and Rosalind Hackett, 228–242. New York, New York University Press.

Fer, Yannick. 2010. "The Holy Spirit and the Pentecostal habitus: elements for a sociology of institution in classical Pentecostalism," *Nordic Journal of Religion and Society* 2: 157–176.

Fer, Yannick. 2005. *Pentecôtisme en Polynésie française: l'évangile relationnel*. Geneva: Labor & Fides.

Grossein, Jean-Pierre, ed. and trans. 1996. *Sociologie des religions*, by Weber, Max, 51–129. Paris: NRF Gallimard.

Hervieu-Léger, Danièle. 2001. "Émile Durkheim (1858–1917): le sacré et la religion." In *Sociologie et religion: approches classiques en sciences sociales des religions*, edited by Danièle Hervieu-Léger and Jean Paul Willaime, 147–196. Paris: Presses Universitaires de France.

Hervieu-Léger, Danièle. (1990a) 1993. "Present-day emotional revivals." In *A future for religion*, edited by W.H. Swatos, 129–148. Sage Focus Editions, Volume 151. London: Sage.

Hervieu-Léger, Danièle. 1990b. "Renouveaux émotionnels contemporains: fin de la sécularisation ou fin de la religion?" In *De l'émotion en religion: renouveaux et traditions*, edited by Françoise Champion and Danièle Hervieu-Léger, 217–248. Paris: Centurion.

Heurtin, Jean-Philippe. 2014. "Max Weber lecteur de Rudolph Sohm, et l'inachèvement du concept de charisme de function." In *Que faire du charisme? Retours sur une notion de Max Weber*, edited by V. Bernadou, F. Blanc, R. Laignoux, and F. Roa Bastos, 55–79. Rennes: Presses Universitaires de Rennes.

Isambert, François-André. 1992. "Sur trois interprétations de la religion dans la pensée de Durkheim," *Revue Française de Sociologie* 33(3): 443–462.

Ladous, Régis. 1995. « Etats-Unis ». In *Histoire du christianisme des origines à nos jours* tome XI : « Libéralisme, industrialisation, expansion européenne (1830–1914) », edited by Jacques Gadille and Jean-Marie Mayeur, 853–932. Paris: Desclée de Brouwer.

Laignoux, Raphaëlle. 2014. "Pour une réévaluation du charisme et de ses usages en sciences sociales." In *Que faire du charisme? Retours sur une notion de Max Weber*, edited by V. Bernadou, F. Blanc, R. Laignoux, and F. Roa Bastos, 13–25. Rennes: Presses Universitaires de Rennes.

Lassave, Pierre. 2012. "Les *formes* dans les *archives*: filiation, refondation, référence," *Archives de Sciences Sociales des Religions* 159: 89–111.

Lutz, Catherine A., and Lila Abu-Lughod, eds. 1990. *Language and the politics of émotion*. Cambridge; Paris: Cambridge University Press and Éditions de la Maison des Sciences de l'Homme.

Lutz, Catherine. 1988. *Unnatural Emotions: Everyday Sentiments on a Micronesian Atoll and Their Challenge to Western Theory*. Chicago : University of Chicago Press.

Lutz, Catherine, and Geoffrey White. 1986. "The anthropology of emotions," *Annual Review of Anthropology* 15: 405–436.

Mellor, Philip A. 2007. "Embodiment, emotion and religious experience: religion, culture and the charismatic body." *The Sage handbook of the sociology of religion*, In James A. Beckford and N.J. Demerath, 587–607. London: Sage.

Mellor, Philip A. 2001. "Sacred contagion and social vitality: collective effervescence in *Les formes élémentaires de la vie religieuse*." In *Emile Durkheim: Critical Assessments of Leading Sociologists*, Third Series, Volume 2, edited by W.S.F. Pickering, 167–188. London; New York: Routledge.

Neveu, Erik. 2001. *Une société de communication?* Paris: Montchrétien.

Nussbaum, Martha. 1992. "Emotions as Judgements of Value," *The Yale Journal of Criticism* 5(2): 201–212.

Passeron, Jean-Claude. 1996. "L'espace Wébérien du raisonnement comparatif." In *Sociologie des religions*, by Weber, Max, 1–49. Paris: NRF Gallimard.

Percy, Martyn. 1996. *Words, wonder and power*. London: SPCK.

Radkau, Joachim. 2011. *Max Weber: a biography*. Cambridge: Polity.

Rao Bastos, Francisco. 2014. "En finir avec le charisme ?" In *Que faire du charisme? Retours sur une notion de Max Weber*, edited by V. Bernadou, F. Blanc, R. Laignoux, and F. Roa Bastos, 217–235. Rennes: Presses Universitaires de Rennes.

Rey, Terry. 2007. *Bourdieu on religion: imposing faith and legitimacy*. London; Oakville: Equinox.

Riis, Ole, and Linda Woodhead, eds. 2010. *A sociology of religious emotion*. Oxford: Oxford University Press.

Rosaldo, Michele Z. 1984. "Toward an anthropology of self and feeling." In *Culture theory: essays on mind, self and emotion*, edited by R.A. Shweder and R.A. Le Vine, 137–157. Cambridge: Cambridge University Press.

Schweder, Richard A., and Robert A. LeVine, eds. 1984. *Culture theory: essays on mind, self and emotion*. Cambridge: Cambridge University Press.

Selzner, Cyril. 2010. *Conscience, réforme et revolution: les transformations de la conscience morale dans la Réforme et le puritanisme anglais aux XVIe et XVIIe siècles*. Thèse de doctorat en philosophie, Université Paris I Panthéon-Sorbonne.

Venditti, Lena, and Nicolas Venditti. 1996. *Formation du disciple: en suivant Jésus dans un service fidèle, INSTE premier niveau, préparation au service.* Des Moines: Open Bible Standard Churches / Department of International Ministries.

Vincent-Buffault, Anne. 1986. *Histoire des larmes, XVIIIe–XIXe siècle.* Paris: Rivages.

Weber, Max. 1993. *The sociology of religion.* Boston: Beacon Press.

Weber, Max. 1978. *Economy and society: an outline of interpretive sociology.* Berkeley; Los Angeles; London: University of California Press.

Willaime, Jean-Paul. 2005. *Sociologie du protestantisme.* Paris: Presses Universitaires de France coll.

Willaime, Jean-Paul. 2001. "Max Weber (1864–1920): genèse religieuse de la modernité occidentale, rationalisation et charisme" In *Sociologie et religion: approches classiques en sciences sociales des religions,* edited by Danièle Hervieu-Léger and Jean-Paul Willaime, 59–109. Paris: Presses Universitaires de France.

Willaime, Jean-Paul. 1999. "Le pentecôtisme: contours et paradoxes d'un protestantisme émotionnel," *Archives des Sciences Sociales des Religions* 105: 5–28.

Willaime, Jean-Paul. 1992. *La précarité protestante: sociologie du protestantisme contemporain.* Geneva: Labor et Fides.

Wood, Matthew. 2009. "The nonformative elements of religious life: questioning the 'sociology of spirituality' paradigm," *Social Compass* 56(2): 237–248.

Woodward, Kathleen. 1996. "Global cooling and academic warming: long-term shifts in emotional weather," *American Literary History* 8(4): 759–779.

Wouters, Cas. 2011. "How civilizing processes continued: towards an informalization of manners and a third nature personality," *Sociological Review* 59 (Supplement s1): 140–159.

CHAPTER 7

"Reverse Mission": A Critical Approach for a Problematic Subject

Eric Morier-Genoud

The topic of "reverse mission" (or "return mission") emerged as a fashionable topic in theology and the social sciences in the late 1990s. It was concerned with a perceived flow of missionaries coming to the global North from the global South when in the past, missionaries left Europe and the Americas to evangelize the South (known successively as the colonial world and the Third World). The subject of reverse mission rapidly gained momentum in the literature, and in 2007 it was "crowned" with an entry in Jonathan Bonk's *Encyclopedia of Mission and Missionaries* (Ojo, 2007). Academics and church people alike debate what reverse mission is, what it should be, whether it is succeeding, and whether it is a key element of the future of Christianity, especially given the contemporary secularisation of the global North. Existing definitions of "reverse" and "return mission" are contradictory and approximate, and debates often conflate social science with theology and normative elements. While this has helped widen the discussion (into issues of migration, the transnationalisation of faith, and the globalisation of churches), it has blurred academic borders and weakened the scientific understanding of the issue.

What is "reverse mission" or "return mission"? Where does the term come from? What can it encompass and what not? How should we understand and analyse it? This chapter revisits the issue of reverse mission from a critical vantage point. In view of the approximate nature of existing definitions and the blurring of disciplines (between theology and the social sciences in particular), there is an urgent need to pause, deconstruct the subject, and reconstruct it critically. Adopting a social scientific approach, the chapter starts by analysing existing definitions of reverse mission, unpacking the term, and trying to find a scientific angle from which to approach it. In the second section, it uncovers the origins of the term and the various discussions around it – pointing to an historical, sociological, and theological archaeology of discourses. The third and last section investigates how reverse mission is understood and used in discourse by European, African, Asian, and Latin American Christians and their churches. Such an exploration will reveal much about theology, the praxis of Christians and their institutions, and the dynamics of scientific debates about religion.

Through this exercise, the chapter engages in a classic problem in the social sciences, namely the epistemological question of how one constructs an object of study and elaborates concepts. It argues that the topic of reverse mission is a typical case of analysts confusing reality with a discourse on reality, and a typical case of adopting uncritically an actor's category as a scientific concept. Against this approach, against the normativeness such an approach introduces, and because the term reverse mission cannot be translated into a scientific category, the present investigation shifts from looking at the content of the term reverse mission to an analysis of the discourses employing the term. It asks where these discourses come from, what their functions are, and what their performativity is. That is to say, the chapter aims at understanding why people use these discourses and what impact they have on reality. Between the lines, it suggests the consequences of adopting as a scientific concept a term used by actors, without reflecting on it.

Definitions, Concepts and Concept-Making

What is "reverse mission" or "return mission"? (Note that from here on, I will equate the terms and mostly use the former for purposes of clarity.) Two definitions predominate in the field. The first emerged in the 1990s when the number of African and Asian migrants grew in Europe and the United States, and some of these migrants began to practice Christian proselytism in their host society. Succinctly articulated by Hun Kim, this definition says "reverse mission is when non-Western churches return with the gospel to societies that initially brought the gospel to them" (Kim, 2011b: 148). In his encyclopaedia entry, Matthews Ojo offers a similar but longer definition:

> "Reverse mission" refers to the sending of missionaries to Europe and North America by churches and Christians from the non-Western world, particularly Africa, Asia and Latin American, which were at the receiving end of Catholic and Protestant missions as mission fields from the sixteenth to the later twentieth century.
>
> OJO, 2007: 380

In another version, Israel Olofinjana says, "African Christians ministering in the UK now are directly or indirectly a harvest of seeds sown by the early missionaries to Africa" (Olofinjana, 2010: 2). In short, in this understanding, reverse mission occurs when those who were converted by missionaries travel or migrate to the missionaries' society to proselytise there.

Such a definition entails two main problems. The first is about time and links. Most definitions presuppose reverse mission is the consequence of earlier (North-South) missionary movements. In general terms, the proposed definition is clear, but it becomes fuzzy as soon as we try to pin down its details. Can we consider the proselytism of *any* African, Asian, or Latin American in the North to be the consequence of earlier European or American missionary work in Africa, Asia, or Latin America? Or should it only be when the person who engages in evangelisation is the son or daughter (or grandson / granddaughter) of a person directly converted by a European or North American missionary? A medium-term solution could be anyone who comes from a church or country linked historically through missionary work to the country where they are now doing their own evangelical work. If we go for any African, Asian, or Latin American, the definition becomes so broad that we may have to say that 19th-century European and American missionary work in the Middle East and North Africa is missionary work in reverse in relation to the expansion of early Christianity from the Middle East and North Africa into Europe and the Americas. If we adopt a narrow definition, the term reverse mission would hardly ever apply, and the medium term definition would not apply very often.

The second problem relates to ethnicity. Implicit in many definitions is that Africans, Asians, and Latin Americans are converting Europeans or North Americans. It is easy to picture as reverse missionary activity an Asian or African migrant proselytising white people in Europe or the Americas. But when these same missionaries try to convert non-white individuals in the global North, the term reverse mission is not used and authors talk instead of "migrant mission" or "diaspora mission" (Wan, 2011; see also Saelee, 2011; Kay and Dyer, 2011). This has led Israel Olofinjana to wonder whether ethnicity is the determining factor to define reverse mission. He asks: "[Is] reverse mission only validated when an ethnic pastor is leading a white congregation?" (Olofinjana, 2004). The question is most pertinent and useful as a critique of the un-thought, if not prejudiced, elements in most understandings of reverse mission. It is also a powerful critique of how approximately the term is usually defined. Nevertheless, an ethnic or racial definition of reverse mission would be just as problematic. If ethnicity were used as the central criterion, we would need to consider as reverse mission only non-White churches and clergy engaged in evangelization among Whites, and this would drastically reduce the number of cases we could consider. There would be an historical problem too. How could we consider Black on White evangelisation as reverse mission if Christianity is originally from the Middle East, i.e. not a White religion in the first place? We do not need to push the argument much further to agree that such a definition does not work – the concept of reverse mission is approximate and normative, as noted by Olodinjana.

A second and older definition of reverse mission draws from a discussion in mission circles in the 1970s about how European and American institutions should react and adapt after Third World churches had asked for a moratorium on missionary work by Northern countries (see next section for more details). In 1979, Gregory Sumtko advocated a format of reverse mission which would encourage American and Canadian missionaries working in South and Central America to influence the public and policy makers back home to make people hear "the silenced cries of many of their brothers and sisters who suffer the evils of an ever increasing state of poverty and injustice" (Sumtko, 1979: 117). More recently, Faye Abram, John Slosar and Rose Walls have defined reverse mission in a similar manner, by saying:

> Instead of teaching, preaching and trying to convert people of another country or community, reverse mission emphasizes learning from indigenous people and their leaders, raising missionaries' and sojourners' level of consciousness and advocating for changes in one's home country.
> ABRAM, SLOSAR, and WALLS, 2005: 161

In a shorter version, Paul Stevens and Brian Stelck argue that reverse mission is about "equipping equippers cross-culturally" (1993: 34). Even more recently, in *Reverse mission: Transnational religious communities and the making of US foreign policy*, political scientist Timothy Byrnes says reverse mission is

> any process through which members of religious communities speak in the United States for their brothers and sisters living abroad who, though profoundly affected by US foreign policy, have no political platform in the United States from which to speak for themselves.
> BYRNES, 2011: 2

Like the first definition given above, this second definition of reverse mission is problematic. We can get the gist of its meaning generally, but it encompasses four quite different elements. Two mention equipping missionaries cross-culturally and two talk about passing to those back home "the cries" of those who suffer abroad or speaking back home on behalf of people abroad. In addition, two use borders as a defining criterion, as if international borders changed the nature of things. Indeed, it is debatable whether there is a substantive difference between relaying the cries of those who suffer poverty and injustice *abroad* and relaying similar cries from those who suffer poverty *at home*. Similarly, is speaking on behalf of someone abroad substantively different from speaking on behalf of someone at home? If so, what is this difference, and would Canada operate as an "abroad" in the same way as a country in Latin America or Africa? Once again, the proposition holds in general terms but not when we try to pin it down in some detail.

A last problem with reverse mission is that all definitions cited here (in both sets) are programmatic and/or descriptive. Reverse mission is a program whereby missionaries act in the world and change reality, not an analytical concept or tool to help capture and understand reality. While such concepts may be acceptable, if not useful, in theology, they do not help social scientists understand what is going on, if they do not actually prevent us from analysing reality outside and beyond the discourse of actors.

What can we draw from the analysis of these two sets of definitions of reverse mission? First, the term is very uncertain. There are two sets of definitions, which is problematic in and of itself. The first set has probably more currency today than the second, but the latter is still influential, and we cannot discard one or the other. Yet running several definitions of the same concept at the same time runs the risk of additional confusion and lack of clarity. Second, both sets of definitions have serious and quite similar problems; they are approximate, descriptive, and normative. What they refer to is uncertain and vague – in terms of criteria, period, ethnicity, etc. Third, both sets refer to intentions, if not theological programs, rather than existing realities. In a best case scenario, they describe reality as defined by and lensed through a discourse when scientific concepts should (help) *explain* reality, without any mediation, particularly from actors. In short, the term reverse mission has little heuristic value; it does not help our understanding of reality, even if it has great value to spark our imagination and stimulate debates about justice, immigration, diaspora, globalisation, or world Christianity (e.g. debates about whether reverse mission is the good side of immigration, or whether it is the way to stop Christianity declining in the global North) (see among others, Spindler and Lenoble-Bart, 2000; Jenkins, 2011).

Looking at the literature on reverse missions, we see little effort to conceptualise reverse mission methodically. Some authors have expressed doubts about the validity of the term. For example, theologian Hun Kim declares that "'receiving mission' or 'reverse mission' is an issue of controversy in the modern mission era, mainly because there are variations on the terminology and their meaning" [sic], adding in the conclusion of his article, that the term cannot "accommodate whole issues with satisfaction" (Kim, 2011a: 62). Historian of religion Afe Adogame (2007) refers to reverse mission as a "rhetoric" – though he later calls it also "a process," the origin of which he goes on to trace.

The only author who seems to have tried to bring some method to the subject is missiologist Mechteld Jansen. Writing about Indonesian and Moluccan immigrant churches in the Netherlands, she defines reverse mission as a "missionary strategy which seems to mirror the 19th en [sic: and] 20th century strategies of North Atlantic missions to the South" (Jansen, 2016: 11). Taking a Weberian approach, she advances the following criteria for an ideal-type of reverse mission: "mother and daughter churches, well-educated pastors being sent out, financial support, gradual independence, and tensions between daughter coming of age and mothers fearing to lose control" (11). The ideal-type is loose and debatable (e.g., What needs to be mirrored and what needs to be reproduced? What is a "mother church" or a "daughter church"?). Worse yet, it does not work well. Jansen says in her conclusion that her case study does not match the reverse mission ideal-type she has built, mainly because there is no mother/daughter relationship between Oceanian and Dutch churches and because class is undermined by culture and race (Jansen, 2016: 11). While she concludes her case differs importantly from the ideal-type, it is just as possible, if not probable, that the problems derive not from the case, but from the way she constructed her ideal-typical concept.

In the social sciences, concepts are abstractions constructed methodically from reality (inductive approach) or derived from theory (deductive approach). In the present case, the term reverse mission has usually not been derived (or deducted) from theory, but from a mix of theological debates and church programs (I discuss this genealogy in the next section). This is problematic because, to do social sciences, we need to think against common perceptions and the discourse of actors – and theologians are actors of church affairs and mission work. Pierre Bourdieu calls scientists to adopt a critical stance and build "scientific reflexivity." That is, he asks us to make an "epistemic break" from the positions taken by actors. Otherwise, he says, we risk aligning ourselves with positions taken by actors, not engaging in a scientific analysis but adopting ideological positions within a game played by actors (Bourdieu, 1992; Wood and Altglas, 2010).

There is no social scientific theory from which one could deduct the concept of reverse mission. As to the inductive method, we have seen how the attempt by Jansen to build an ideal-type following a Weberian approach is limited, if it does not simply fail. Whilst worthy and interesting, the attempt is inherently flawed because the ideal-typical concept is not built from an analysis of reality, as it should be, but from a discourse about reality (encapsulated by the term and discourse on reverse mission). And this is the crux of the problem: reverse mission is, as noted by several authors, just a discourse. Accordingly, if we want to do social sciences, we need either to ditch the term and start investigating the issues raised by the term reverse mission, or else we need to analyse the term for what it is, namely a *discourse*, i.e. "a way of speaking which gives meaning to experiences from a particular perspective" (Jørgensen and Phillips, 2002: 66).

Two authors have already noted that reverse mission is discourse or rhetoric, but their analyses are not satisfying. Although Adogame defines reverse mission as rhetoric, he engages nonetheless in an analysis of the origins of this type of mission as if it existed in reality and was not simply a discourse after all. By the same token, sociologist Paul Freston refers to reverse mission as discourse and rhetoric. Oddly, however, after discussing definitions of reverse mission and the problems of each definition, he goes on to ask whether this type of mission is practiced in reality, with what success and with what prospect – again as if reverse mission were not a discourse after all, but an actual reality. Like Adogame, Freston conflates discourse and reality and mixes both in the same article. Freston goes as far as to argue that reality should actually catch up with the discourse – a rather theological position for a sociologist (Freston, 2010).

Against both these authors, I propose that if reverse mission is *discourse*, then we must engage in... *discourse analysis!* Because no discourse analysis has ever tackled the subject of reverse mission, it seems best not to start with a textual analysis, a syntactic analysis, or discursive psychology. Instead, I will engage in a *critical discourse analysis* whereby I will investigate the history of the discourse and analyse the context of its emergence, before studying the discursive practices around the term reverse mission and analysing the performativity of the discourse (i.e. its impact on reality) (Jørgensen and Phillips, 2002: Ch.3).

Origin and Context of the Discourse on Reverse Mission

To understand the discourse on reverse mission, we need to identify its origin and context. In general terms, it originates, as previously mentioned, in Christian theology and, more specifically, in debates among missiologists in the 1960s and 1970s about what missions were and what they should be in the future. The term also appeared within the context of decolonisation, the end of the European empires, and the globalisation of Christianity – a context featuring major debates and struggles about what role the Third World has and should have in the future. From this general point, we need to engage in an archaeology of the discourse on reverse mission to uncover the enunciative dynamics leading to the invention of the term and the shaping of the ensuing discussions and debates. Accordingly, this section will reconstruct the genealogy of the discourse on reverse mission, starting with a short excursion into how mission was understood before the term reverse mission emerged.

Missionary work in the 19th and 20th centuries was mostly about Europeans and Americans going to Africa and Asia to extend the Kingdom of God on earth. Their early discourse was about the "Great Commission" (Matthew 28:18–20), a description popularised in the late 19th century which aimed at evangelizing "pagans," something which, within a colonial context, was as much about culture and politics as it was about faith (Porter, 2004; Stanley, 1990; Prudhomme, 2004). Missionaries travelled great distances to do missionary work and set up "indigenous churches." Such churches were the logical development and result of missionary work. They were to eventually become independent, when the time was "ripe," taking over the Christian works initiated by the missionaries who would withdraw. Needless to say, the reality differed substantially from the discourse, as Europeans struggled to hand over power, and as Africans, Asians, and Latin Americans appropriated the Christian message and established their own churches and movements outside missionary control.

National churches had to be set up before they could become independent. By World War II, many indigenous "daughter churches" existed in Africa and Asia and were moving towards autonomy if not independence, but they frequently remained dependent on foreign support both theologically and financially. The case of the Catholic Church was slightly different in that there was no "daughter churches," but the teleological discourse remained the same – national churches were created and had to become independent (within the global Church). In Latin America, the dynamic differed somewhat, with national independence occurring in the 19th century, but the "maturing" of national churches seems to have taken place in the 20th century nonetheless.

After World War II, decolonisation accelerated worldwide, and the issue of the relationship between missionaries and "daughter churches" (re-labelled "young churches") became a topic of debate. At the 1947 International Missionary Council (IMC) conference in Whitby, Canada, participants agreed the missionary task remained very important, but something had to change in the relationship between churches. Accordingly, they decided to adopt a program for missionary organisations and young churches to work together in a "Partnership in obedience." The partnership was decided by the missionaries alone; it asked everyone to submit to the task of the Great Commission, i.e. the obedience element of the partnership was imposed on young churches.

Structures were not challenged, and finances continued to flow mostly from the North to the South. In Mexico City in 1963, the World Council of Churches (WCC, founded in 1947 out of IMC) decided to abolish the distinction between Christendom and the "non-Christian world," something that transformed, by the whim of a definition, all six continents into lands of mission. Mission work was thereafter no longer something for the Northern Christian churches to do in Southern "pagan" territories, but something for *everyone* to do *everywhere*. Translating this idea into action, the WCC ran a program between 1959 and 1973 called "Joint Action for Mission." For all their worth, these ideas and this programme still did not challenge the structures of power and finance put in place in the 19th century by Northern churches, although they laid the ground for discussions to come, not least those on reverse mission (Blaser, 1998: 84).

A turning point eventually occurred in 1971. At a mission festival in the United States, the head of the Presbyterian Church of East Africa, John Gatu, proposed a "moratorium" on foreign missionaries and funds to the Third World. He explained:

> [Our] present problems can only be solved if all missionaries can be withdrawn in order to allow a period of not less than five years for each side to rethink and formulate what is going to be their future relationship... The churches of the Third world must be allowed to find their own identity, and the continuation of the present missionary movement is a hindrance to this selfhood of the church.
>
> GATU, 1971, cited in ANDERSON, 1974

The same year in the Philippines, Emérito Nacpil, president of Union Theological Seminary, made a similar call, saying that missionaries were "a symbol of the universality of Western imperialism" and "the most *missionary* service a missionary under the present system can do today in Asia is to go home" (cited in Reese, 2014: 245; see also Kwiyani, 2014: Ch.2). In other words, using the language of the churches, the "young" institutions were claiming their adulthood and telling their parents to let them live independently.

The issue went mainstream in Protestantism at the World Council of Church's Bangkok gathering in January 1973 and at the All African Conference of Churches (AACC) meeting in 1974. After discussing the issue at length, the AACC issued a call which stated:

> To enable the African Church to achieve the power of becoming a true instrument of liberating and reconciling the African people, as well as finding solutions to economic and social dependency, our option as a

matter of policy has to be a moratorium on external assistance in money and personnel.

AACC, 1974, cited in REESE, 2014: 248

A major debate ensued in missionary circles. What we need to note about it at this point is that some defended a disconnection of Southern churches from Northern churches so the former could become really independent – mostly Southern pastors with some Northern theologians. Others did not necessarily oppose independence *per se*, but they were worried about the effect of the moratorium on missionary work. For example, the General Secretary of the Dutch Missionary Council Johannes Verkuyl argued the moratorium was de-mobilising potential missionaries in Europe and destroying the *élan* to gather funds for missionary work in the world (Reese, 2014: 245–246). This debate is of present interest because an important discussion of the responsibility of missionary work emerged from it. Western missionaries realised their own society needed missionisation as secularisation grew. For their part, Third World churches became aware of their responsibility to assume the mission-ary work hitherto done by westerners. As noted by Klauspeter Blaser, however, this discussion did not last long; liberationist theologies gained momentum and discussion shifted from missionary work to issues of liberation, justice and development (Blaser, 1998: 92). Still the issue of the global South's role in mis-sionary work had been raised – the next time it was discussed publically would be within the framework of reverse mission.

Three social and sociological transformations took place before the discus-sion of the mission work of Third World churches morphed into one about re-verse mission or return mission. The first was the deepening secularisation of Northern societies. True or not (is it secularization or the privatisation of faith, etc.), the perception developed that western societies were becoming less reli-gious. Concerned churches and theologians looked for a means to reverse this perceived decline in faith. In the 1980s and 1990s, the growth of Southern Chris-tianity came to be seen as a sign of hope, and its missionary work a possible solution for re-Christianisation of the North. The second transformation was a significant migration of African and Asian Christians into Europe and North America from the 1980s onwards. Franca di Lecce says that in Italy, Christians represented 52.5% of all immigration from the South in 1966 – and presumably thereafter – leading to a renewal of European churches and the establishment of new communities, if not new churches (di Lecce, 1989: 276). Matthew Ojo notes on his side that there were 1000 migrant community churches in Ger-many in the 2000s, while the number in the United Kingdom went from fewer than 100 in the 1970s to over 1000 in the late 1990s (Ojo, 2007: 381). The third transformation occurred in the 1980s and 1990s when transnational African, Asian, and Latin American churches (Nigerian, Korean, and Brazilian, in particular) opened branches in the global North and engaged in missionary work there. Institutions such as the Nigerian Redeemed Church of God not only gained "market shares" in the United Kingdom, but also developed an agenda to do mission work in societies they perceived as secularised, if not neo-pagan. Such dynamics challenged Northern churches and theologians, and in the 1990s and 2000s, they started to discuss the role of Southern Christianity in the North. The term reverse mission captured the three processes just described and was used from the 1990s onwards as a tool to debate whether these processes were good or not, to be supported or not, to be controlled or not.

The debate about the missionary undertaking of Southern churches unfolds mostly in the Protestant world. The societal changes mentioned above affected the Catholic institution too, but there is little discussion of these themes under the label "reverse mission" within the Catholic Church. The Church is one and catholic, with Southern churches part of the whole institution, not a series of independent competitors. Evangelisation is done together systematically, following a plan centrally agreed upon in Rome. In 1975, the Pope reminded the faithful of this in an Apostolic Exhortation, *Evangelii Nuntiandi*, saying that "evangelization is for no one an individual and isolated act; it is one that is deeply ecclesial"; it is always "in union with the mission of the Church and in her name" (Pope Paul VI, 1975). That is to say, by definition, all Catholics work together towards the same aim. As for migration, the Catholic institution has long dealt with the issue internally through pastoral work, chaplaincies, ethnic parishes, and linguistic missions (Odem, 2004; Lopez, 2004). The arrival of African, Asian, and Latin American migrants in the 1990s has therefore not led to substantial changes. Possibly the biggest alteration has been the novel involvement of missionary congregations in pastoral work "at home" with migrants from the land where priests did missionary work, e.g. the Missionaries of Africa developing new pastoral work for Africans in Switzerland (Ballif, 2014). This said, the flow of personnel from the global South to the global North has also created problems in this church, including issues of exploitation, racism, and a clash of religious traditions. To deal with these issues, the Congregation for the Evangelization of Peoples put out a regulatory document in 2001 called "Instructions on the sending abroad and sojourn of diocesan priests from mission territories." As he launched the document, the head of the Congregation for Evangelization explained that the migration of Southern personnel to the North needed to be regulated because it undermined the good functioning and expansion of Southern dioceses (Allen, 2009: 44–45). Said differently, secularization, migration, and new religious movements exist in the Catholic Church too, but they are dealt with within the institution and regulated by the Vatican who keeps an eye on the global dynamics. There has consequently been no discussion of reverse mission (except in the first version of the term of voicing "at home" the agenda of people "abroad").

Discursive Practices and Performativity

The debate about reverse mission emerged with some force in the 1990s, as mentioned earlier, mostly under the meaning of Southern missionaries coming to do mission work in the North. It is unclear who developed the term in the newer sense – whether Southern or Northern theologians. Be this as it may, the discussion surfaced in the 1990s, and this was within a particular context. I noted the growing secularisation of the global North, along with the arrival of African and Asian immigrants and their transnational churches. A fourth issue, linking the three previous ones and making the whole extremely sensitive, was the "asylum crisis" affecting Europe and the USA from the early 1980s on. The number of immigrants labelled "refugees" rose significantly and tolerance for foreigners declined (Hein, 1993). How was the term used, by whom, for what purpose, and with what effect within this new context? This section considers these questions in a bid to clarify the discursive practices of reverse mission and their impact on reality (i.e. their performativity).

The function of the discourse on reverse mission (or the function of the use of the term reverse mission) has been and remains multi-fold. Generally speaking, its main role is to frame perceptions and situate the subject in both time and space. Geographically, it places the centre of the discussion in the North. Speakers talk about missionaries reversing a North-South dynamic, meaning they are looking at missionaries coming *from* the South (Asia, Africa, and Latin America) and going *to* the North (Europe and the Americas) and not any other missionary movements, whether East-West (e.g. Eastern Europe to Western Europe) or South-South (e.g. Brazil to Africa). In terms of periodisation, the use of the term reverse mission places the phenomenon on a time continuum beginning with European and American missionaries going South in the 16th or 19th century and ending today with Southern missionaries "reversing" the dynamic. By connecting time and geography in this way, reverse mission and discussions using this term create a genealogy of (a process of) new missionaries coming to the global North in contradistinction to the old missionaries going to the global South (to "the colonies" or pagan lands). Implicit in the term is a causation, whereby one process would have triggered the other. As we have just seen (above and in the previous section), the genealogy and the causality are fuzzy, but they capture the imagination. They give continuity to, and the impression of a revival of, an old Northern missionary process, which many thought had died out. They also build a narrative about decolonization which is coming to a happy close as the South "comes of age," engages in its own missionary work, and even now challenges Northern societies.

On top of framing discussions in time and space, the term reverse mission provides a moral compass. Philip Jenkins (an historian with a religious agenda), for example, uses it to provide a positive outlook on immigrant missionary work. He says the arrival of Christian immigrants and transnational churches in the global North constitutes a "coming home," and he hopes Southern Christianity will not just help the secularised North revive its faith, but also contribute to the rise of a new global Christendom. Both space and time are at work here in a scenario Jenkins recognises could turn out to be negative, but which he clearly hopes will be positive – a new Christendom. Geographically, his use of "coming home" implies Christian immigrants not only have a right to come to Europe and the Americas; they also have a right to live and work there as if Europe and America were their original homes (Jenkins, 2011: 224).

Paul Freston develops a similar approach – equally hopeful of a return of Christendom. In his article on reverse missions (already discussed), he looks positively at the missionary work of immigrants for the re-evangelisation of the global North. Whereas Jenkins sees external challenges facing immigrant missionaries (racism, theological differences, and the risk of schism), Freston focuses on internal challenges of the movement as he reckons an uncritical praising of reverse mission may lead to a "romantic perception of the south as the salvation for the tired West" (Freston, 2010: 172). In Freston's view, reverse mission is not very efficient or, at least, not as efficient as it should be. Reverse mission tends to be practiced mostly among diaspora communities, he argues, and this leads to very few conversions of Americans or Europeans – a reality noted by other scholars (Maxwell, 2007: Ch.7). Like Jenkins, then, Freston uses the term reverse mission to express a positive outlook on migrants' evangelising work in the global North; his take is more critical, however, as he considers the evangelisation drive is not strong or efficient enough.

Many African and Asian Christian migrants have adopted the term reverse mission in a similarly favourable and optimistic fashion. They use it to bolster their claims to be allowed to do church work in the global North, in countries where, more often than not, they face disrespect, discrimination, and racism. The term reverse mission has a function here of imparting empowerment and legitimacy. As reported by Maïté Masken, migrants use the term "reverse missionaries" to transform themselves from being perceived as "job stealers" into "prophets of their time" (Masken, 2008: 60–61). More speculatively, André Mary argues migrants use the term to transform "the original biblical malediction of the sons of Cham taught by the missionaries" into "a messianic destiny" and, thus, to turn "Africa into a continent of salvation" (Mary, 2008: 25). According to these authors, migrants use the term reverse mission to valorise themselves and their work. Needless to say, the term normalises, even belittles, their host societies; instead of simply being secularized societies, Europe and America become spiritually dead ones, in need of help and re-moralisation. Interestingly, historian David Maxwell says African missionaries in England use terms very similar to those used in Africa by ethnocentric Victorian missionaries a century ago (Maxwell, 2007: 175).

Danielle Koning best captures the function of the discourse of reverse mission for African, Asian, and Latin American religious practitioners. She explains it is an "identity discourse" which allows migrants to establish an ideal place, mark a concrete space, and challenge the relations of authority existing in the host religious milieu and society (Konig, 2009). As we have just seen, the discourse of some social scientists and theologians contributes to this legitimising function. Conflating discourse and reality, several authors have looked for the historical origins of reverse mission – not the origins of the discourse, but the origins of the alleged "reality." Paul Freston cites a statement by Edward Blyden from 1880 saying Africans may one day have a role of re-spiritualising Europe, and he identifies as "reverse missionary" a Jamaican evangelist in Britain in 1880 (Freston, 2010: 157). Similarly, Batatunde Adedibu finds as precursors of Black majority churches and reverse mission in Britain a Black pastor in 1906 and a Black church in 1907 – before the term or idea of reverse mission had ever been thought about (Adedibu, 2013: 95). Both authors thus legitimise and give historical depth to reverse mission as a reality and thereby bolster the claims of actors who use such discourse to reinforce their rights and legitimacy to be in the global North doing missionary work.

The term reverse mission can also have much less favourable moral implications and functions. It can imply a hierarchy between old and new missionaries, evoking obligations of the "younger missionaries" to "older missionaries," such as showing respect or having a duty to learn (rather than claiming knowledge and teaching older missionaries). This meaning has been pushed by several actors in connection with the integration of Christian immigrants and new churches in the global North. Tensions between immigrant Christians and host societies are many – linguistic, ethnic, cultural, and religious (see Masken, 2008; Koning, 2009). Many immigrant Christians and transnational churches see western societies as spiritually deficient and sinful, and they promote a proselytizing and conservative religious stance with little tolerance for liberalism, ecumenism, gender equality, or gay rights (Maxwell, 2007: Ch.7; Koning,

2009: 62; Fancello, 2010). Within such a context, using the term reverse mission can be a way to challenge how immigrants and transnational pastors act in host societies. A comment from the head of the German Association of Protestant Churches and Missions is illustrative:

> Another question is how far we want to accept "reverse mission," conducted by people coming from the global South. Migration is a fact. Churches in the North should be happy and offer hospitality. But some of the churches from the global South describe the commission their members have for mission in the North in a quite aggressive, non-dialogical way. Such views affect people of other faiths, but also Christians living in Germany, especially when, for example, they read on some church websites that "they have lost a lively, committed faith in Christ or never really had one." Missionaries and local churches from the global South sometimes consider these Christians in Germany to have gone in false directions or to be lost, and they see it as their obligation to "save" them. This seems to show that they are not interested in the contextuality of the Christian witness in this country. Because of its conflict potential, this kind of reverse mission is regarded sceptically, not only by local German churches but also by other religious communities and persons of no religious affiliation.
>
> ANDERS, 2014:107

The issues raised in this statement, and others along the same lines, are multiple – truth, orthodoxy, ecclesiastical pluralism, collegiality, co-operation, and Christian unity, among others (see Wahrisch-Oblau, 2000; Simon, 2010; Parris, 2014). Reference to reverse mission allows actors, in this case Northern actors, to frame the discussion in a non-theological way, putting migrant missionaries as guests in a society where they should understand and respect rather than challenge. The need to learn and respect is not just an informal issue for many church leaders and organisations; many ask publically for the re-training of immigrant pastors and missionaries in the global North. In Switzerland, for example, an influential pastor recommended the training of immigrant pastors in "classic courses" of theology, inter-culturality, good management, collegiality (because immigration pastors would be too individualistic), and immigration issues (particularly in relation to their children, the so-called *segundos*) (Hoegger, 2006, 2012).

In the same vein, in 1998, missionary organisations in Germany set up a Program for Cooperation between German and Immigrant Congregations. The first (and main?) task of the program was to put together a list of immigrant congregations in the country so as to establish a list of those deemed adequate and to be able to negotiate for them a legal recognition with the government. As stated by Claudia Wahrisch-Oblau (involved in the program), the ultimate goal was to move immigrant churches from "reverse mission to common mission" (Wahrisch-Oblau, 2000: 474–478; see also Simon, 2010; Parris, 2014). Here, using the term reverse mission allowed Northern Christians to avoid discussing theology, culture, and ecumenism, and instead assert their authority, ask immigrant Christians to respect their "elders," and make an effort to fit in with existing structures and ways of practising faith in the global North – a global North which would have "evolved," if not "progressed," since the times when Northern Christians were themselves engaged in aggressive and un-ecumenical missionary work in the South.

This preliminary analysis of discursive practices suggests the term reverse mission has several functions and meanings which allow actors to intervene in and defend different points of view and positions and to participate in debates of the legitimacy, place, and role of immigrants in evangelisation and the practice of faith in Europe and the Americas. While many immigrant Christians (and their supporters) use reverse mission to assert their position, their legitimacy, and their work in the global North, some Northern Christians use the same term to do the reverse, that is to assert their dominance and to make demands on immigrant Christians (including social and theological re-training). The debate and struggle are most heated when different currents of Christianity are opposed, especially immigrant Pentecostals and established liberal Northern churches.

The polysemy of the term reverse mission which we saw as a scientific problem earlier on (to establish a concept) reveals itself as a strength in practice, as different actors can use the term in different ways, all useful to them, and thus add to the intensity of the debate. More importantly, reverse mission is not just rhetoric or discourse. It is a *performative discourse*, that is, a discourse with a direct impact on reality. It shapes particular understandings of real issues. It shapes policy, whether of states or religious organisations (notably in relation to official recognition and re-training), and it shapes the action and legitimacy of Christians themselves (are they entitled to their own practice and to evangelise?). Just as noted in the literature on discourse analysis, such discourses "contribute to the creation and reproduction of unequal power relations between social groups" (Jørgensen and Phillips, 2002: 63). The fact that the term continues to be used and debated to this day suggests the issues are important for Christians in the North and in the South. It will therefore continue to have currency among religious actors for some time – though hopefully not among social scientists.

Conclusion

What has this investigation uncovered? First, reverse mission represents a discourse on reality used to discuss issues of migration, the evangelisation work of foreigner Christians, and what is proper Christian theology and praxis. Second, the term reverse mission and debates around it emerged in the 1970s after decolonisation led to a rethinking of the relationship between Southern and Northern churches. Third, debates about reverse mission understood as Southern Christians "returning" to the North to do evangelisation work appeared in the 1990s after an increase in the migration of Southerners to the North, the rise of Southern transnational churches, and an alleged "refugee crisis." Fourth, discourse analysis reveals the term reverse mission (or return mission) has several functions within struggles of orthodoxy, power, and identity in faith institutions and practices in the global North. Finally, the term structures perceptions and creates knowledge and meaning which, on the one hand, contribute to social identities and social relations and, on the other hand, structure the action of actors (including churches and states) and change power relations between social groups.

The chapter highlighted also a methodological issue. Many authors conflate discourse and reality and/or use the categories of actors without due care. They align themselves, knowingly or not, with the discourse and the interests of certain actors in the religious field and produce uncritical and unhelpful social sciences. This may be acceptable and unproblematic in a church milieu, but it is un-rigorous social science. To build and practice serious social science, we cannot simply adopt terms used by actors (including theologians) as social scientific concepts. We need to apply "scientific reflexivity" and make an "epistemic break" with the discourse of actors, as recommended by Bourdieu, else we risk not only aligning with certain actors and reinforcing their positions, but also weakening the scientific understanding of the issue at stake.

References

Abram, Faye Y., John A. Slosar, and Rose Walls. 2005. "Reverse mission: a model for international social work education and transformative intra-national practice," *International Social Work* 48(2):161–176.

Adedibu, Batatunde. 2013. "Origin, migration, globalisation and the missionary encounter of Britain's black majority churches," *Studies in World Christian History* 19(1): 93–113.

Adogame, Afe. 2007. "The rhetoric of reverse mission: African Christianity and the changing dynamics of religious expansion in Europe." Draft of lecture for *South moving North: revised mission and its implication* Conference, 26 September, Protestant Landelijk Dienstencentrum, Utrecht.

Allen Jr., John L. 2009. *The future church: how ten trends are revolutionizing the Catholic church*. New York: Image.

Anders, Christoph. 2014. "Christian witness in a multi-religious world: a German perspective," *International Review of Mission* 103(1):103–109.

Anderson, Gerald H. 1974. "A moratorium on missionaries," *Christian Century*, 16 January, accessed 19 November 2009, from http://www.religion-online.org.

Ballif, Edmée. 2014. "Les Africains, origine et avenir de l'Eglise catholique suisse? Réflexions sur les discours des organisateurs du pèlerinage aux saintes et saints d'Afrique à St-Maurice," ethnographiques.org 28, accessed 26 May 2016, from http://www.ethnographiques.org/2014/Ballif.

Blaser, Klauspeter. 1998. "Fait missionnaire: formes et mutations récentes," *Le Fait Missionnaire* 6: 71–107.

Bourdieu, Pierre. 1992. "The practice of reflexive sociology (the Paris workshop)." In *An invitation to reflexive sociology*, edited by Pierre Bourdieu and Löic J.D. Wacquant, 217–260. Cambridge: Polity.

Byrnes, Timothy. 2011. *Reverse mission: transnational religious communities and the making of US foreign policy*. Washington DC: Georgetown University Press.

di Lecce, Franca. 1989. "Etre ensemble l'église." In *Chrétiens d'outre-mer en Europe: un autre visage de l'immigration*, edited by Marc Spindler and Annie Lenoble-Bart, 275–281, Mémoire d'Eglises Series. Paris: Karthala.

Fancello, Sandra. 2010. "'Afrique élève l'Europe.' Pentecôtisme, afrocentrisme et démocratie." In *Chrétiens africains en Europe: prophétismes, pentecôtismes et politique des nations*, edited by Sandra Fancello and André Mary, 206–241. Paris: Karthala.

Freston, Paul. 2010. "Reverse mission: a discourse in search of reality?" *PentecoStudies* 9(2): 153–174.

Hein, Jeremy. 1993. "Refugees, immigrants, and the state," *Annual Review of Sociology* 19: 43–59.

Hoegger, Martin. 2012. "Les besoins en formation théologique des Eglises protestantes: issues de la migration," accessed 22 March 2016, from http://www.dialogueoecumenique.old.eerv.ch/files/Les-besoins-en-formation-the%CC%81ologique-des-Eglises-protestantes-de-la-migration.pdf.

Hoegger, Martin. 2006. "Eglises africaines en Suisse: l'explosion," *Protestinfo*, 29 March, accessed 1 May 2014, from http://protestinfo.ch/200603293485/eglises-africaine-en-suisse-l-explosion.

Jansen, Mechteld. 2016. "Reverse or revised mission: Indonesian and Moluccan immigrant churches in the Netherlands." Paper for ISSRC conference, 9–12 July, Princeton.

Jenkins, Philip. 2011. *The next Christendom: the coming of global Christianity.* Oxford: Oxford University Press.

Jørgensen, Marianne W., and Louise Phillips. 2002. *Discourse analysis as theory and method.* London: Sage.

Kay, William, and Annie Dyer, eds. 2011. *European Pentecostalism.* Leiden: Brill.

Kim, Hun. 2011a. "Receiving mission: reflection on reversed phenomena in mission by migrant workers from the global churches to the western society," *Transformation* 28(1): 62–67.

Kim, Hun. 2011b. "Migrant workers and 'reverse mission' in the west." In *Korean diaspora and Christian mission,* edited by S. Hun Kim and Wunsuk Ma, 146–152. Eugene: Wipf and Stock.

Koning, Danielle. 2009. "Place, space, and authority: the mission and reversed mission of the Ghanaian seventh-day Adventist church in Amsterdam," *African Diaspora* 2(2): 203–226.

Kwiyani, Harvey C. 2014. *Sent forth: African missionary work in the west.* Maryknoll: Orbis Books.

Lopez, Javier. 2004. "'Il n'y a pas d'étrangers dans l'Eglise'? Les missions catholiques espagnoles dans le diocèse de Lausanne, Genève et Fribourg (1960–1980)." MA thesis, Department of History, University of Fribourg, Switzerland.

Mary, André. 2008. "Introduction. Africanité et christianité: une interaction première," *Archives de Sciences Sociales des Religions* 143: 9–30.

Masken, Maïté. 2008. "Migration et pentecôtisme à Bruxelles: expériences croisées," *Archives des Sciences Sociales des Religions* 143: 49–68.

Maxwell, David. 2007. *African gifts of the spirit: Pentecostalism and the rise of a Zimbabwean transnational religious movement.* Oxford: James Currey.

Odem, Mary E. 2004. "Our Lady of Guadalupe in the new south: Latino immigrants and the politics of integration in the Catholic Church," *Journal of American Ethnic History* 24(1): 27–31.

Ojo, Matthews A. 2007. "Reverse mission." In *Encyclopedia of mission and missionaries,* edited by Jonathan J. Bonk, 380–382. London; New York: Routledge.

Olofinjana, Israel. 2010. *Reverse ministry and mission: Africans in the dark continent of Europe.* Milton Keynes: AuthorHouse.

Olofinjana, Israel. 2004. "'Reverse mission: a sign of arrogance or gratitude?" accessed 14 May 2014, from http://www.ethicsdaily.com/reverse-mission-is-it-rhetoric-or-reality--cms-21385.

Parris, Garnet. 2014. "The stranger in our midst: issues of misunderstanding between African migrant churches in Germany and the mainstream German churches." In

The public face of African new religious movements in diaspora: imagining the religious "other," edited by Afe Adogame, 275–286. Farnham: Ashgate.

Pope Paul VI. 1975. "Evengelii nuntiandi: apostolic exhortation of his Holiness Pope Paul VI," accessed 6 April 2016, from http://w2.vatican.va/content/paul-vi/en/apost_exhortations/documents/hf_p-vi_exh_19751208_evangelii-nuntiandi.html.

Porter, Andrew. 2004. *Religion versus empire? British Protestant missionaries and overseas expansion.* Manchester: Manchester University Press.

Prudhomme, Claude. 2004. *Missions chrétiennes et colonisation XVIe–XXe siècles*, Histoire du Christianisme Series. Paris: Le Cerf.

Reese, Robert. 2014. "John Gatu and the moratorium on missionaries," *Missiology* 42(3): 245–256, accessed 23 February 2016, from http://www.edsmither.com/uploads/5/6/4/6/564614/reese_ems_2012.pdf.

Saelee, Terri. 2011. "Migration and adventist mission," *Journal of Adventist Mission Studies* 7(2): 64–74.

Simon, Benjamin. 2010. *From migrants to missionaries: Christians of African origin in Germany.* Bern: Peter Lang.

Smutko, Gregory. 1979. "Reverse mission: consciousness-raising in North America," *Missiology* 7(1): 117–118.

Spindler, Marc, and Annie Lenoble-Bart, eds. 2000. *Chrétiens d'outre-mer en Europe: un autre visage de l'immigration*, Mémoire d'Eglises Series. Paris: Karthala.

Stanley, Brian. 1990. *The bible and the flag: Protestant missions and British imperialism in the nineteenth and twentieth centuries.* Leicester: Apollos.

Stevens, R. Paul, and Brian Stelck. 1993. "Equipping equippers cross-culturally: an experiment in the appropriate globalization of theological education," *Missiology* 21(1): 31–40.

Wahrisch-Oblau, Claudia. 2000. "From reverse mission to common mission...We hope: immigrant protestant churches and the 'programme for cooperation between German and immigrant congregations' of the United Evangelical Mission," *International Review of Mission* 89(354); 467–483.

Wan, Enoch. 2011. "Diaspora missiology in the context of the 21st century," *Transformation: An International Journal of Holistic Mission Studies* 28(1): 3–13.

Wood, Matthew, and Véronique Altglas. 2010. "Reflexivity, scientificity and the sociology of religion: Pierre Bourdieu in debate," *Nordic Journal of Religion and Society* 23(1): 9–26.

CHAPTER 8

"We are Peace-Loving People." Sufism, Orientalist Constructions of Islam and Radicalization

Alix Philippon

Introduction

Axiological neutrality is supposed to be the first commandment of research and teaching in social sciences. However, some objects of research are more prone to axiological discourses, axiomatic assumptions, or even political interferences than others, and that is very much the case with Islam today. Since 9/11, in the framework of the "War on Terror," the various signifiers designating, *a priori*, the more politicised and violent forms of Islamic expression and mobilisation (Islamism, salafism, wahhabism, jihadism) have experienced an unprecedented proliferation, amalgamation, or even vilification in public debates and academic discourses. Conversely, Sufism, the "mystical" trend of Islam, has gradually been idealised as an apolitical and tolerant religious form constituting an ideological alternative to radical Islamism.

The notion of Sufism has never achieved definitional consensus among the community of scholars. Whilst generally associated with a brotherhood organised on the basis of a master/disciple relationship, Sufism can evade this extremely plastic institutional frame. Despite a quietist reputation, Sufi actors and institutions have long been submitted to multiple processes of politicisation, in the sense of requalification in the political field of discourses, practices, and institutions constituted outside it (Lagroye, 2003: 360–361). We can note the involvement of Sufi orders in anticolonial struggles or modern electoral politics, but even so, no generalisation is possible. Some quietist orders have abstained from playing too active a part in the affairs of this world; yet their visibility, popularity, and social functions make them easy prey to public actions or to the actors of policies, and it proves difficult for them to avoid political interferences (Chodkiewicz, 1996: 541).

Therefore, awarding a normative definition to Sufism often implies skipping the complex genealogy of a concept whose uses are recent and highly prone to controversy. It also implies taking the risk of participating in ideological debates without even knowing it (Ernst, 2000: xvi) or being trapped in the tight net of security concerns based on often biased apprehensions of the Islamist object. The instrumentalisation of Sufi actors for neocolonial ends (for western powers) or for political benefits (for the regimes of the Arab and Muslim world) should not be overlooked.

Based on several years of fieldwork in Pakistan, a frontline state in the War on Terror, in this chapter I question the essentialist and ideological biases weighing down contemporary studies of Islam, specifically Sufism. The first part of the chapter addresses common biases in academic and public policy circles. It attempts to understand the underpinnings of such orientations before deciphering how and why the signifier "Sufism" has become the locus of debates among social, religious, and political actors trying to impose the legitimacy of specific meanings. As this section makes clear, the struggles triggered by the definition of the term have historically plunged it into a semantic precariousness. The very category of "Sufism" has been at stake in the public sphere, caught between contending groups. The section concludes with some suggestions on overcoming recurrent methodological problems. The second part more specifically illustrates what I establish in the first part. It plunges into a Pakistani case study showing the radicalisation of the very Sufi actors who have been promoted to combat radicalism in the framework of the War on Terror. Politics, more than theology, is at stake in the processes of radicalisation involving Sufi, as well as Muslim actors more generally. Thus, far from considering Sufism as an ideal phenomenon, the chapter tries to evade the normative approach that often tends to describe more what some would like it to be than what it actually is. I do so by showing how it has been socially instituted and organised according to contentious contexts marked by specific configurations of political power.

Epistemological Issues

Idealisation, Vilification, Essentialisation

Over the last 30 years, Islamism has been a main object of scrutiny for political scientists, but the importance of the role of Sufi orders in the Islamic revival is generally overlooked. Islamism has long been construed as a category antithetic to Sufism, and this perspective has only sharpened since 9/11. A typical discourse on Sufism and Islamism states:

> The Sufi tradition is a movement of devotion and divine rapture focusing on spiritual experiences. It represents a particular creative and liberal dimension of Islam characterised by practiced tolerance, humanism, peace,

and the accommodation of differences.... It can be generally recognised as a "softer" alternative to the authoritarian voices of formal scriptural religion and of Islamist movements.

FREMBGEN, 2007: ix

The idea of the Sufi tradition as an "alternative" to Islamism – or to other more "authoritarian" Islamic movements – and the focus on their opposition rather than their interaction, often postulating their different nature in normative ways, are widespread in specific academic fields, notably Islamic studies and anthropology, even though some publications, more or less recent, have questioned them (Ridgeon, 2015). This is not so surprising, for as Woodward et al. point out:

> The academic literature on Sufism tends to focus on classical texts by Rabi'a al-Adawiyya (713–801), Muhyi'l-Din ibn'l-Arabi (1165–1240), Jalaluddin al-Rumi (1207–1273) and other gnostic Sufis whose major themes were the love of God, the quest for union with the divine and the equivalence of all religions. This orientation is mirrored in the anthropological literature that champions popular *Sufism* for acceptance of local cultures and the role of peaceful *Sufi syechs* and merchants in the spread of Islam.

WOODWARD et al., 2013: 58

It is also worth noting that Muslim scholars (including converts) with a strong Sufi inclination have strengthened the sense of a Sufi/Islamist dichotomy. A collective book by western Muslim scholars mostly specialising in Islamic studies and edited by famous scholar and Sufi shaykh Seyyed Hossein Nasr, *Islam, Fundamentalism and the Betrayal of Tradition*, analyses current issues in the Muslim world and suggests solutions on the basis of Islamic traditional teachings (including Sufism) and the rejection of the modern and ideological versions of Islam ("fundamentalism" and "radical Puritan reformism") propounded by a minority and perceived as having no legitimacy (Lumbard, 2004).

My point is not to say these approaches are necessarily wrong or invalid in the absolute, but they are essentialist, and they might preclude the descriptive analysis required by the complexity and the diversity of the phenomenon. Narrowing Sufism down to merely the traditional mystical trend within Islam that is antithetical to Islamism or Salafism, the "soft core of Islam," a "path of love" (Frembgen, 2009: vii) or even a devotional movement focused on spiritual experiences, does not allow enough leeway for an adequate understanding of its more social and political dimensions as they can be encountered within its institutional form, the Sufi order. In fact, besides their religious function, the Sufi orders have, throughout history, fulfilled various other functions, ranging from economic to military mobilisation.

Sufi orders have often been called on to fuel other forms of mobilisation as well, including Islamism. The structure of the brotherhood, one of the most widespread organisational formats in the Muslim world, has influenced many Islamist movements, such as the Egyptian Muslim Brotherhood or the Pakistani Jama'at-e Islami. As a plastic mobilising structure available to activists, it can be creatively reinvented and put to other uses than a strictly religious one. Hassan Al Banna, founder of the Egyptian Muslim Brotherhood, Abu Ala Mawdudi, founder of the Pakistani Jama'at-e Islami, and Sheikh Abdessalam Yassine, founder of the Moroccan Al Adl wal Ihsan, were all initiated into Sufism before establishing an arm's length relationship with it, albeit in an ambivalent way.

Conversely, pressured by both the constraints of modernity and the attacks of reformists and modernists alike, Sufi orders have operated their own *aggiornamento*. Indeed, whilst Sufi traditions in Islam are not generally acknowledged as compatible with modern life, research has recently made new inroads and called into question this hypothetical incompatibility (Van Bruinessen and Howell, 2007). Admittedly, monographs on certain orders have not generally focused very closely on the political dimension of Sufism, and the political position of Sufis or even the controversy between Sufis and anti-Sufis has garnered little attention from scholars (Sirriyeh, 1999). When it has, the conclusions are sometimes surprising. To provide an example, an academic conference organised in 2002 in Italy, "The role of Sufism and Sufi orders in contemporary Islam: an alternative to political Islam?" gathered together prominent specialists of Sufism (Alexandre Popovic, Thierry Zarcone, Marc Gaborieau, and Itzchak Weissman) who generally give a balanced view of Sufi orders in their respective fields. However, organiser Marietta Stepanyants, a philosopher with obvious normative inclinations, thought it urgent to evaluate the potential of Sufism as an alternative to the danger of fundamentalist Islam. On the one hand, she argued Sufism offers different qualities, such as tolerance, universality, and anti-dogmatism. On the other hand, in a sweeping generalisation reminiscent of some orientalist positions of the 1960s, she concluded:

> Sufism is unable to render real ethical motivations for radical transformations of Islamic societies in conformity with the challenges of our days. In other words, Islamic mysticism can not bring that rethinking of Islam

which can not only defeat fundamentalism, but, what is more essential, will lead the Muslims away from social degradation or backwardness.
    STEPANYANTS, 2003

This is not the same normative conclusion reached by think tanks and governments in their new search for a "good Islam." Sufism has gradually come to be considered by both authoritarian regimes in the Muslim world and western policy makers as a force to be supported and financed to counter the tide of terrorism. In their endeavours to elucidate how Sufism could relate to US foreign policy goals with respect to terrorism, western think tanks have often sought the help of academics. Such scholars mainly belong to the field of religious studies, are well-known orientalist scholars, or are Sufi actors settled in the US. For instance, a report entitled "Understanding Sufi Islam and its potential role in US foreign policy" gives a precise account of a conference hosted in 2003 in Washington by the International Security Program of the Nixon Center. The keynote speakers were famous historian and orientalist Bernard Lewis and deputy leader of the Naqshbandi Haqqani Sufi order Shaykh Muhammad Hisham Kabbani. The latter is described in the report as "the first Muslim leader to warn the United States about the imminent threat posed by Osama bin Laden and the al-Qaeda terrorist network" and the one who "led the Muslim world in immediately condemning the attacks of September 11th" (Baran, 2004). As for the former, his address betrays a normative and essentialist approach to Sufism that deserves to be partially reproduced here:

> But Sufism is remarkable. It offers something better than tolerance. ... There is an Indian Sufi, Shaykh Sarafaddin, who ... says "Offenses against people are worse than offenses against God. If you commit an offense against God, you are not doing God any harm and God can, in his way, forgive you. If you do things against other people, you are doing them real harm which may be irreparable. The question of forgiveness then becomes much more complicated." It seems to me that this is an interesting contribution to the moral debate of the highest value.
>   BARAN, 2005:18

Since then, academic articles on this issue have flourished, exploring how "Sufism" could be "an answer to global terrorism" (Gauri, 2010), "how and why Sufism" could "help combat Islamic extremism" (Jamali, 2012), or how "the support of Sufism" could be "a counterweight to radicalization" (Sedgwick, 2015). As we will see later in the chapter, in the case of Pakistan, the idealisation of Sufism in public policies might actually have had serious counter-productive effects in spreading love and tolerance. For it to be fruitful, unlike what Bernard Lewis thinks, the debate should be much less "moral" and more axiologically neutral and descriptive of socio-political processes.

These essentialist, normative, and/or generalising views of a "good" and a "bad" Islam, have generally given way to convenient *religious* keys to understanding current conflicts that have influenced public policies in both the Muslim world and the West. These ways of defining Islam and Sufism are not harmless; they attempt to define some Muslims as inherently prone to violence and others as predisposed to tolerant and moderate attitudes because of different theological orientations. Furthermore, they tend to view the relations between Sufism and the various forms of reformism as psychomachias, abstract and rival entities, thus obfuscating the numerous forms of interactions between Sufism and Islamism throughout history, as well as the social and political factors that might explain, among others, their modes of action, organisation, and transformation. Hence, they depoliticise both terrorism and Sufism and prevent their sociological analysis.

As Mahmoud Mamdani puts it, "culture talk," that is to say "the predilection to define cultures according to their presumed 'essential' characteristics, especially as regards politics," has some troublesome side effects: it tends "to read Islamist politics as an effect of Islamic civilization" and it "dehistoricizes the construction of political identities" (Mamdani, 2002: 766). Besides being culturalist, such an approach completely conceals the responsibility of western powers' policies in the production of terrorism. And it leads to the construction of largely ahistorical and meaningless categories trying to encapsulate Muslim groups and actors. Thus, the "good Sufi Muslim" is only possible through a negative contrast with the "bad Islam" as embodied in Islamists. However, if some Sufis overcome the "Islam of resentment" (Roy, 1992:242) that Islamism is supposed to be, others do not. They can be as "radical" in their ideology or their modes of action as their purported opponents. They can display a worldview hostile to alternative perspectives, draw sharp boundaries with enemies, or even have recourse to violence. So what are we to do as researchers? Brand these "resentful Sufis" "fake Sufis" or simply ignore them because they have the audacity not to fit in our categories? Obviously not.

Historicising the Category of Sufism

Fundamentally, we should not *a priori* present a monolithic image of Sufism and its relation to society and politics. Constructing it as a homogeneous reality devoid of internal diversity is methodologically problematic. Given the extremely diverse heritage and the great hermeneutic plasticity of Sufism, it seems best to use the word in a descriptive way to avoid getting trapped in one ideological discourse or another. In addition, individuals, groups, and organisations pursuing political objectives can appropriate Sufism differently. Determining the nature of Sufism is an act of power, adding to the already existing power relations marking the politicisation of the very definition of the term that has gradually become the locus of debate between competing groups within the public sphere.

Therefore, defining *ex ante* a hypothetical Sufi essence does not seem to be methodologically satisfying, as we are confronted with tremendous variations in beliefs, practices, institutions, and actors. Similarly, defining Islam has never been a prerequisite for political scientists aiming at deciphering what James Piscatori and Dale Eickelman call "Muslim politics," a symbolic politics translating into debates on the traditions, values, ideas, and institutions making up Islam (Eickelman and Piscatori, 1996). One methodological trick (Becker, 2002) would be to study this phenomenon in the network of relations of the different groups within which these definitions have been constituted and historically used. Sufism has been the successive and ambivalent target of reformism, colonialism, modernism, and more recently Islamism and objectified by being named a new category (Ernst, 2000: 199), making it the subject of a plethora of competing discourses. It is thus essential to historicise the semantic trajectories of the Sufi object within the different discursive strategies of observers, academics, and competing political or religious actors in the Muslim world and beyond.

The word "Sufi" appeared in the 9th or 10th century in Arabic literature to designate the ethical and mystical aims of a growing movement (Ernst, 2000: 20–21). However, the concept of "Sufism" that is supposed to correspond to the Arabic *tasawwuf*, inducing a process of becoming Sufi, has more recent origins and owes its crystallisation into a doctrine (-ism) and its introduction to the academic world to the cultural needs and imperatives of modern Europe. Michel Chodkiewicz (2002: iv) locates its first appearance (*Sufismus*) in a European book in Latin written by a German clergyman, Friedrich August Tholluck, in 1821. For Carl Ernst, the invention of the modern concept of Sufism goes back to the 18th century as "an appropriation of those portions of 'Oriental' culture that Europeans found attractive" (Ernst, 2000: 9). It gradually emerged from the written works of European travellers and orientalists in the exotic image of a sect having little relation with Islam (Ernst, 2000: 9). The dance, music, and poetry of these Sufi "freethinkers" were reminiscent of an abstract philosophy closer to Christianity or Greek philosophy than to the faith set up by Muhammad. Interestingly, this distinction between Sufism and Islam is still popular today, notably, but not only, in New Age publications. However, those who started to be designated as Sufis from the 9th century onward have mostly defined themselves as belonging to the Islamic tradition.

Conversely, in the Indian subcontinent, the figure of the saint, whether a Hindu *sadhu* or a Muslim *fakir*, became the target of a negative orientalism. Because of their indifference to colonial authority and because they themselves were alternative sources of authority, these "wandering dervishes" became the symbolic instruments of a hegemonic policy aiming at building an inferior colonised culture and identity. The orientalist discourse tried to neutralise and ridicule these subversive holy figures by creating the myth of a golden age of "true" spirituality safely located in the past. It helped delegitimise the contemporary mystical actors who bore the stigma of corruption and were perceived as having no relation to "pure" and "pristine" Sufism (Ewing, 1997: 62–63). Some elements of this colonial discourse have been appropriated by Muslim actors and have played a role in the ideological debates of the creation and identity of Pakistan, founded in the name of Islam, which was partitioned from India in 1947 (Ewing, 1997: 47–49).

In a different geographical context, notably in Maghreb, far from being belittled for their "charlatanism," Sufi actors who mobilised against the colonial invaders were criminalised. There was a time when the "Islamic peril" was not identified with Salafi Jihadists, such as Osama Bin Laden or Abu Umar al-Baghdadi, but with the leaders of Sufi orders who spearheaded the resistance to European powers. In the context of colonialism, the term Sufism resonated as a threat, a "fanatic resistance" to European domination (Triaud, 1995: 19). The "brotherhood peril" gradually became the new European concept, fuelled by the fashionable model of the "politico-religious secret society" (Triaud, 1995: 12). The category of "Muslim brotherhood" suggested a society with secret and subversive objectives. From India to Algeria, Sufi orders leading jihads against colonial powers became the objects of the paranoia of European administrations (Triaud, 1995: 19). Ironically, later French studies on maraboutism in Maghreb elaborated an influential theory portraying Sufism as completely opposed to fundamentalism, thus ignoring the role of these orders in reislamisation (Roy, 1992: 47).

Since the 1950s and 1960s, Sufi orders have been relegated to the backyard of history and assimilated in the academic world as non-objects of folkloric or historical interest only (Coulon, 1981: 2). Sufism has been analysed as a dying rural tradition of Muslim societies confronted by social change and as a backward force unable to adapt to the social and political conditions of modernity. One of the most influential analyses of the era is by Michael Gilsenan (1973) on Egypt. In his view, Sufi orders' only functions in the new circumstances of modernity are the maintenance of security and stability of tradition in a hostile new world and the granting of religious status to all those lacking social standing; in short, a crutch for those who cannot keep up with modernity. For Gilsenan or Trimingham (1971), Sufis, even the most reformist ones, are "about to leave" the social scene, as they are outstripped on the field of social and political mobilisation by Islamist movements.

Muslim elites of postcolonial states converting to western models of development and the hegemonic discourse opposing tradition and modernity have often appropriated scientific western theses and anti-Sufi Islamist discourses, postulating the inadequacy of Sufi orders in the face of modernity. However, the West and its allies from the South have not been the only ones to objectivise "Sufism" and the Sufi consciousness; Muslim reformists have done the same.

As early as the 18th century, often presented as a dark era in Islamic history, in reaction to the feeling of moral and intellectual decline and to the dynamics of political fragmentation and weakening, Islamic orthodox renewal movements tried to formulate an ideological response to the ills of their community. In their bid to purify Islam from all "blameable" innovations leading to the Islamic decline, and in their ambition to reform the faithful to become true Muslims, they called for a rejection of Sufism. It was identified as the traditionalist pole of Muslim societies, as a cultural accretion dragged along by history and as a deviation from the authentic Islam of the golden age. The controversy surrounding Sufism continued to swell, leading in the 19th century "to a greater variety of self-questioning among Muslims" (Sirriyeh, 1999: ix). Modern Islamist movements, as the heirs of earlier reformist actors, have often stigmatised Sufism as a sort of traditionalism outside Islam and a withdrawal from the political sphere. For numerous Islamist leaders and theoreticians, Sufism is responsible for the stagnation and decline of Islam throughout history (Burgat, 1988: 16). Yet interactions between Sufism and Islamism can be observed throughout the Muslim world.

At any rate, a rhetoric of decline, decadence, and, at times, downright condemnation has long dominated the public discourse on "Sufism," particularly concerning the system of meaning and practices centred on shrines, Sufi saints, and their much criticised descendants, and still more specifically, on the cult of the saints. However, analysing Sufism only as a doctrinal position would be incomplete and inaccurate. Admittedly, there are rivalries among competing interpretations of Islam, but competing authorities searching for popular legitimacy and attempting to constitute their own clientele are also implicated. Carl Ernst rightly points out that whereas the controversy is formulated in a doctrinal language, the struggle is actually a political one

(Ernst, 2000:79). If Islamists, among others, have often identified Sufis as their "enemies," it might also be because Sufis have been powerful institutional actors within Muslim societies, making them potent rivals in any bid to reform the sociopolitical order.

Analysing Sufism as a Tradition and a Symbol

To avoid essentialist constructions, Sufism may be analysed as a "tradition" and as a "symbol." Both are useful conceptual tools to analyse the competing discourses and debates in the public sphere, notably those centring on religious legitimacy, authority, and identity, and to examine the power relations inherent in and conflicts surrounding the definition of what it means to be a Sufi. Tradition is all about language games and practices allowing individuals to construct themselves as subjects, but a political community can also constitute itself by reinventing the meanings encapsulated in a tradition. Far from being a static universe of meaning and action, "tradition" is mobile. It enables the researcher to conceptually view politics as the creation of new semantic uses for the key terms of a tradition and their constant recycling in new language games to render possible new forms of life (Mouffe, 1994: 39). Talal Asad proposes the notion of "discursive tradition" be applied to the study of Islam:

> A tradition consists essentially of discourses that seek to instruct practitioners regarding the correct form and purpose of a given practice that, precisely because it is established, has a history.... An Islamic discursive tradition is simply a tradition of Muslim discourse that addresses itself to conceptions of the Islamic past and future, with reference to a particular Islamic practice in the present.
>
> ASAD quoted in ZAMAN, 2004:6

This could equally apply to the study of Sufism.

Sufism could also be apprehended as a symbol, in the sense suggested by Philippe Braud (1996) in his work on emotions in politics. A symbol never possesses a single meaning that needs to be uncovered. It is uncertain, fluid, and ambiguous, and it gives way to competing interpretations. It is a signifier that is efficient in mobilising powerful emotional projections. This efficiency can be analysed through the capacity to structure social issues and societal concerns, (de)legitimise social powers, and mobilise supports and resources.

Sufism in the Muslim world has proved diversely efficient in structuring social issues, offering a repertoire to articulate political claims and mobilise for collective action. As a prominent repertoire of Islamic language, Sufism has been a component of identity politics, used by groups and individuals to negotiate and articulate their identity, often in highly inconsistent ways. It has been tapped as a political resource and instrumentalised as a legitimising tool by state and non-state actors. Generally speaking, it has played a role in ideological debates on the place of Islam in the state and society in the Muslim world. As the contested so-called "mystical" aspect of faith, it has become part of the "ideologisation of Islam" and represents a fertile approach to "Muslim politics."

The language of Islam, its normative codes, and its symbols have been used in the Muslim world in conflicting ways by actors willing to take part in political life and participate in debates in the public sphere. This has led to a great "fragmentation of authority" (Eickelman and Piscatori, 1996: 58), even to violence, as no one has the monopoly on the "right" interpretation of Islam. Even so, more and more actors feel legitimised to speak in its name. Muslim symbolic politics often implies the construction of identity frontiers between contending actors.

In the next section, I turn to Pakistan where rivalries have set certain Islamist groups against others and/or the state in a complex dynamics of politicisation of Islam from the bottom up and from the top down. In this process, Pakistan has become a dangerous field where violence, be it "proactive" or "reactive," is a widely used political repertoire and where interactions between contending actors seeking power and influence in the name of Islam do not always occur through compromises and negotiations. Rather, the symbolic politics of Islam has hardened the constitution of identity frontiers between antagonistic actors. The section focuses on the Barelwi movement, as it is rooted in the Sufi tradition and, at the same time, is an active player in the Islamist field.

Sufi Politics in Pakistan

The Barelwi Movement in the Islamist Field

Within the Pakistani Islamist field, comprised mainly of the Deobandi Jamiyyat-e Ulama-e Islam (JUI), the Jama'at-e Islami (JI), and the Barelwi Jamiyyat-e Ulama-e Pakistan (JUP), the Barelwi[1] movement has most loudly proclaimed its affiliation to a Sufi identity. Often overlooked by scholars, this theological school was founded in the 19th century in colonial India in reaction to the "orthodox" assaults of reformist movements, such as the Deobandis

---

1   The Barelwis also call themselves Ahl-e Sunnat Wal Jama'at, "the people of the Tradition of the prophet and of the community of believers."

and the Ahl-e Hadith. Usually presented merely as a counter-crusade against the repeated attacks against Sufis (*pirs*) and shrines, or as a passionate defence of the Sufi status quo, this movement can be considered a reform movement in itself. As historian Usha Sanyal points out in one of the only monographs devoted to the Barelwis to date, the founder Ahmed Reza Khan "promoted reformist religious methods in order to enable his disciples to become better traditionalists" and "more individualistic" (Sanyal, 2006:xii). This movement has played a widely ignored role in the politics of Pakistan, through party politics, social movements, and the Islamisation of society (Philippon, 2011). This section draws on fieldwork conducted in Pakistan from 2004 to 2009 during which I carried out numerous interviews and performed participant observation of Barelwi groups.

In the 1940s, within the framework of an organisation called the All India Sunni Conference, Barelwi *pirs* and *ulamas* supported the movement for Pakistan led by nationalist leader Muhammad Ali Jinnah. Even today, the Barelwis consider themselves key nationalist actors, unlike the Deobandis who were generally not in favour of the creation of Pakistan. In the newly created state, the Barelwi politico-religious group of reference is the Jamiyyat-e Ulama-e Pakistan founded in 1948. Up to the 1970s, it remained a religious pressure group supportive of the elites in power. In the 1970s, it became an oppositional party under the dynamic leadership of Shah Ahmed Nurani, a Sufi, *alim*, and politician in his own right, who remained head of the party until his death in 2003. Throughout the 1970s, the JUP earned more votes and seats in the Assembly than the Jama'at-e Islami, becoming a notable political force thanks to its connections to the *madrasas*, shrines, and *pirs* of Penjab and Sindh. However, it went into decline in the 1980s in the context of the Zia-ul Haq regime, which promoted a more Deobandi form of Islam and marginalised the Barelwis, for example, by barring them from participating in the jihad in Afghanistan against Soviet troops.

From this decade onward, new Barelwi organisations have proliferated in Pakistan, partly because of the fragmentation of the movement and partly in reaction to its marginalisation in favour of Deobandi Islam. The first two organisations were created in 1981: the Minhaj-ul Quran founded by the Sufi and *alim* Tahir-ul Qadri in Lahore and the Dawat-e Islami founded by the Sufi and *alim* Ilyas Qadri in Karachi. They remain the most popular religious and revivalist Barelwi organisations. In 1990, a disciple of Ilyas Qadri, Saleem Qadri, created the Sunni Tehreek, a sectarian group that considers violence a legitimate tool to respond to Deobandi violence, defend the Barelwi creed, and take control of some Deobandi mosques.

As their names indicate, the founders of these organisations belong to the Qadiriyya, one of the main four Sufi orders in Pakistan (the others are the

Surhawardiyya, Chishtiyya, and Naqshbandiyya). Hence, we cannot apply Hervé Bleuchot's (1996) sociological explanation of Sufi politicisation to the Sufi orders in Pakistan. Looking at the case of Sudan, he asks why the two Sufi orders engaging in politics by creating a party were the reformist Mahdiyya and Khatmiyya and not the others. He believes the internal features of the orders allowed them to elaborate a "differential sociology." According to him, the degree of mysticism, secularisation, and involvement in the world, which he calls the "nature of the order," depends on the thoughts of the founder and the rules and traditions he establishes. Bleuchot says the main aim of the Qadiriyya is the love of God, not a terrestrial mission.

However, this essentialist approach fails to explain the politicisation of the Qadiriyya in other settings, such as Pakistan. Indeed, as we have seen, many of the shaykhs of the Barelwi revival in the 1980s belonged to the Qadiriyya. In this case, the "entrepreneurs of salvation goods," including the charismatic leaders, the sociopolitical grievances, the resources of the organisations, and the structure of political opportunities, played a larger role in the politicisation of the movement than the "nature" of the Qadiri order. They were much more involved in the affairs of this world than Bleuchot suggests. In other words, we must be careful not to freeze the features of a given order, as these may take on different forms, functions, and contents in different contexts. As Hobsbawm and Ranger show, traditions can be invented or quite recent in history, even though they "use history as a legitimator of action and cement of group cohesion" (Hobsbawm and Ranger, 1983: 12). Therefore, social movement theory, as well as the sociology of collective action and mobilisation, could be of great help to analyse Sufi orders. As John O. Voll argues, "In general terms, one might view the whole effort to maintain an authentic sense of Islamic faith and identity in the dramatically new contexts of modernity as a 'social movement'" (2007: 284)

The form of authority exercised by these Barelwi leaders, at least Tahir-ul Qadri and Ilyas Qadri, is a charismatic one; that is to say, their devotees believe them to be the "heirs of the Prophet," endowed with Baraka and the ability to win salvation on the Day of Judgment. Interestingly, the names of these groups do not allude to their Sufi identity. As a matter of fact, they do not always recruit solely on the basis of the *qadiri* identity, nor do they systematically impose the oath of allegiance with the Sufi master which is compulsory in most Sufi orders. Whilst claiming to be the representatives of the majority of Sufi Islam (the cult of Sufi saints and the Prophet), Barelwi actors feel they have paradoxically become a political minority. Throughout history, they have stigmatised other Sunni sects (the Deobandis and Ahl-e Hadith) as deviant religious "minorities" who are deemed responsible for "terrorism" and patronised by the state.

Thus, the enemy is clearly identified as part of the "Wahhabi" trend, thereby promoting a purified Islam rejecting traditions and customs associated with Sufism. But despite their hostile discourse when speaking of their Deobandi or Ahl-e hadith counterparts, these Barelwi groups have actually imitated them. The Dawat-e Islami has asserted itself as the Barelwi counterpart of the fundamentalist Deobandi Tablighi Jama'at, one of the biggest Islamic preaching movements in the world. The efficient organisational model of the Jama'at-e Islami has been emulated by the Minhaj-ul Quran. The reformist positions of Tahir-ul Qadri are such that he has been marginalised by other Barelwi groups and is often presented as the "Mawdudi[2] of the Barelwis." The Sunni Tehreek's radical modes of action are also a novelty among Barelwis, making it a foil to the most sectarian "Wahhabi" groups. All these groups claim to be very orthodox and to follow the Quran and the Tradition (*sunna*) of the Prophet. In addition, most are located in urban centres and can compete directly with their rivals. They mostly recruit among the urban middle-classes. These "neo Sufi orders" (Roy, 2002) have developed different strategies to defend their version of Islam and fight for an Islamic State, an endeavour they call the system of the Prophet (*Nizam-e Mustafa*). Today, there are dozens of Barelwi organisations differently involved in processes of politicisation, protest, and radicalisation.

To designate such groups, like the Barelwis, claiming Sufism and Sufi identity as a register for Islamist mobilisation, I have coined the concept "Sufislamism." Besides enabling an enhanced analysis of the various interactions between Sufism and Islamism, this concept may improve our understanding of the highly fissile politicisation of the doctrinal fractures inside the Islamist field in Pakistan, thus helping to chart the deep waters of identity politics, especially those relevant to "intra-Sunni sectarianism."

Sufism has taken on an ideological dimension among new organisations, formalising their doctrinal differences to transform their specific religious identity into a political resource and a sectarian stance. As a matter of fact, the Barelwi movement is scripted into the sectarian dynamics that have grown in Pakistan since the 1980s. Islamism in Pakistan should be conceptualised as a "field" if we apply Pierre Bourdieu's seminal concept of a field as a complex and conflicting political space of positions, including both alliances and common stakes but also competition (Bourdieu, 2002: 113).

Surprisingly enough, the Barelwi movement has been identified by the US and successive Pakistani governments as a potential ally in the fight against terrorism since 9/11. A delegation of Barelwi leaders was welcomed in Washington

---

2   Abu Ala Mawdudi is the founder of the Jama'at-e Islami and is considered one of the most influential Islamist ideologues in the Muslim world.

in April 2010; the group met representatives of the State Department, Department of Defense, Congress, USAID, think tanks, and NGOs (Mirahmadi et al., 2010). This initiative was launched by a NGO called WORDE (World Organization for Resource Development and Education); it argued that only a partnership with the Barelwi networks, leaders and institutions in Pakistan would lead to a long term solution to terrorism. In WORDE's view, the legitimacy of the Barelwis as a "moderate religious voice," their deep insertion in the social fabric through their networks of madrasas, mosques, and shrines, and their will to eradicate the threat of Talibanisation made them natural "allies" of the United States, especially as the US was facing an unusually high level of anti-Americanism and looking to change its image in Pakistan. WORDE suggested offering financial help to Barelwi institutions to empower them and strengthen their legitimacy in the face of jihadi networks that had proved efficient in building their support base by providing social services to the most disenfranchised citizens.

At the same time, Sufism was being promoted by the Musharraf regime as an alternative to radical Islamism (Philippon, 2014). This attempt to redefine Sufism along liberal, modern, and moderate lines in order to show an "enlightened" version of Islam to the world did not receive an enthusiastic welcome in all Sufi quarters. Being a "moderate" Sufi Muslim was clearly understood by some Pakistani Sufi actors as being a supporter of US foreign policy. And as matter of fact, after 9/11, the distinction between "moderate" and "radical" assumed a specific meaning linked to security concerns. As Ahmad points out, moderates are those with whom the West can do business, whereas radicals are generally those who are reluctant to cooperate (Ahmad, 2010: 6). A disciple of a Naqshbandi order says:

> Sufism has become Washington's agenda. They think Sufism will take people away from violent struggles, that it will liberalize them, modernize them, but it is not so. Sufism will only bring you closer to Islam. It will make you more radical, more fundamentalist.
>
> Interview with the author, December 2006, Lahore

Besides being a striking example of the antagonistic representations of Sufism in contemporary Pakistan, these contradictory views illustrate the way Sufism has been politicised: those in power have an interest in politicising practices, issues, or even social mobilisations that might become resources for their specific activities and goals (Lagroye, 2003: 366). However, this approach ignores the complex religious sociology of Pakistan. Barelwis are not at all as "liberal" or "moderate" as they are currently portrayed.

The emergence of the Barelwi School in the 19th century can be explained in relational terms, as a reaction to the Deobandi and Ahl-e Hadith schools' adoption of more reformist positions. An interactionist approach can also guide analysis of the movement in the late 20th and early 21st century, notably its sectarian expression. An analysis of ethnicity, understood as a form of social interaction and as a process of opposition between insiders and outsiders, seems relevant as well. It shows how identity construction and identification with a community of belonging can operate through an allocation of otherness. In this approach, a "constitutive exterior" (Mouffe, 1994:13) is understood to help build identity. As Mouffe notes, the intervention of the external other in identity construction explains

> the permanence of antagonism as well as its conditions of emergence. Indeed, in the realm of collective identifications – where it is about creating a *we* through the delimitation of a *them* – there is always the possibility of this relation we/them transforming into a friend/enemy relation, so it can become the locus of an antagonism. The other ... starts being perceived as negating our identity and as questioning our very existence.
> MOUFFE, 1994:13

This approach sheds light on sectarian dynamics and the potential passage to violence.

Radicalisation of the Barelwi Movement

Barelwi leaders define Sufism as the tolerant face of Islam and present themselves as peaceful actors who have never been responsible for the violence plaguing Pakistan. As a matter of fact, the majority of Pakistani radical groups, whether sectarian or jihadi, are not Barelwi. Apart from the prominent Barelwi leader Nurani who encouraged his disciples to perform jihad in Afghanistan as early as 2001 (this rapprochement with Taliban was not appreciated by other Barelwi actors), or certain jihadi groups in Kashmir and some militant ones in the tribal areas, the Sunni Tehreek is probably the only example of a massively militarised organisation among the Barelwis. As a result, the Wahhabis are denounced as the "real culprits" and the only actors in the current wave of "terrorism." Sufi identity is claimed as a major criterion discriminating "them" and "us." In this view, Sufis belonging to other schools are considered impostors, pretending to be Sufis but cooperating with other sectarian and jihadi groups, as well as with the Taliban and Al Qaeda.

In contrast, the leaders of the Sunni Tehreek (ST) appeal to their Sufi identity to clear their name of "Wahhabi terrorism," despite radical modes of action. Their violence is portrayed as defensive or reactive:

> The Sunni Tehreek is not a terrorist organization. We are the followers of the Sufis, we have never been terrorists in the past and never will be in the future. We are peace-loving people. We simply protect our religion and our mosques.
>
> MOHAMMAD SHAHEED GHAURY, ST Central Executive Committee, interview, May 2008, Islamabad

The ST was created in 1990 in Karachi by Saleem Qadri; its official aim is to defend the Barelwi school "practically." Among other things, this aim implies defending the mosques belonging to the Barelwi sect. The sectarian dimension of this group is detectable in its name: the Sunni Movement, with "Sunni" meaning "Barelwi." The paranoid world vision of the ST centres on sectarian affiliation, in fact, and the group has been placed under surveillance in the context of the War against Terror. It is also involved in the urban guerrilla warfare in Karachi against "Wahhabi" groups and against the secular Mohajir party, the Muttahida Qaumi Movement, an organisation perceived by the ST as the invisible hand behind the bomb attack that killed its whole leadership in February 2006, along with 60 other people.

Saleem Qadri was not educated in a Barelwi mosque and was not a religious scholar. Generally speaking, therefore, the group's militants are not limited to religious scholars and laymen identifying with the Barelwis. The three successive leaders of the ST, Saleem Qadri, Abbas Qadri and Serwat Qadri, were businessmen but also disciples of the leader of Dawat-e Islami, Ilyas Qadri, making them members of the Qadiriyya Sufi Order.

Before being directed towards one of the three branches of the organisation, each new member of the ST benefits from a general formation bordering on indoctrination, where he has to listen to numerous recorded speeches of the leader (known as "the voice of the Ahl-e Sunnat"). Then, the profile of the member is assessed, and he is sent to one of the departments, three of which are politics, welfare, and preaching (*tabligh*).

The preaching section educates members in religious matters: they take Kuranic lessons, get to know the commentaries on the Koran (*tafsir*), and study its translation into Urdu. They help organise religious events such as the celebration of the birth of the Prophet (*milad-e mustapha*) or gatherings for religious causes such as *Tahafuz namuz-i risalat*, the protection of the prestige of the prophet:

> The Jews and the Christians insult our Prophet a lot. They write literature
> against our religion, and they make caricatures. We want to put an end
> to these things, and if we have to make use of force, we are ready to give
> our lives for that.
>
> Internal brochure, "Aims of ST"

The preaching department also proposes 15 days of religious education at the
provincial and city levels.

The welfare department comprises the service committee (*khidmat*), located in the headquarters of the ST in Karachi. It operates thanks to compulsory alms-giving (*zakat*) and the charity of the Ahl-e Sunnat, but also, as is the
case of numerous other Islamic charities, thanks to the sale of the leather from
animals sacrificed during the religious feast of '*eid*. This committee takes care
of orphans, has created a computer institute, has founded religious schools
(madrasas) to educate poor children, and has built a hospital in Karachi. The
committee also pays the dowry of future brides, distributes wheat and rice to
the poor, and is planning to build a library.

Despite its origins as a social and religious movement, the ST has attempted
to move into the political arena. In 2002, its leadership decided to participate
in the general elections in Karachi to "serve the Ahl-e Sunnat, even in politics"
(Alvi Haider, interview, May 2008, Pindi). The will to "change the system of the
country" is thought possible only through "the power of the ballots" (Serwat
Ejaz Qadri, open letter). The manifesto of the party aims at establishing a "true
Islamic Welfare State" and promoting "national harmony" and "brotherhood"
among people, but will not compromise on the "ideology of Pakistan," whereby
"all Muslims are considered as a nation." Once the group is in power, the manifesto says, all laws contradicting this ideology will be amended or nullified.
Whilst the manifesto aims at working for "harmony," it also aims at protecting
"the real faith and real Islamic rights," that is to say, the faith and rights of the
Ahl-e Sunnat. It says, "All the anti-Islamic forces leading people astray" will be
combated. We can recognize these "forces" as the "Wahhabis."

In essence, the ST founder, Saleem Qadri, perceived the political dimension
of the plight of Barelwis in Pakistan and wanted to commit more actively and
more violently to the defense of his school of thought. Qadri and his followers saw the Barelwis as too accommodating and unconscious of the danger of
disappearance. As explained by a cadre:

> The Ahl-e Sunnat thought: "if someone occupies our mosques, it doesn't
> matter, we will build new ones." But this is not the solution. The ST thinks

that those who occupy our mosques and our shrines can change people's ideology.

ALVI HAIDER, interview, May 2008, Pindi

Hence, the ST is a group on the defensive, ready to sacrifice for "the rights of the Ahl-e Sunnat":

> The main difference between Sunni Tehreek and other Barelwi groups is that we defend all the groups which are only doing preaching. We preach but we also defend the Ahl-e Sunnat. Wherever Ahl-e Sunnat groups or people need us, we go.
>
> ALVI HAIDER, interview, May 2008, Pindi

In an "open letter" to his followers (literature internal to the organization), Saleem Qadri expresses his ambition to mobilise more people to confront the "enemies" and save future generations from the disappearance of their school of thought. Qadri evokes the Prophet, who is venerated by the Barelwis, to justify the expansion of his organisation and to galvanise his readers:

> If we don't do anything, these people [the Wahhabis] will win against us and will change the young generations. When I see these things, my heart bleeds. We are facing numerous problems so, my friends, wake up! If one suffers, he cannot sleep. If I have the power, I will wake all of you up. In this predicament, I need people who are willing to give their lives and I need brave people who can solve these problems by force. Those who are ready to sacrifice their lives must create problems to these people and threaten them. My brothers, if we love the Prophet and are his servants, then we will open our movement to the whole world to lighten it up and we will preach concerning our school. I pray God that He gives us a chance. We will take our responsibilities in the right path and will defend our school from our enemies. We will also defend those who are led astray. So that in the Day of Judgment, we will be able to give answers to God and the Prophet.
>
> SALEEM QADRI, open letter

The emotional dimension of Qadri's commitment is clear in his rhetoric. "My heart bleeds" is an expression repeated by militants when they explain what inspired them to commit themselves to the Sunni Tehreek. One says, "I wanted to become a member of ST after hearing the speeches of Saleem Qadri.

My heart softened for ST" (Alvi Haider, interview, May 2008, Pindi). Saleem
Qadri's rhetoric and the group's resources seduced potential recruits; the STs'
intentions and its modes of action became radicalised, and its militants were
absolutely committed, ready to die for the cause of the Ahl-e Sunnat.

In 2001, Saleem Qadri was killed in an attack that provoked riots in the already unstable city of Karachi. Hundreds of young Barelwis, some of them
masked, poured into the streets soon after Qadri's death was announced; they
set on fire and threw stones at cars. Qadri's funeral gathered a huge crowd, the
biggest of the kind for a very long time (20,000 people according to official
sources, 30,000 according to journalistic sources). This pointed to the growing importance of a phenomenon that had so far gone unnoticed: the great
capacity for mobilisation of Barelwi groups. The ST ended up with a martyred
leader, thus empowering the group to strengthen the cause of Barelwis. In an
open letter to the Ahl-e Sunnat, Abbas Qadri, the successor to Saleem Qadri,
presents the martyrdom of the ST founder as an enviable destiny, an ideal for
every militant to emulate in order to exterminate the "enemies":

> The Sunni Tehreek counts many martyrs, especially our leader Saleem
> Qadri. These people are lovers of the prophet. These people are brave,
> they have walked in front of Wahhabis and Deobandis with defiance....
> Even if an enemy of Ahl-e Sunnat is alive, we are ready to fight with him
> until death.... You have to work hard to reach the aim of our martyred
> amir (leader). We have to complete his mission, and work night and day.
> Let us pray that God will defend us and will help us to complete our mis-
> sion so that we can recover our rights.
>   ST propaganda literature

The Sunni Tehreek is not exactly a "moderate" group. However, in May 2009
during the yearly festival of the Sufi saint Shah Rukn-e Alam, Pakistan's Foreign
Minister officially announced the mobilisation of the Barelwis against the
"Talibanisation" of the country. Several meetings organised by the government
had already taken place with the leaders of the ST and other Barelwi groups
to encourage them to lead a social movement against the insurgents of the
Swat Valley in the north of the country (Rasul Bakhsh Rais, Professor in Political Science, LUMS University, interview, July 2009, Islamabad). The insurgents
belonged to the Taliban Movement of Pakistan (Tehreek-e Taliban Pakistan)[3]

---

3 The genesis of this movement goes back to 2003, with the first intrusions of the Pakistani army in tribal areas to hunt the Afghan Taliban and al-Qaeda militants. But in 2007,
   the movement came into its own as an entity, under the leadership of Beitullah Mehsud.

and were suspected of being close to al-Qaeda. The militants wanted to impose a judicial system founded on Islamic law, the *sharia*. The day following Qureishi's speech, the Sunni Tehreek demonstrated in Peshawar; this was followed by the launching of the campaign "Save Pakistan" by Barelwi forces, just before a Barelwi eight-party alliance was formed.

Feeling threatened by the Taliban phenomenon, Barelwi leaders have tried to formulate a common platform. The Taliban insurrection in the north allowed the convergence of Barelwi sectarian interests with government and military interests. In fact, the radical militants have targeted not only official figures and institutions but also Sufi leaders and shrines. Barelwi actors close to the regime are waging a semantic and identity battle over the definition of "real Islam." The state is manipulating sectarian conflicts between the Barelwis and Deobandis to strengthen its fight against radical Islam, even though some Barelwi actors might be just as "radical" as their Deobandi counterparts. Conversely, this war serves the interests of the Barelwis in their own fight against those identified as terrorists. Although the Barelwis are anti-imperialists, the struggle against western powers and their collaborators has been monopolised by their challengers. Hence, the Barelwis have prioritised the sectarian struggle and instrumentalised the state to strengthen their position in the Islamist field – as much as they have been instrumentalised by it.

Nevertheless, apart from the Sunni Tehreek, armed radicalism remains relatively unimportant among Barelwi groups who unanimously reject suicide attacks and privatised jihad. So how are we to analyse this differential use of violence between the Barelwis and their challengers? Is the explanation to be found in the different ways Islam has been turned into a political ideology? Maybe, but only if we consider that hermeneutics and ideology are at least partly the results of an identity constructed through interactions with other groups and in larger contexts. The doctrinal element is a legitimising tool used in identity strategies aiming at distinguishing the "enemies" according to a specific position in the political field. As Bourdieu writes: "The principle of taking a position is linked to the occupation of a position in a space of positions" (Bourdieu, 2000). Contending interests are defined inside the political field. It is the structure of oppositions and relations that matters. A stand can only be understood relationally, in the difference from and the "distinctive gap" with the challenger.

The radical circles in Pakistan seem to be multi-organisational comprised of dozens of more or less autonomous groups (Pashtuns, Penjabi, and foreign militants) but they share common strategic, financial, and even ideological interests.

What would the Barelwi groups have become if they had benefitted early on, like the Deobandis, from the foreign funding of Saudi Arabia and the patronage of the Pakistani state? The existence of armed groups is an indication of the radical potential of the Barelwis. This has remained limited partly because of identity constraints, but also because Barelwi actors lacked the symbolic (legitimisation of their functioning by the state) and material resources that allowed their challengers to flourish in the 1980s. In short, "policy makers and policy-oriented scholars would be well advised to abandon the quest for theological roots of violence and theological tools for combating it" (Woodward et al., 2013: 77).

Conclusion

> Could it be that a person that takes his or her religion literally is a potential terrorist? That only someone who thinks of a religious text as not literal, but as metaphorical or figurative, is better suited to civic life and the tolerance it calls for?
>
> MAMDANI, 2002:767

I respond to this slightly ironic question, alluding to the Sufi/Salafi dichotomy and their purported differential approaches to violence, with a resounding no. By shifting the focus from doctrine and culture to history and politics as Mamdani suggests, I have shown in this chapter that this idealised category of Sufism is a western product that has changed meanings in history according to the needs and imperatives of the West with regards to its colonies or neo-colonies. I have deconstructed an approach that has contaminated studies on political Islam by over-emphasising ideology and doctrine and building on the opposition between good and bad Muslims. This culturalist/essentialist bias has often led to the depoliticisation of both Sufism and violent activism, but neither can be reduced to its ideological/doctrinal components: "Violence is part of a process and is an ever-evolving option, constrained by a number of variables that are not principally ideological" (Bonnefoy, Burgat, and Ménoret, 2011: 128).

My focus on the Barelwi movement in Pakistan highlights at least three ideas: first, Sufi actors and groups can fight for the establishment of an Islamic State and be part of the Islamist field; second, the radicalisation process and the recourse to violent modes of action can take place within movements officially promoted because they are considered "Sufi" (i.e. tolerant, peaceful, moderate etc.); third, this process of radicalisation can be apprehended partly as identity politics and partly as counter-violence in response to perceived structural discrimination (an Islamisation from the top down, marginalising Barelwi Islam). But this political frame of "good Sufism" is not only a fantasy of the West or of an illegitimate regime in search of political resources and allies. It is also manifest amongst the Barelwi actors themselves when they highlight the tolerant dimension of the message of Sufi saints. They may have internalised western policy makers' discourses on Sufism, but the use of violence constitutes a criterion of identity distinguishing them from the "Wahhabi."

More generally, at the level of the larger Muslim world, neither Sufism nor Islamism is a static entity immutably locked in a specific trend. Many mainstream Islamist parties reject recourse to violence and have undergone a process of "embourgeoisement," whilst some Sufi actors and groups have undergone a process of politicisation or even radicalisation. These evolutions have to be understood with the help of variables that have nothing to do with Islam *per se*. Political, social, and cultural claims might be hiding behind religious slogans and their screening effects. Doctrine is often secondary, falling behind such profane factors as national identity, western imperialism, economy, social status, etc. (Eickelman and Piscatori, 1996:5). Olivier Roy reminds us that analyses of Islamism have had a tendency to overdetermine Islam as an explanatory factor. What really counts is what Muslims say about what the Qur'an says; that is to say, the interpretations that circulate and the conflicts that emerge between these interpretations. The concepts of discursive tradition and symbol are great resources to decipher those processes. Interpretations, circulations, and conflicts of interpretations never happen in a social or a political vacuum. So in any case we have to come back to Muslims and their concrete practices rooted in specific social and political contexts (Roy, 2002:13).

References

Ahmad, Irfan. 2010. *Islamism and democracy in India: the transformation of Jama'at-e Islami*. New Delhi: Permanent Black.

Baran, Zeyno, ed. 2004. *Understanding Sufism and its potential role in US policy,* Nixon Centre Conference Report, Washington, accessed 11 May 2016, from http://www.islamawareness.net/Sufism/sufism_us_policy.pdf.

Becker, Howard. 2002. *Les ficelles du métier: comment conduire sa recherche en sciences sociales*. Paris: La découverte.

Bleuchot, Hervé. 1996. "Les confréries religieuses et leurs partis au Soudan: évolution ou mutation?" In *Les institutions traditionnelles dans le monde arabe*, edited by Hervé Bleuchot, 151–171. Paris: Karthala.

Bonnefoy, Laurent, François Burgat, and Pascal Ménoret. 2011. "Introduction," *Social Compass*, Special issue "From structural violence to violent activism around the Persian Gulf," 101(2), 125–129.

Bourdieu, Pierre. 2002. *Questions de sociologie*. Paris: Editions de Minuit.

Bourdieu, Pierre. 2000. *Propos sur le champ politique*. Lyon: Presses Universitaires de Lyon.

Braud, Philippe 1996. *L'émotion en politique*. Paris: Presses de la Fondation Nationale des Sciences Politique.

Bruinessen, Martin Van, and Julia Day Howell, eds. 2007. *Sufism and the "modern" in Islam*. London; New York: I.B. Tauris.

Burgat, François. 1988. *L'islamisme au Maghreb: la voix du sud*. Paris: Karthala.

Chodkiewicz, Michel. 2002. "Préface." In *Le soufisme, al-tasawwuf et la spiritualité islamique*, edited by C. Bonaud, i–xii. Paris: Maisonneuve et Larose.

Chodkiewicz, Michel. 1996. "Le soufisme au XXIe siècle." In *Les voies d'Allah, les ordres mystiques dans le monde musulman des origines à aujourd'hui*, edited by Alexandre Popovic and G. Veinstein, 25–47. Paris: Fayard.

Coulon, Christian. 1981. *Le marabout et le prince, Islam et pouvoir au Sénégal*, Paris: Éditions A. Pedone.

Eickelman, Dale, and James Piscatori. 1996. *Muslim politics*. Princeton: Princeton University Press.

Ernst, Carl. 2000. *Sufism: an essential introduction to the philosophy and practice of the mystical tradition of Islam*. Boston: Shambhala South Asia Editions.

Ewing, Katherine Pratt. 1997. *Arguing sainthood: modernity, psychoanalysis, and Islam*. Durham and London: Duke University Press.

Frembgen, Jürgen Wasim. 2009. *Journey to god: Sufis and dervishes in Islam*. Karachi: Oxford University Press.

Frembgen, Jürgen Wasim. 2007. *The friends of god: Sufi saints in Islam*. Karachi: Oxford University Press.

Gauri, Sharma. 2010. "Sufism: an answer to global terrorism," *International Journal of Interdisciplinary Social Sciences* 5(7): 223–230.

Gilsenan, Michael. 1973. *Saint and Sufi in modern Egypt: an essay in the sociology of religion*. Oxford: Clarendon Press.

Hobsbawm, Eric, and Terence Ranger, eds. 1983. *The invention of tradition*. Cambridge: New York Cambridge University Press.

Jamali, Jehangir Ali. 2012. *How and why Sufism can help combat Islamic extremism*. Kalamazoo: Kalamazoo College.

Lagroye, Jacques. 2003. "Les processus de politisation." In *La politisation*, edited by Jacques Lagroye, 360–361. Paris: Belin.

Lumbard, Joseph, ed. 2004. *Islam, fundamentalism, and the betrayal of tradition: essays by western Muslim scholars*. Indiana: World Wisdom.

Mamdani, Mahmood. 2002. "Good Muslim, bad Muslim: a political perspective on culture and terrorism," *American Anthropologist* 104(3): 766–775.

Mirahmadi, Hedieh, Mehreen Farooq and Waleed Zia. 2010. "Traditional Muslim networks: Pakistan's untapped resource in the fight against terrorism," Report of WORDE, World Organization for Resource Development and Education, accessed 12 May 2016, from http://www.worde.org/files/WhitePapers/WORDE%20White%20Paper%20-%20Traditional%20Muslim%20Networks.pdf.

Mouffe, Chantal. 1994. *Le politique et ses enjeux: pour une démocratie plurielle*, Paris: La Découverte.

Philippon, Alix. 2014. "A sublime, yet disputed, object of political ideology? Sufism in Pakistan at the crossroads," *Journal of Commonwealth and Comparative Politics* 52(2): 271–292.

Philippon, Alix. 2011. *Soufisme et politique au Pakistan: le mouvement barelwi à l'heure de la "guerre contre le terrorisme."* Paris: Karthala.

Ridgeon, Lloyd, ed. 2015. *Sufis and Salafis in the contemporary age.* London: Bloomsbury.

Roy, Olivier. 2002. *L'Islam mondialisé.* Paris: Seuil.

Roy, Olivier. 1992. *L'échec de l'Islam politique.* Paris: Seuil.

Sanyal, Usha. 2006. *Ahmad Riza Khan Barelwi: in the path of the prophet.* Oxford: Oneworld.

Sedgwick, Mark. 2015. "The support of Sufism as a counterweight to radicalization." In *Countering radicalization and violent extemism among youth to prevent terrorism*, edited by Marco Lombardi, 113–119. Amsterdam: IOS Press.

Sirriyeh, Elizabeth. 1999. *Sufis and anti-Sufis.* Richmond: Curzon Press.

Stepanyant, Marietta, ed. 2003. *Sufismo e confraternite nell'islam contemporaneo: il difficile equilibrio tra mistica e politica.* Turin: Edizioni della Fondazione Giovanni Agnelli.

Triaud, Jean-Louis. 1995. *La légende noire de la Sanûsiyya: une confrérie musulmane saharienne sous le regard français (1840–1930).* Paris: Éditions de la Maison des Sciences de l'Homme.

Trimingham, Spencer. 1971. *The Sufi orders in Islam.* Oxford: Clarendon Press.

Voll, John. 2007. "Contemporary Sufism and social theory," In *Sufism and the 'modern' in Islam*, edited by Martin Van Bruinessen and Julia Day Howell, 281–298. London; New York: I.B. Tauris.

Woodward, Mark, Mauhammad Sani Umar, Inayah Rohmaniyah and Mariani Yahya. 2013. "Salafi violence and Sufi tolerance? Rethinking conventional wisdom," *Perspectives on Terrorism* 7(6): 58–78.

Zaman, Muhammad Qasim. 2004. *The ulama in contemporary Islam, Custodians of change.* Princeton Studies in Muslim Politics. Princeton: Princeton University Press.

Index

CPSIA information can be obtained
at www.ICGtesting.com
Printed in the USA
LVHW082329200819
627996LV00006B/13/P

9 781642 590753